CROSSCURRENTS *Modern Critiques*

CROSSCURRENTS *Modern Critiques*
Harry T. Moore, *General Editor*

EDITED BY

Robert Hogan and *Michael J. O'Neill*

Joseph Holloway's Abbey Theatre

A SELECTION FROM HIS

UNPUBLISHED JOURNAL

Impressions of a Dublin Playgoer

89898

WITH A PREFACE BY

Harry T. Moore

PN 2602
.D 82
A 26 H7

Carbondale and Edwardsville

SOUTHERN ILLINOIS UNIVERSITY PRESS

FEFFER & SIMONS, INC.

London and Amsterdam

THIS IS AN exciting book, an exciting publishing project. Indeed, it might be called a publisher's dream.

For many years, including those of the great period of the Abbey Theatre, Joseph Holloway kept a diary in which he recorded not only his reactions to the plays but also his descriptions of Dublin's leading figures: W. B. Yeats, Sean O'Casey, and hundreds of other compelling personalities who cross and recross Holloway's pages. He wrote of all this with a consistency and thoroughness which might be called a kind of magic pedantry. For he has left us a treasure-house of comment and fact.

This diary has had an underground reputation, and for years scholars have consulted the manuscript in the National Library of Ireland. And now an important series of selections from it has been culled by Robert Hogan and Michael J. O'Neill, whose names have an appropriate Irish tang. Mr. Hogan, who teaches at the University of California at Davis, is no stranger to Southern Illinois University Press and its Crosscurrents/Modern Critiques: for this series he has written The Independence of Elmer Rice, which is not only an interesting critical study but also a valuable collection of previously unpublished documents. Mr. Hogan has, in addition, written a book on Sean O'Casey and has helped edit an anthology of plays. Similarly, Mr. O'Neill is no stranger to Southern Illinois University Press, for which he edited one of the James Joyce miscellanies, in collaboration with Marvin Magalaner. Mr. O'Neill, who was born in Dublin, teaches at the University of Ottawa.

In putting the present volume together, these editors have had to be highly selective since the manuscript of the diary runs to some 25 million words jotted down hastily on more than 100,000 pages. That it will ever be published in its entirety is doubtful; hence the present redaction has a special value.

Holloway was not a perfect commentator; the editors deal with him fairly critically in their introduction, and they even quote some rather uncomplimentary remarks about him. On the other hand, they appreciate his good points, which they discuss at length. They have, in presenting the heart of the diary, performed a great service to modern literature. And they have enough excellent material of the same kind left over to make another volume the size of the present one, if it is well received— as it certainly should be.

Mr. Hogan and Mr. O'Neill in their introduction provide a lively sketch of Joseph Holloway himself, so I will say nothing further about him. It is now time for the reader to turn to that introduction. Afterward he can get into the journal itself and walk the grey streets of Dublin with Holloway—a rewarding journey—can sit with him through Abbey performances of all kinds, and can then accompany him through all the backstage intimacies and intrigues. As I said before, this is an exciting book.

HARRY T. MOORE

Southern Illinois University
November 24, 1966

ACKNOWLEDGMENTS

A BOOK OF THIS NATURE can scarcely be assembled without the active cooperation of many people. In particular, we would like to acknowledge the kind and invaluable assistance of Ronald Ayling; of Ernest Blythe of the Abbey Theatre; of Mrs. M. M. F. Boothroyd who allowed us to quote letters from her father-in-law, William Boyle; of Paul Vincent Carroll; of Padraic Colum; Sister Marie-Therese Courteney; Elizabeth Coxhead; of Gerard Fay for permission to quote letters from his father, Frank J. Fay, and uncle, William G. Fay; of Dermot Guinan; of the Rt. Hon. Lord Hemphill for permission to quote letters from Edward Martyn; of Professor J. J. Hogan; of Denis Johnston; Mrs. Eileen Judge (Eileen Crowe); of Bernard Kelly; Michael J. Lennon and Ignatius Lyons; of Mary Frances, Isabel, and Florence McHugh for permission to quote letters from their father, Martin J. McHugh; of Dr. Roger McHugh; of Dr. Mícheál Mac Liammóir and the late Anew McMaster (whose death was a great loss to the Irish stage) for helpful reminiscences; of Eva Murray for much help and for permission to quote letters from her father, T. C. Murray; of Seumus O'Brien; of Sean O'Casey for much kind discouragement and for permission to quote various letters to the press; of Frank O'Connor; Frank Hugh O'Donnell; Sean O'Faolain; Eoin O'Mahony, K.M.; Myles Purcell; John and Dorothy Robbie for innumerable kindnesses; of the late Lennox Robinson and of Mrs. Dolly Robinson for permission to quote material by her husband; of Diarmuid Russell for permission to quote letters from his father, AE; of Dr. Owen Sheehy-Skeffington for much helpful information and for permission to quote some letters to the press written by his mother, Mrs. Hannah Sheehy-Skeffington; of Professor John L. Synge for great courtesy and trouble; and of Mrs. W. B. Yeats for permission to quote various materials written by her husband.

We are also indebted to the London Express News and Feature Services for allowing us to include material that originally appeared in *The Daily Express* and *The Sunday Express*, and to *The Irish Times* for permission to use materials which originally appeared within its pages, and to *The Dubliner* (now called *The Dublin Magazine*) where appeared in somewhat different form the Introduction to this volume.

We owe a special debt to Mr. Holloway's niece, Mrs. E. M. Gordon, for permission to edit the journals and for much helpful information about her uncle.

Of the various officials of the National Library of Ireland, in which the Holloway papers are housed, we made extraordinary demands for facilities and information, and we received every kindness and courtesy. We are particularly indebted to the Council of Trustees for permission to publish this extract from the Holloway papers, to the Director of the Library, Dr. R. J. Hayes, to Patrick Henchy, and Alf. Mac Lochlainn.

This volume could not have come into existence without a Guggenheim Fellowship awarded to Robert Hogan and a United States Government GI Grant awarded to Michael J. O'Neill. To both of these benevolent institutions, our deepest gratitude.

Finally, we must mention our wives, Betty Hogan and Delia O'Neill, whose contribution was of such a nature that it probably should have been listed first.

R. H.

June 30, 1966   M. J. O'N.

CONTENTS

IN EVERY WAY BUT ONE, Joseph Holloway of Dublin was a thoroughly unremarkable man, but in that one way he was, without exaggeration, astounding. For most of his almost eighty-four years, he was a man as completely dedicated to art as his country had ever seen. His interest embraced music, painting, and, above all, the theatre. People who knew him toward the end of his life, in the 1930's and early 1940's when he had achieved a mild local notoriety as a Dublin character, would have seen him at every art exhibition, every concert, every lecture, and every theatrical first night. In appearance he was then a short, slightly portly old gentleman with a bowler hat set squarely upon his head, with a mane of thick gray hair, a straggling moustache, drooping jowls, bright and inquisitive blue eyes, and a kindly and benevolent manner.

If one knew him slightly better, one might have thought him a trifle eccentric. The basis for this unjust judgment was that he was known to be an indefatigable collector who for over fifty years had filled his house to bursting with everything even remotely connected with the theatre: books, playscripts, prompt copies, playbills, scrapbooks filled with clippings, letters from actors and playwrights—a vast pile of theatrical refuse garnered from a half-century of devoted playgoing. He covered the walls of his house from floor to ceiling with paintings, sketches, and drawings that he had commissioned young artists to make of Irish theatrical and literary figures. Ultimately, the walls became so completely covered that many of the pictures had to be merely stacked in heaps against the baseboards. In his later years, his study became so cluttered with his books and journals that one could only move through it along two or three narrow pathways. Once his study table collapsed under the weight of material upon it, and, rather than disturb the orderly disorder of the room, it was more convenient to let it lie undisturbed for a couple of years than to extricate it. When, toward the end of his life, he contributed most of his books and pictures to the Municipal Gallery and the National Library, lorryload after lorryload was hauled away before making a significant dent in the trove.

The size of the collection may have been a bit overwhelming, but the collection itself was scarcely foolish. Holloway was prompted by a purposeful and methodical devotion rather than by a whimsical eccentricity, and for the historian the material is a gold mine of information, much of which would almost certainly have been lost had not Holloway preserved it.

The most remarkable memorial that Holloway left was not, however, his collection, but an immense manuscript journal called "Impressions of a Dublin Playgoer," which covers in minute detail practically everything that he saw and did for a period of over fifty years. This journal is composed of 221 bulky manuscript volumes housed in the National Library of Ireland. The volumes contain over 100,000 pages upon which are semilegibly written approximately 25 million words. This vast journal was the great work of Holloway's life. In style and in artistry it is probably one of the worst books ever written, but in scope and in content it is one of the most valuable and fascinating documents to emerge from the greatest period of Irish letters.

Holloway was born on March 21, 1861, at 71 Lower Camden Street, where his father operated a bakery shop. While Holloway was attending St. Vincent's College,

Castleknock, his father, who had already retired, died in January, 1874. For the next few years, Holloway went to various schools and lived with sundry relatives until finally moving with his mother and sister to 21 Northumberland Road where he lived for the rest of his life.

He attended the School of Art in Kildare Street for several years, and when he was nineteen entered the office of J. J. O'Callaghan, an architect. There Holloway remained until he set up for himself as a practicing architect in 1896.

Architecture did not, however, occupy a great deal of his time and attention, and he found himself increasingly attracted by the many flourishing cultural societies and clubs in Dublin and increasingly attracted by, although not to, the theatre. He was a member of the National Literary Society, the Association of Elocutionists, and the Literary, Musical, and Dramatic Society, and at all of these societies he often read papers about the stage or gave recitations. Under a pen name, he wrote drama criticism for local periodicals.

This great ferment of little groups and cultural societies in Dublin around the turn of the century arose partly from the ardent desire for, and the almost complete lack of any really excellent Irish expression in the arts. There had been a fine flowering of Irish literature in the first half of the nineteenth century. Those years had been made memorable by the great figure of William Carleton, as well as by Maria Edgeworth, Lady Morgan, the Banim brothers, Gerald Griffin, Lever, Lover, and later Le Fanu, and the poets Ferguson, Mangan, and Tom Moore. But by the Famine years of the 1840's, by the time of the collapse of the Young Ireland movement, many of these writers had either died or done their best work. There was a kind of cultural hiatus that lasted until the final years of the century, but then the early theatrical efforts of Yeats and his colleagues found a small but already eager audience.

Holloway was one of the first and most enthusiastic supporters of the Irish dramatic movement, and his life-long involvement with it was assured when he was hired by Miss A. E. F. Horniman to renovate the old Mechanics Theatre on Abbey Street for Yeats and the National Theatre Society.

Holloway practiced architecture in a desultory fashion until the First World War when, as he told Sean O'Casey, "The War killed for the time domestic architecture, and my work ceased to exist." He was not greatly perturbed by the fact, for he had a sufficient income to allow him to pursue the real work of his life — the appreciation of art, music, and the theatre, the accumulation of his collection, and the writing of his journal. He was a creature of habit — a quiet, courteous, and for the most part kindly man, who helped in countless ways scores of artists, authors, and actors. Perhaps two comments will suffice. Micheál Mac Liammóir, the well-known Irish actor, wrote to us, "Dear Joseph Holloway . . . was the first man to welcome me on my return to Ireland — I mean with permanency in my mind — in 1917. . . . I will never forget his kindness to me, a lanky boy back from ten years of London." And Miss Eva Murray, the daughter of Holloway's longtime friend, T. C. Murray the dramatist, wrote, "To me Mr. Holloway typified the perfect gentleman of the old school. I never remember him other than kind, simple and courtly. . . . He had a very special place in our hearts." Fortunately for the interest of his journal, his basic kindness was marred by small streaks of cattiness and mild malice that once or twice rose to vehement vituperation. It would be difficult for an individual so inordinately addicted to gossip — it would be difficult for a Dubliner — to avoid such foibles, but they make his journal only the more lively without essentially detracting from the man's basic goodness of heart.

He died shortly before his eighty-fourth birthday, in 1944.

Holloway's journal, *Impressions of a Dublin Playgoer*, has great fascination for devotees of the theatre and of Irish literature. He saw practically every great actor and every interesting play that appeared in Dublin in his adult lifetime, and he knew more or less intimately practically every writer, actor, or artist worth knowing in the Ireland of his time. In his journal he records how Irving, Bernhardt, Duse, Salvini, Coquelin, Tree, Forbes-Robertson, Ellen Terry, Mrs. Patrick Campbell, the Fays, Sara Allgood, Barry Fitzgerald, F. J. McCormick, Micheál Mac Liammóir, Orson Welles, Sybil Thorndike, and Cyril Cusack (to mention only a few) acted in some of their greatest successes and some of their worst failures. He records with something approaching total recall innumerable conversations that he had with the great writers of the Irish Renaissance: Yeats, AE, Lady Gregory, John Synge, Edward Martyn, Padraic Colum, James Joyce, George Moore, Sean O'Casey, Frank O'Connor, Sean O'Faolain, and many others. He copies into his journal hundreds of letters written to him or to his friends by Yeats, Lady Gregory, Frank and Willie Fay, Dudley Digges, William Boyle, T. C. Murray, and many others. He copies out critiques of plays which Yeats, Synge, Lady Gregory, Lennox Robinson, and Ernest Blythe had sent to aspiring Abbey Theatre dramatists who were his friends. He even copies out letters and notices from newspapers and magazines, and some of these were never reprinted by Yeats, Shaw, and O'Casey. He was present and describes for us what happened when John McCormack and James Joyce sang on the same platform, when the Abbey Theatre audience rioted over *The Playboy of the Western World*, when the General Post Office was under fire during the Rising of Easter Week, 1916, and when another Abbey audience rioted over *The Plough and the Stars*. In fact, Holloway's journal contains so much that it would require a longer essay than this to describe it.

We have studied the journal in an attempt to select the heart of it, for it would be an impossible and unprofitable task to publish the whole of it. In fact, a good number of intelligent people consider it impossible and unprofitable to publish any of it. Frank O'Connor described the journal to us as "that donkey's detritus," and Sean O'Casey remarked to us that "The Diary of Holloway is an impossible pile of rubbish. . . . Why it was taken by the Library is another example of Eire's love of triviality. To edit it would be a sinful, woeful waste of time, and, in the end, impossible. More profitable to edit *Mrs. Dale's Diary* spurted out from the B.B.C. for years."

When one is familiar with the entire Holloway journal, such a view seems entirely unjustified. People who have dipped into the journal at the obvious dramatic points — such as the Abbey riots — have found that Holloway was almost lividly bigoted in his opposition to the Synge and O'Casey plays, and have concluded that Holloway was a narrow Philistine whose opinions on literary matters were invariably wrong. That view does Holloway great injustice, for most of the great modern Irish actors and many of the best modern Irish playwrights valued his opinions highly. And the complete journal makes it clear that he was a man whose knowledge of the theatre was so catholic and complete that the knowledge of many scholars seems trifling by comparison.

Actually, Holloway was opposed to the Synge and O'Casey plays primarily for patriotic reasons. He felt that *The Playboy* was an inaccurate, malicious, and, therefore, inartistic representation of the Irish peasant. He felt that the artistic worth of *The Plough* was severely limited because it seemed to debase the patriotic ideals of the 1916 Rising by counterpointing to them what seemed to him examples of immorality. His reasons for censuring these two plays were not aesthetically valid, but, given the time and the place, they were quite understandable. Even a very great critic like Samuel Johnson was sometimes more strongly swayed by the tenor of his time than by the standards of the ages, and certainly some of Holloway's more notable contemporaries were guilty of misjudgments that arose from similar critical blindspots. W. B. Yeats, for instance, had a prime hand in rejecting for the Abbey Theatre such masterly work as *John Bull's Other Island,*

The Silver Tassie, and *The Old Lady Says, "No!"*; Edward Martyn had a bias in favor of the "intellectual" or Ibsenite drama and had a low opinion of the poetic drama. The young Joyce contemptuously dismissed the Irish Literary Theatre for having surrendered "to the trolls." And even the sanest and soundest modern critic of them all, Bernard Shaw, was capable of the wildest and most impossible of opinions.

It is fairer to censure Holloway for being too easily swayed by the opinions of people around him. For instance, his glimpses of *The Plough and the Stars* in rehearsal did not convince him that the play was an excellent one, but neither did they throw him into a tizzy of moral indignation. His views were colored by the curiously rabid indignation of his friend James Montgomery, the Film Censor and a well-known Dublin wit, and they were given added impetus by the purely patriotic protests of Mrs. Sheehy-Skeffington and the group of ladies who impelled the initial outbursts against the play. Later, when the heat of the moment had cooled, he came round to a juster and saner view of both *The Playboy and The Plough,* and this re-evaluation is much to his credit.

In a less dramatic fashion, his moral and patriotic biases caused him frequently to do an injustice to much of the work of—for instance—Lennox Robinson, St. John Ervine, and Denis Johnston, which dealt with material that he found repugnant. Conversely, he came to value at more than their true worth a number of "sweet" plays like *The Two Shepherds* and *The Cradle Song* of Martinez Sierra. Nevertheless, even though he sometimes undervalued an excellent play, he rarely overvalued a poor one. Finally, it is impossible to dismiss as a narrow Philistine a man who was so enthusiastically appreciative of such esoteric fare as Yeats's *The Shadowy Waters,* Maeterlinck's *Pelleas and Melisande,* and Eliot's *Murder in the Cathedral.*

If, then, we allow that any critic has his biases, and that these do not necessarily make him *hors de combat,* we shall be able to read with profit not only a great critic like

Samuel Johnson but also a minor critic like Joseph Holloway. His views on the majority of plays that he saw were
quite sound and specific, and they were valued by many
practicing dramatists who frequently sought out his opinions on their own work. He was not a deep or a penetrating critic, and his opinions were best when concerned
with what was and what was not theatrically effective.
"He had," as Padraic Colum remarked to us, "the shrewd-
ness of a first-nighter, but had, I should say, no real
literary judgment." As the drama has been traditionally
overburdened with literary judgments from Aristotle to
Eric Bentley, it is perhaps refreshing to find one critic who
can make a purely theatrical judgment.

Holloway's opinions of actors and acting were considerably sounder than his opinions of playwrights and plays.
The Irish actress Maire nic Shiubhlaigh remarked that he
was "essentially a man of the theatre," and that he "was
the finger which we, as players, kept upon the pulse of
Dublin." Edward Martyn once wrote him that "You and
I, my dear sir, are epicures in the theatre." That excellent
actor, the late Anew McMaster, wrote to us that "He
was the most indefatigable playgoer I have ever met, with
the possible exception of my late friend, Eddie Marsh.
. . . He was most helpful in his criticism of artistes; indeed, I have a letter from him after a performance of
Oedipus, in which he told me I jumped too suddenly
from pianissimo to fortissimo, and I have through the
years tried to correct the fault."

Holloway's description of acting and actors, then, is his
strongest and soundest point. Occasionally one feels that
he undervalues or overvalues a player or performance
slightly, but it is difficult to find in the entire journal a
judgment on acting where he went entirely astray. It
would be too much to suggest that he had discovered an
excellent and ultimately appropriate way to describe acting, and he himself occasionally remarked this failure.
Still, it is a failure that he shares with every other dramatic critic. His most specific failing as a critic of acting is
his tendency to make quick general judgments in a phrase

or two, and his chief excellence is when he details what an actor did. When he is engaged in this latter business, his judgment seems sure and his taste impeccable. He recognized that the criticism of the actor is quite as important and integral as the criticism of the play. For this salutary realization and for the chronicling of what individual actors specifically did in certain parts, playgoers must be grateful.

His standard of judgment for acting rested basically upon the same premises that he applied to plays: a faithfulness to reality, a holding of the mirror up to nature. He was swift to sense when a player by mannerism or exaggeration jumped, as he put it, out of the picture. Nevertheless, as he tacitly realized, such a standard must be a flexible one when applied to either plays or players, and it is a trifle confusing to find him silently shifting his standards although using the same terms. He was able to appreciate the acting of Henry Irving in *The Bells* and the acting of Barry Fitzgerald in *Juno and the Paycock*; and he was able to appreciate a piece like Lady Gregory's Wonder Play, *The Dragon*, and at the same time a realistic play like Padraic Colum's *The Land*. Apparent, if not stated, in the appreciation of such opposites is an understanding of conventions that exist on a continuum from stylization or fantasy to realization or photography. The failure to be real which Holloway might criticize in Beerbolm Tree's playing of "Svengali" is not the same failure he would criticize in Arthur Sinclair's unreal playing of "The Eloquent Dempsy." One might have wished that he had been more explicit about his standards, but, if he was not, it was not because they were nonexistent; the reason was that he quite simply was not interested in aesthetics or dramatic theory, but in plays and players.

His diary is not weaker for that fact. After all, he has succeeded in putting on paper more than literary or dramatic criticism. Holloway's journal is an invaluable and, we think, an enduring book because it contains the people and their personalities, the arguments, the preoccupations, the gossip, and the flavor of more than fifty exciting years. In many, many ways Holloway's journal is a very faulty book, but any book through whose pages stride the violent and combative figures of Shaw, Yeats, O'Casey, and scores of their opinionated contemporaries has some claim to greatness. If one might choose to relive any fifty years of literary history, one would probably first consider the Athens of Pericles or the London of Shakespeare, but the Dublin of Holloway would not be such a bad choice either.

The problem of editing a selection from Holloway's journals was somewhat gigantic, and for those interested in such matters here is an explanation of our procedure and an apologia for our occasional malprocedure. Reading the millions of words that make up the Holloway journals is to reach (at times) the conclusion that here is, as O'Casey suggested, a gigantic repository of trivia rendered in a style that makes the reading sometimes an almost unendurable agony. After extensive reading of the journals, one is really impelled to plunge into Milton, or Shelley, or Dylan Thomas in order to remind oneself of the noble capabilities of the English language. Still, if one persists—and one does, for Holloway has something of the hypnotic fascination of the Ancient Mariner—one finds nuggets and often veins of real and sometimes inestimable worth.

There are, however, problems. For one thing, relatively little personal interest attaches to Holloway himself. Almost completely lacking in the engaging foibles of a Boswell or a Pepys, he lived a long, placid bachelor life of simple and unvarying routine. If any of the fiercer passions raged within him, they ruffled neither the pages of his journal nor the kindly and benevolent exterior he presented to the world.

Also, despite the fact that Holloway reports many long and fascinating conversations with some of the most interesting people of his time, he also reports many other conversations that were of monumental dullness and insignificance. Although we see W. B. Yeats raging from the

Abbey stage that an Irish audience has disgraced itself
again, we see him also relating a tedious story about a man
who collects hotel keys. Although we see Bernard Shaw
denouncing Ireland in a witty speech, we also see Sean
O'Faolain asking if he might come to the Film Censor's
office to view *Snow White and the Seven Dwarfs*. Although we see Lord Dunsany eloquently condemning the
Irish theatre, we also see Padraic Colum haggling with a
bookseller over sixpence, and Sean O'Casey talking about
buying shirts, and Edward Martyn discussing his house-
keeper's bread. We see Oliver Gogarty, the comrade of
Joyce, whom George Moore called the wittiest man in
Dublin, appearing as a rather ponderous bore, and we see
the eloquent Moore himself discussing the weather.

Sometimes Holloway is almost superb. There is his
graphic and painful account of the fighting in O'Connell
Street during the Rising. There are his long conversations
with O'Casey and his sparring with Yeats. There is the
fine scene of the night, early in the history of the Irish
National Theatre Society, when John Synge, in the ram-
shackle rehearsal hall in Camden Street, read to the company for the first time *The Well of the Saints*. Or the
scene during the rehearsal of *Deirdre* at the Abbey when
Mrs. Patrick Campbell, with that rare tact and charm of
which she was sometimes capable, gently ushered Yeats
off his own stage. Or those scenes in which the crafty
Yeats squelches his dislike of Holloway, and in his round-
about way attempts to persuade him to woo William Boyle
back to the theatre. Or that poignant scene of Yeats
wandering alone in Mount Jerome Cemetery after the
death of Synge. But despite many such passages, Holloway's impressions often suffer from a brevity and a casual-
ness of phrasing that considerably limit their interest.
Sometimes he will without elaboration make an irritating
remark like "Mr. Synge and I had a long chat."

The problem of the scholar confronted with such a
work is doubtless similar to the problem of the scholar
confronted with a variant reading of a line by Keats, but it
is magnified to such an enormous degree that it seems

almost a problem of a different nature. The Keats scholar must use his knowledge, his taste, and his empathy into the mind of the poet in order to make a judgment which is to a certain extent artistic. He must touch up a small fault upon a virtually completed, virtually unblemished work of art. The scholar confronted with a problem like the Holloway journal must make the same kind of decision not once but a million times. He must turn a massive, unreadable volume into an only moderately bulky, interesting one. It is the difference between being given a nearly completed statue and told to determine the shape of the earlobe and being given a block of valuable marble and told to produce the statue.

We found that an extract from Holloway's entire journal, in which we had kept the bare essentials, ran to 1500 pages. So, we have temporized here and made another extract dealing primarily with the great years of the Abbey Theatre, from its founding in 1899 to the departure of Sean O'Casey in 1926. We have done this with considerable misgivings, conscious that what we have left out is as valuable as what we have kept in. Even so, this extract of about half of the Holloway journals provides, we think, a closer, a fuller, and a longer view of theatrical and literary life in the great period of Irish writing than is available anywhere else. It would have been ideal if a clever man with a flair for words had written the Holloway journals. A George Moore, for instance, would have been superb. But, on the other hand, a clever man—clever in the narrow, witty, caustic, Dublin sense of the word—probably could not have done it. Holloway has, of course, a touch of cleverness; indeed, he could not have been a Dubliner without a touch of this malicious eye for the absurd, and it appears occasionally in his remarks about Yeats and Lennox Robinson. Basically, however, he was a humble and ordinary man who in a most un-Dublin-like way never gave a thought to his manner—either to his manner of life or to the manner of his journal.

Consequently, we have allowed ourselves some latitude with regard to his style. Despite excellent and even eloquent passages, the usual style ranges from the undistinguished to the rather garbled. His syntax is sometimes awkward and sometimes baffling, and his system of punctuation, although it relies largely on the exclamation mark and the parentheses, is primarily guided by whim. We have not hesitated to untangle the occasional sentence in order to make the sense clear, and we have not hesitated to throw out several million exclamation marks and to make the punctuation throughout somewhat more functional. For the most part, we have rectified any spelling lapses, and the paragraphing is largely our own, as Holloway utilized the paragraph only in the rarest of instances. On infrequent occasions we have supplied without brackets an omitted word or phrase which was necessary for clarity, and we have silently corrected any errors we found of dates or names. Taken all in all, our work might seem to exceed the usual scholarly limitations. To have made a literal transcription, however, would have produced a painfully tedious book which scholars might have braved, but which would scarcely have had the broader interest inherent in the material. We were not, after all, dealing with a Shakespeare or a Shaw whose very mistakes might be worth preserving, but with a very ordinary man who did not consider his journal a polished and finished book and who did not regard any of his minor errors and flaws as sacrosanct. We have not finally transmuted Holloway, but merely tidied him up in a way which he himself thought would be necessary and which will allow the real excellence of his great accomplishment to appear unblemished by a mass of inessential and trivial flaws. Holloway was a humble man, and he would not have minded.

Indeed, he was humble and ordinary enough so that even his immense store of erudition sat lightly on his shoulders. Probably the last remark one could make about the Holloway journal is that it proves how close a really ordinary man could come to greatness.

ROBERT HOGAN
MICHAEL J. O'NEILL

June 30, 1966

Joseph Holloway's Abbey Theatre
A SELECTION FROM HIS
UNPUBLISHED JOURNAL

PREFACE

[The following preface was written by Joseph Holloway in January 1897, but was inserted in his manuscript for the year 1896.]

I FEEL STRONGLY on everything connected with the stage and the art of speech from the audience's point of view, and have an unfortunate habit of expressing truthfully what I feel, whether it pleases or not. I have no prejudices nor fads; all performers appeal to me only on their merits as performers, whether they pose as comedians, tragedians, vocalists, elocutionists, music hall artistes or lecturers. To see whether the mirror has been held up to Nature is the object I always keep before my mind in writing. . . . It is as an ordinary play-goer, and not in the capacity of a professional critic, that I have given expression to my thoughts. . . . I love the theatre as I love my existence and rejoice exceedingly when I witness art displayed in any of its branches. I am catholic in my tastes, not pre-ferring tragedy to comedy, grand opera to musical farce, provided that they are equally good of their respective kinds.

With this pronouncement of faith, I open my diary.

Joseph Holloway

1899

Thursday, January 5. Went to the Catholic Commercial Club where I heard Mr. P. H. Pearse deliver a lecture on "Irish Saga Literature." The lecturer is quite a young man with a peculiar, jerky, pistol-shot-like delivery that becomes trying to listen to after a time, as it makes him hack his sentences into single words and destroys the sense of his remarks. . . . He was indiscriminantly eulogistic to absurdity over his subject, and the adjectives he employed to describe the extracts which he read from the Sagas were beyond the beyonds of reason when the stuff so praised became known to his listeners. Woeful exaggeration or absurd grotesqueness were the only merits they possessed as far as I could see, but then I am not a Gaelic speaking maniac. . . . It is this absurd, unmeaning, almost fanatical praise that makes the few lovers of the Irish language left us so unbearable and impractical to all broadminded people.

Monday, January 9. Amid most artistic surroundings the members of the National Literary Society held the first Conversazione in the Leinster Lecture Hall. . . . Mr. W. B. Yeats explained to us his scheme for a national theatre for the production of Celtic drama under the title of "The Irish Literary Theatre," and said it was the intention of the promoters to produce a medieval Celtic drama in verse, and a modern Celtic drama in prose in Dublin in May next. That the scheme may be successful is my ardent wish. If enthusiasm can command success, then it is assured, as nothing could be more enthusiastic than the manner in which Mr. Yeats has taken up the idea.

Saturday, May 6.   Attended Mr. W. B. Yeats's rambling discourse on "Dramatic Ideals and the Irish Literary Theatre," delivered at No. 6 Stephen's Green, under the auspices of the National Literary Society before a fashionable and literary audience. Dr. Sigerson presiding.

First of all, Mr. Yeats answered effectively the attacks that had been and are being made upon his play, *The Countess Cathleen,* by Frank Hugh O'Donnell [1] and *The Daily Nation,* and read a letter from an eminent divine re the correctness and inoffensiveness of its ideas from the Roman Catholic point of view, on which ground it had been bitterly assailed—for personal reasons it would seem.

Then Mr. Yeats rambled off without notes to speak of the drama, and mistook the actor's calling for that of the orator or elocutionist in his ideas of how drama ought to be presented. He advocated that poetry should be rhymed or chanted, and that scenery and dress should be subordinated to the words spoken; in short, that good literary writing should appeal to the mind and not the eye, and that acting should not be acting but recitation of the old sing-song order.

Certainly Mr. Yeats in speaking acts up to his opinions, as he chants most of his remarks in a monotonous recitative most slumberful in result; only he is so erratic or overladen with ideas, that he continually breaks off at a tangent from a rhymed idea to a commonplace quite foreign to the previous sentence. . . . I assure you that three gentlemen on the line of chairs with me were almost lulled to rest and peacefully closed their eyes as Mr. Yeats's chanting fell on their ears. . . .

Count Plunkett proposed in his usual pause-between-each-word-dreamy-way the vote of thanks, and Mr. George Russell (AE) seconded it and went for Mr. Yeats's spiteful detractors and castigated the poor spite of

those who published and circulated attacks on his work
out of pure malice. Dr. Sigerson in putting the vote also
had a go at the geese who will always screech, especially
those of Celtic breed.

Monday, May 8.   At last the Irish Literary Theatre is
become an actuality, and the red letter occurrence in the
annals of the Irish Literary movement took place in the
Antient Concert Rooms where a large and most fashionable audience filled the hall. There a pretty little miniature
stage, perfectly appointed, had been erected. W. B.
Yeats's miracle play in four acts, *The Countess Cathleen*,
was the work selected to inaugurate the Theatre, and from
one cause or another the event was looked forward to with
considerable excitement and interest, owing to the hostil-
ity exhibited in certain quarters to the author.

Expectation was satisfied, as an organised claque of
about twenty brainless, beardless, idiotic-looking youths [2]
did all they knew to interfere with the progress of the play
by their meaningless automatic hissing and senseless comments—and only succeeded in showing what poor things
mortals can become when the seat of reason is knocked
awry by animus, spite, and bigotry. Thomas Davis seemed
to be the particular "bee in their bonnets," as they frequently made reference to the poet. That some disturbance should take place had been expected for weeks long
back as a comment of W. B. Yeats on that vigorous poet's
work had got Davis' admirers' backs up some time ago.
. . . Their "poor spite" was completely frustrated by enthusiastic applause which drowned their empty-headed
expressions of dissension.

But enough of this, and let me record without further
delay the gratifying success of the undertaking. Yeats's
beautiful narrative poem in dramatic form, *The Countess
Cathleen*, as the literary world knew for years past, reads
admirably, but that it would make a good actable play as
well its performance to-night incontestably proved. It was
weirdly, fantastically, pathetically, or picturesquely effective by turns; and, as I followed its progress, Poe's words,

"All that we see or seem is but a dream within a dream," floated in on my mind, and a spiritual, half-mystic, visionary sensation crept over my senses as I watched enraptured, as if I were in fairy land, the merchant-demons trafficking in the immortal souls of the poor starving peasants—until the benevolent, beautiful, self-sacrificing "Countess Cathleen" barters her own to save the others, and dies broken-hearted, to be awarded a crown of glory "for so supreme a sacrifice."

As to the interpretation, it was not acting in the ordinary sense, but a laudable attempt "to lend to the beauty of the poet's rhyme the music of the voice" in half chant-like tones, and that the artists wholly succeeded . . . I cannot truthfully say . . . as indistinctness was the result of their efforts; but then the official journal of the Irish Literary Theatre, *Beltaine*, says, "the speaking of poetic words, whether to music or not, is, however, so perfectly among the lost arts that it will take a long time before our actors, no matter how willing, will be able to forget the ordinary methods of the stage or to perfect a new method.". . .

Miss May Whitty made an ideal "Countess Cathleen," sympathetic and lovable in manner, and spoke her lines with a delicious, natural, sweet-musical cadence expressively and most distinctly, looking the "rare and radiant maiden" of the poet's dream to the life, and always using simple yet graceful and picturesque gestures, and posing artistically yet never artificially in every episode so as to create many memorable and beautiful stage pictures. . . . Miss Florence Farr as "Aleel," a bard, declaimed all her lines in majestic, beautiful, rhythmic manner grand to listen to—most impressive if occasionally indistinct. . . .

Much of the last act was spoiled by a creaky door, and the too liberal use of palpable tin-tray-created thunder claps. The staging was good if unpretentious, and the dresses excellent; and the piece went without a hitch, although the stage room was somewhat scanty. . . .

The twenty would-be immovable obstructions presented a sorry sight at the end as the thunders of applause which greeted the play, players, and author simply wiped their ill-timed efforts out. By the way, in taking his call, Mr. Yeats seemed most embarrassed and did not know what to do until, prompted by the "devil" in the person of Mr. Trevor Lowe, he took Miss Whitty's hand and shook it heartily, and afterwards that of Miss Farr which he treated similarly. My, Yeats must have felt very proud at the complete triumphing over his enemies!

Note. Chanting is hard to follow until the ear grows accustomed to listening to measured rhythm. Many of the artists failed to allow those in front to clearly understand what they spoke. This should not be, of course, as the first essential of effective stage work is the clearness of articulation in the speech of the actors.

Tuesday, May 9.   To-night the second dramatic work prepared for our delight by the Irish Literary Theatre was presented, and completely captured the listeners' attention at once and held them almost breathlessly mute to its tragic climax, with the exception of well-timed oases of enthusiastic applause after almost every exit. A more absorbing play than Mr. Edward Martyn's *The Heather Field* I have not witnessed for a long time. When I read the piece last week at the National Library, I became deeply interested in its development, as the dialogue was so natural, yet full of beauty and keen observation, and the action ever culminating and well sustained; but my interest in the work was intensified considerably in following its working out on the stage, and the admirable manner in which it was acted and the grip it got on the highly cultured and fashionable gathering present proved it to be a work of real dramatic grit. The influence of the giant Norwegian dramatist, Ibsen, was distinctly traceable in Mr. Martyn's clever and splendidly characterised play, and the master's *The Enemy of the People* was brought to my mind in watching "Carden Tyrrell's" anxiety about the success of his reclaimed heather field.

Evidently the unruly youths of last night had no crow to pluck with Mr. Martyn as they remained elsewhere, and the audience was allowed to listen to the performance without any disturbance whatever. For which relief, much thanks. . . .

One cannot give any idea of the amount of pathos and tenderness the dramatist has worked round the incidents leading up to the tragedy of this dreamer whose mind gives way on hearing that his dream has turned out naught but a dream, after all. His love for his brother, son, and friend were beautifully indicated, and his utter hopelessness in trying to make his wife understand him one little bit was also admirably hit off. As a character study, the part of "Carden Tyrrell" would be hard to better, and his every phase of emotion was simply and clearly brought out with rare dramatic skill by Mr. Thomas Kingston who gained the complete sympathy of the house for the poor misunderstood visionary. There was no chanting in this play, but the mirror was held up to nature rigidly, and nature beheld herself reflected therein without flattery or exaggeration in speech or manner. . . .

The play was effectively staged and must be recorded a triumphant success as an acting drama. The applause was immense at the conclusion, and the actors were called and recalled several times, and finally Mr. Edward Martyn appeared on the scene several times to receive the homage deservedly due to him, ere the delighted spectators dispersed. Beyond a doubt, the admirable performance of *The Heather Field* has made the Irish Literary Theatre an unmistakably established fact, and an institution which all Irish people of culture and refinement ought to be justly proud of.

1900

Monday, February 19.[1]   Whatever may be the literary
worth of the two pieces presented by the Irish Literary
Theatre at the Gaiety to-night, their unsuitability as stage
plays is beyond all doubt . . . as witness to-night the
utter failure of *Maeve* to impress. . . . Why the fact of
the matter was that "Maeve's" cold inanimate manner
and wistful, far-away look and visionary talk only created
laughter among a most kindly disposed audience. On
occasion they could not refrain from irreverent mirth at
the daft behaviour of this eminently unloveable young
woman, and one old play-goer was heard to remark as he
left the theatre that "They ought to have clapped that
one into an asylum. . . ."

I must candidly confess that when I read Mr. Martyn's
piece a little while ago, I thought it would have made a
better stage play than it did, but all the weird fascination
conjured up in the reading vanished in the stage representation, and the complete lack of human interest in the
unsatisfactory working out of the symbolic idea ruined its
chance of success as a work of stagecraft. I know little or
nothing of "symbols" and "psychology," but I know a
good acting play when I see one, and this fairy tale
symbolising the unspannable gulf between Irish and English ideals undoubtedly is not one. It was a frost that killed
poor, ever-dreaming "Maeve" as she fell asleep on the
balcony, and *Maeve*, as a play, is a "killing" frost. . . .

Miss Alice Milligan's twenty minutes' peep into the

legendary past of the Ossianic period of Irish folklore entitled *The Last Feast of the Fianna* (why *feast* by the way, as there was nothing visible on the stage, only a huge fire of heaped-up faggots? "Famine" . . . would have been a much more appropriate word) was picturesque and might have proved dramatically acceptable if the actors taking part were as good as the ladies.

Thursday, February 22.   Mr. George Moore's brilliantly written political squib was produced by the Irish Literary Theatre at the Gaiety, thinly disguised as a comedy of manners in five acts under the title of *The Bending of the Bough*,[2] and was quite dramatic in parts though slow as a whole, while the "curtains" with the exception of that of Act I were very tame and ineffective. In fact, at the end of Act II, the man in charge of the curtain appealed to the actor on the stage if he was to lower the drop, and on receiving a distinctly audible "Yes!" down it came. No wonder this man did not imagine the act concluded, so unfinished appeared the situation on which he was called upon to shut off the stage from the audience.

Everyone knows by this that the differences between the corporations of Northaven and Southaven treated of in this work are meant to represent none other than poor Ireland's struggle against mighty England, and the various characters introduced are merely types employed to work out that idea. The audience was fully aware that this construction was to be put on the actions and sayings of the various characters, and applauded many of the passages right heartily on that account, as they discovered clever home thrusts in them. The piece much resembled an Ibsen drama in its working out, but many of the long speeches put into the mouths of "Jasper Dean" and "Ralf Kirwan" became most unreal when spoken as dialogue. This was especially noticeable at the commencement of Act III where these two characters stand apart and, facing the audience, repeat long passage after passage gazing fixedly at nothing in particular when they are supposed to be addressing their remarks to each other. This irritating

fault of addressing the house seems to be the rule instead
of the exception at the Irish Literary Theatre performances and particularly in this piece. . . . The final moments of the comedy were made to appear supremely
ridiculous to me by the way these two actors got one to
each side of the stage, and, fixing their heads to one
side . . . as if boils at the top of their collars were irritating their necks, commenced spouting yards of artificial,
fanciful thoughts, as they stood transfixed gazing vacantly
into space. If this is the art of acting, I'll be blowed. . . .

The scene in the Meeting Hall of the corporation was
very animated and effective especially towards the climax,
and many fine dramatic passages here and there throughout the comedy caught a grip on me. The audience (not a
very large one) was thoroughly delighted with the work
and wanted the author out afterwards, but he wisely
declined the honour.

Friday, November 30.   "Mr. Oscar Wilde, the dramatist
and author, died at Paris of meningitis." Thus briefly is
his death announced who only a few short years ago had
the world at his feet. . . . Oh, the emptiness of the
whole thing, when a man's literary fame vanishes with his
good name!

1901

Monday, October 21. The Irish Literary Theatre is
with us again for the third season. The Gaiety Theatre is
again the scene of operation, and the Benson Company
and members of the Gaelic Amateur Dramatic Society the
operators. In the first place, a really splendid house assembled. Everybody who is anybody in Dublin seemed to
be there, and the attention paid to the plays was remarkable in its intensity. A few years ago no one could conceive
it would be possible to produce a play in Irish on the
Dublin stage and interest all beholders, yet such was the
case to-night when Dr. Douglas Hyde's little Gaelic piece
The Twisting of the Rope was produced for the first time
by Gaelic speaking amateurs.[1] And though their efforts
were crude from an acting point of view, the "old tongue"
flowed so expressively and musically from their lips as to
send a thrill of pleasure through one's veins, and make
one regret that most Irishmen (including myself) have
been brought up in utter ignorance of their own language. . . .

The play is founded on an old folk-tale and tells of how
"Hanrahan," a wandering poet from Connaught, enters a
farmer's house in Munster while a dance is in progress and
gains the ear, by his soft talk, of the farmer's daughter,
"Oona," who is engaged to "Sheamus O'Heran." And the
people are afraid to eject this poet from the house by force
as he has the reputation of having a "curse that would
split the trees," and it would be dangerous to meddle with

his liberty. However, they put their heads together and concoct a little plan which has the desired effect of placing the unwelcome guest on the outside of the door. By a pious fraud they say that a coach has been overturned down the road and that a "sugaun," or hay rope, is required to tie up the damaged portions; and they persuade "Hanrahan," who refuses to leave "Oona," to twist the rope, and in his doing so he gets on the outside of the door which is slammed on him; and as he curses to his heart's content they proceed with the dance, and "Oona" becomes reconciled to "Sheamus" again when the sweet-tongued wanderer has disappeared.

Dr. Douglas Hyde, the author, as "Hanrahan," though villainously made up, made love very persuasively, and rated those who would deprive him of the young maiden with delightful glibness and sincerely expressed abuse. I have always been told that Irish is a splendid language to make love in or abuse, and having heard Dr. Hyde I can well believe it. His "soft talk" and "hard words" flowed with equal freedom and apparent ease from his slippery tongue. . . .

There was a simple naturalness about the whole scene that was refreshing, and the double four-hand reel on which the curtain closed was danced with vigour and surprising lightness of step. The applause was great at the end, and the curtain was raised several times amid continual approval.

Messrs. George Moore and W. B. Yeats's romantic three-act play, *Diarmuid and Grania*, enacted entirely by members of the Benson Company opened the programme, and on the whole is a beautiful piece full of weird suggestiveness, but lacking here and there in dramatic action. The lackadaisical manner and eternal attitudinising of Mrs. Benson as the fickle "Grania," together with her almost uniform die-away inaudibleness nearly wrecked the play. Mr. T. O'Neill Russell summed her performance up as "d——d bad," and I am compelled to say "hear, hear!" to his verdict. The jaunty way she moved about and sprawled limply all over the place was enough to spoil any play. Oh, for a Miss Lily Brayton in the part.

The legend of "Diarmuid's" flight with "Grania" and subsequent death from the wound of a wild boar was clearly and graphically told, and over all the glamour of poetry was distinctly felt. The second act was dramatically the strongest, and the flight of "Diarmuid" and the attendant ceremonies were most impressive. The Funeral March by Dr. E. Elgar added greatly to the solemnity of the procession on which the dramatists rang down the curtain. The last scene—the wooded slopes of Ben Bulben —was picturesque, but the others I thought only so-so, while the lighting of the stage was very erratic at all times. . . .

General verdict favourable if not enthusiastic. Everything went surprisingly well for a first night. All was over by 11:20. The gods whiled away the interval with Gaelic songs and choruses cleverly sung.

1902

Thursday, April 3. Was present at the second performance of *Deirdre* and *Cathleen ni Houlihan* at St. Teresa's Hall, and were it not for the unseemly and distracting noises, such as snatches of popular songs, erratic dance steps, and the continual sound of billiard balls coming in contact with each other, wafted from an adjoining room, so that most of what the performers said was lost to me . . . , I would have spent a thoroughly delightful evening. . . .

There was quite a poetic glamour over AE's (George Russell) fanciful and beautiful rendering into dramatic form of the "Deirdre" legend, and the gauze curtain between the audience and the performers added much to the weird and dreamy effect of the play upon the listeners. And, by the way, the audience was a most attentive and appreciative one! Most of the performers chanted their lines after the monotonous method of the "Ghost" in *Hamlet,* and a few having very marked accents, the effect produced at times was not impressive, to put it mildly. . . .

Miss Maire T. Quinn (a true daughter of Ulster by her accent) looked picturesque and chanted her lines in agreeable, if monotonous, monotone as the beautiful "Deirdre," and Mr. J. Dudley Digges made an admirable "Naisi," realising the role with excellent dramatic impressiveness and telling declamatory effect as the text demanded. Mr. F. J. Fay as the treacherous "King Conco-

bar" acted capitally also. The "Fergus" of Mr. P. J. Kelly
pleased me as he spoke well, and Miss Maire nic Shiubhlaigh [Mary Walker] was commendable as "Lavarcam,"
"Deirdre's" foster-mother. The others were not up to
much, and a few were very bad indeed. There was something about the play which took my fancy very much, but
what it was evades me as I write!

The interval music was supplied by the string band of
the Workman's Club, York Street, and much resembled
that supplied each evening at the Queen's Theatre. The
author and all the performers were enthusiastically called
at the end of *Deirdre*.

The scene of Mr. W. B. Yeats's one-act play, *Cathleen
ni Houlihan*, was laid in a cottage close to Killala in 1798,
at the time of the landing of the French. We are introduced to the family of "Gillan" whose eldest son is about
to marry "Delia Cahel" in the morning; and to the cottage comes a mysterious old lady—"Cathleen ni Houlihan"—who so plays on the feelings of the coming bridegroom that he gives up his bride and follows her to strike
a blow for ould Ireland, whom she symbolises. The matter-of-fact ways of the household and the weird, uncanny
conduct of the strange visitor make a very agreeable con-
coction. And as the piece was admirably played, it made a
deep impression. Most of the sayings of the mysterious
"Cathleen" (a part realised with creepy realism by the tall
and willowy Miss Maud Gonne, who chanted her lines
with rare musical effect, and crooned fascinatingly, if
somewhat indistinctly, some lyrics) found ready and apt
interpretation from the audience who understood that
Erin spoke in "Cathleen," and they applauded each red-
hot patriotic sentiment right heartily, and enthusiastically
called for the author at the end, and had their wish
gratified. . . .

The whole performance was very creditable to Mr.
W. G. Fay's Irish National Dramatic Company, and the
scenery by AE and W. G. Fay was very effective, while the
dresses made from designs of AE were appropriate as well
as picturesque.

Saturday, August 16.   I met Mr. Fay, who told me that his company was rehearsing several new Irish plays in the English language for production this coming season and had taken a hall in Camden Street for the purpose. This is cheery news to the Irish playgoers with a combined love of country and art.

Friday, October 31.   In the evening, I spent a delightful time witnessing three little plays at the Antient Concert Rooms, produced by the earnest and enthusiastic little band of players, who style themselves the Irish National Dramatic Company. Unfortunately, there were very few present to see their efforts, but those who were spent a happy and enjoyable time, to judge by their applause and hearty laughter. I noticed many well-known people pres-ent—Miss Maud Gonne, W. B. Yeats, George Russell, Sarah Purser, Arthur Hugh Law, M.P., William Field, M.P., D. J. O'Donoghue, Lady Gregory, Dr. Douglas Hyde, etc.

Mr. Seumas O'Cusin's [1] dramatic one-act play of real life in two scenes, *The Racing Lug,* was played for the first time on any stage and received very sympathetic treatment from the hands of the performers, creating quite an impression on the audience. The gloom and dread of coming disaster was admirably conveyed, and the fading out of life of the old fisherman's wife as she awaits her husband's return was pathetically enacted by Marie T. Quinn. . . . This profoundly touching little scene was perfectly realised by the players, and it was some time after the fall of the curtains before the audience clam-oured for the author, such an impression had the little work left on their minds. The setting of the stage and appointments generally were very appropriate, and the loud ticking of the clock added greatly to the intensity of the weary waiting of the wife and daughter. . . .

The second play, a clever skit in two acts on the corrup-tion of Municipal bodies, entitled *The Laving of the Foundations* by Fred Ryan (first produced two nights ago), was capital fun of the most satirical kind. . . . The third play (played in Irish) was a short and bright one, *Eilis agus an Bhean Deirce* by P. T. McGinley.

Saturday, November 1. . . . I went on to the Antient Concert Rooms where I heard Mr. W. B. Yeats lecture on "Speaking to Musical Notes" with Miss Florence Farr (Mrs. Emery) to give examples to the accompaniment of the psaltery (a sort of lyre) made especially for the purpose by Dr. Arnold Dolmetsch, the great authority on old chamber music. The experiment was very interesting, but in no way could it be called *speaking* to musical notes — call it chanting or intoning or what you will, but not speaking. Sometimes it was more like to singing than to aught else, with the exception that the words were always distinctly heard, not like the poet's words when sung in the usual way, "which might as well be," as the lecturer said, "the multiplication table as poetry for aught the listener hears of them."

This lilting, or what you will, to notes, though made quite pleasing and beautiful by Miss Farr for short periods (she gave all short passages or lyrics with slight pauses between), would, I imagine, become very trying if continued for any length of time, even by an artist like Miss Farr. What then would it be in a tyro's charge? Monotonous agony from which Lord deliver us! . . .

The poet-lecturer's contention is that if in the speaking or reading of a poem the verbal music were destroyed, it ceased to be a poem and became instead bad, florid prose, which I in a sense agree with. Poetry being a thing apart from nature must have a law of interpretation all its own. At least, that is Yeats's idea, hence all this pother about speaking it to musical notes which the lecturer endeavoured to instill into the minds of his hearers in his own enthusiastic, excitable, impressionable way, with continuous hand action (though he sneered at the over-gesticulation of trained elocutionists in reciting verse, he himself in speaking is the most extravagant, wind-mill . . . I ever saw!) and fidgety movements. . . .

The lecture and examples were most interesting. There

is an air of unconventionality about Yeats's lectures that
entertains me, and his method of announcing each of
Miss Farr's selections as the lady glided in and out, attired
in Greek flowing robes, had a touch of comedy in it that
amused me internally at all events. Visible laughter would
have been a sacrilege!

Though small, the audience had many interesting peo-
ple in its composition—Edward Martyn, Standish
O'Grady, Maud Gonne, Mrs. Scott Furnell, Dr. Douglas
Hyde, Edith Oldham, etc.

Saturday, December 6.   Again I found myself at the
Camden Street "Theatre," [2] piercing cold and all as the
night was and despite the hall being so villainously cold
and draughty—as I knew it would be by the experience of
Thursday last. But, truth to tell, the temptation of seeing
again real live plays lovingly interpreted by players with
their soul in their work was too strong for me to resist.
. . . In fact, the acting all-round of this little company is
so effective and unconventionally realistic, as to be start-
ling in result. The effects are all gained without the
slightest effort at "point making," and the amount of
business introduced unaccompanied by speech is very
great and always effective. This habit, perhaps, at times
makes the progress appear slow, but the general result
makes for completeness of effect and illusion, so that each
little piece becomes a perfect miniature of unblemished
realisation of the moving scenes enacted therein.

1903

Saturday, March 14. The members of the Irish National Theatre Company have reason to be proud over the success attending their performance in the Molesworth Hall, where W. B. Yeats's one-act morality play, *The Hour Glass*, and Lady Gregory's one-act play, *Twenty-Five*, were performed for the first time on any stage.

The hall was thronged with an audience who listened enthralled to the clearly spoken and simply set representation of *The Hour Glass*—a simple legend beautifully and poetically expressed by our own particular mystic poet, the raven-locked W. B. Yeats. . . . It is wonderful the effect this little allegorical play had on the listeners, and the gentleman beside me inquired, "if a white flame really did appear at the end? For," he assured me, "I saw one. My imagination was so worked up by what had gone before!" This was cheating the imagination into belief with a vengeance, and was a great tribute alike to the power of the poet and the players.

The stage setting was simplicity itself—a background of green unrelieved by any colour with entrances of the same shade; a rude desk with a ponderous tome thereon, a bell pull (that refused to convey its message to the bell on occasion when pulled), and a tiny bracket supporting an hour glass were all the properties, while the costumes of the players were composed of materials that worked in harmony with the said background—"The Angel" and "The Fool" alone being clad in tints with a little warmth in them. The effect of this scheme, in such a piece, I think, heightened the effect and enchained the interest. . . . The result was profoundly impressive!

The acting was in keeping with the subject. Mr. J. Dudley Digges, if one forgot his over-facial expression (he looked like "Richard III" during most of the time) ably and powerfully enacted the role of "The Wise Man." He spoke well and acted finely for the most part. Miss Mary Walker [Miss Maire nic Shiubhlaigh] impersonated "The Angel" in a way that Dante Gabriel Rossetti or Burne-Jones would have loved to limn. Her pose as she stood immoveable at the door was very beautiful and quite after the pre-Raphaelite manner of her measured delivery, most telling and effective. No member of the company has improved so much since I first heard her last year in *Deirdre* at St. Teresa's Hall as the heroine's foster-mother. She seems to me to be a most earnest student and enters the spirit of each part she plays. Enthusiasm and earnestness are bound to come out on top in the end. Mr. F. J. Fay's conception of "The Fool" was A-1, and he scored a big success in the part as the play proceeded. He is another enthusiast who is reaching the top of his ambition also by legitimate hard work. . . .

The homely nature of Lady Gregory's play of *Twenty-Five* was in great contrast to *The Hour Glass*, but the vital incident—the game of cards—scarcely proved convincing. It is hard to imagine a man who is being turned out of his home, sitting calmly down to play at cards for such high stakes as those put down in this play, and taking the winning of such large amounts in such a matter of fact way. This is the weak point in the piece, and, occurring where it should be the strongest, it militated greatly against the complete success of the clever little work. The dialogue is very natural right through, and the characters cleverly suggested. . . .

The setting of the homely cottage scene was completely spoiled for me by the inappropriate side wing that did duty for a screen outside the cottage door, especially as the said cottage door remained open during most of the

piece. Little things—trifles light as air—often completely
mar the illusion of a stage play, no matter what may be
said to the contrary! . . .

By the way, the introduction of presenting flowers to
the performers by the management might be omitted
with advantage, especially as it savours too much of the
commercial theatre, which the promotors of the company
pretend so much to despise. It is a silly habit at best and is
a compliment to no one.

Mr. W. B. Yeats was announced to lecture on "The
Reform of the Theatre" between the two plays, and duly
came forward evidently to do so. In the lower portion of
an unpainted deal dresser could dimly be observed what
purported to be the model of a stage, which after the
lecturer's opening remark was never referred to, strange to
say, but instead of alluding to it he meandered on making
many statements that no sane playgoer could agree with
. . . and trying to prove that acting should be something
other than acting and that stage plays should be something quite different also—in fact, that nothing on the
stage should be as it is. He then went on to puff his own
wares, and said that "those who could not write in Gaelic
should give us of their best in whatever language they
could." Just then a loud crash was heard behind, and the
speaker added that "the properties said 'hear, hear!' to
that." Which showed that poets are not quite devoid of
humour.

Mr. Yeats said little, to my mind, of any value, and
retired dreamily without reference to the little stage
perched on the impromptu table awaiting the explaining
that never came. Shortly after, Mr. Yeats mingled among
the audience, and evidently someone asked him "What
about the model?" for he got on the platform again and
apologised for his completely forgetting to tell them about
his little stage. "But dreamers must be forgiven a little
thing like that!" And so the audience passed it off with a
laugh and settled down to witness Lady Gregory's play.

I think the evening was the turning point in the career
of the Irish National Theatre Company, and has placed

them on the wave of success. May the tide be taken at the flood is my wish! [1]

Friday, July 3.   Attended a rehearsal at Camden Street "Theatre" where I saw Mr. W. Fay put the company through W. B. Yeats's poetic and decorative poem, *The Shadowy Waters*. Mr. Frank Fay and Miss Walker chant musically, but some of the others make lame attempts to sing their lines beautifully. The artificial method adopted by these players in poetic plays is very trying if not properly mastered, and much resembles the sing-song droning of poor preachers. The effect produced is often laughable on this account.

Seeing it merely in rehearsal, I should say *The Shadowy Waters* is more a beautiful mystic poem than an actable play. The final love scene, however, is full of charm, and Frank Fay and Miss Walker struck me as having caught the spirit of the poet's dream perfectly, and even without a background of "dressers," boxes, and all sorts of odds and ends made me forget the incongruous surroundings and listen enraptured to their love duet so musically crooned. Anyone who would be an actor, and failed after the careful and painstaking instruction of Mr. W. G. Fay must be a duffer, indeed!

Friday, August 21.   . . . Visited the Camden Street "Theatre" where I saw Mr. Synge's curious play, *In the Shadow of the Glen*, rehearsed, and also W. B. Yeats's new play in verse, entitled *Seanchan*.[2] I followed the first play with much interest, but as a carpenter was busy sawing, sandpapering, and hammering some "cages" for lights, etc., all the while just behind me, I heard little of the latter work. It certainly was rehearsing under difficulties. . . .

I had a long chat with W. G. Fay re a "tin house" for a home for Irish drama and the probable cost of same. I told him I did not think such a structure as he described could be procured under £250 or thereabouts, and he suggested that some old Methodists' Hall might be picked up cheap on the other side and re-erected here. He also told me he intended making an offer of £50 per annum for three nights a week for the Molesworth Hall with the intention of giving three performances a month—these during the season. He had been speaking to the authorities re the Hall per night, and they told him they would let him have the use of it per night for £1.2.6, if he would guarantee not to play elsewhere during the season. £1.10.0 is the usual charged price per night for the hall. The Camden Street Hall was found impossible for public displays. It is right enough for rehearsing in. £20 a year is the rent they pay for it. It is strange that in a city like Dublin there is no public hall suitable for amateur theatricals.

Friday, September 4.   Attended a rehearsal at the Camden Street "Theatre" where I heard W. B. Yeats's new poetic conceit in dramatic form, *Seanchan*, gone through, and also the weird, humourous, and grimly unconventional little piece, *In the Glen*, in which an old man pretends he is dead in order to spy on his somewhat frivolous young wife's suspected goings-on with a young neighbour. . . . How an audience will receive it I am curious to see, for, as you can well observe, the tone of it is not quite Irish in sentiment at all events, and the wind-up strange, to say the least of it. The dialogue is capital and most amusing in parts. . . .

Seanchan is one of those poetic fancies of Yeats which the National Theatre knows how to interpret so lovingly and poetically. Mr. Frank Fay, as the discarded poet who resolves to starve himself to death on the doorstep of his late master, speaks Yeats's verse extremely musically, and enters the spirit of the poet's thoughts with inspired effectiveness. Mr. W. G. Fay's attempts at the sing-song chanting as "The Mayor" were very crude to my mind, and much resembled the sounds produced by an infant class repeating lessons aloud. He is a born impersonator of tramps and quick-witted beggars. Poetic drama is out of his line. The others are shaping well in their respective roles.

Jack B. Yeats, W. B.'s artist brother, was present at this rehearsal; so was the carpenter with his busy saw and plane.

Thursday, October 8. The Molesworth Hall was crowded to the doors to sample the wares provided by the National Theatre Society for the opening night of the season. Everybody that is anybody in artistic or literary Ireland was there, and W. B. Yeats's new one-act play in verse, *The King's Threshold,* was proved a thing of exceptional beauty to the eye and ear. The chief role, that of the banished poet, "Seanchan," was marvellously well played by F. J. Fay, whose conception and acting of the difficult part were both well nigh perfect. Truly he lent the beauty of the voice to the poet's words; and his delivery of the final speeches was as musical as the songs of birds, and fascinated the senses quite in the same indescribable manner. . . . All this may seem extravagant praise to only an amateur, but let any real judge of the beautiful and true in dramatic art see Mr. Fay play this part and truthfully say otherwise, and I'll give way to his opinion, but not till then. . . .

This was the most ambitious play as yet attempted by the Society—no fewer than seventeen characters were in the cast—and, therefore, all the more praise is due to the admirable manner in which it was carried through to a genuinely successful issue. The grouping, considering the limited space at command, was remarkably effective, and the stage lighting very successful. No footlights were used, but two limelights—one at either side of the stage—and one from the back of the hall, were substituted. By the way, the illumination of the stage before the curtains were drawn aside has a funny effect, as the curtains become transparent under the strong light, and the preparations for the coming scene become visible to those in front. Great laughter was caused when Mr. Roberts as "Dan Burke," the supposed dead man in *The Shadow of the Glen,* was seen getting into bed and arranging his clothes about ere the play commenced.

Mr. J. M. Synge's play in one act, *In the Shadow of the Glen*, purporting to be a true transcript from the peasant life in County Wicklow, met with a mixed reception. The nature of the plot would warrant this result despite the cleverness of the dialogue and the conciseness of the construction. . . . Now this subject, no matter how literary-clad, could never pass with an Irish audience as a "bit of real Irish life," and, though most present applauded the clever interpreters of the literary and dramatic merits of the play, they had little to say in favour of the matter of the story contained therein. The author got a call at the end. . . .

Mr. W. B. Yeats was called after both his plays, and held forth at the end of *Cathleen ni Houlihan* in his usual thumpty-thigh, monotonous, affected, preachy style, and ended by making a fool of himself in "going" for an article that appeared in this morning's *Independent*. He generally makes a mess of it when he orates. Kind friends ought to advise him to hold his tongue.

Friday, October 9.   I am delighted to be able to record that all the minor drawbacks, such as the transparent curtains, W. B. Yeats's oratory, and street noises that slightly marred the perfect enjoyment of the opening night of the National Literary Theatre, were absent at to-night's show, and everything went as merry as the proverbial marriage bell, so that the audience was allowed to enjoy undisturbed each of the three plays presented. And that they did right royally, to judge by their rapt attention to each while in progress, and their hearty bursts of approval in conclusion. . . .

Anything more natural than some of the peasant scenes enacted by these plays I have never seen. Take, for instance, Miss Sara Allgood's realising of "Bridget Gillan" in *Cathleen ni Houlihan*. She was the good-hearted, kindly, motherly housewife in her every turn, and her love for her big, strong, manly boy, "Michael," was tenderly and beautiful expressed. . . . And her eyes lit up with the true love-light of motherly idolatry as she looked at her big-framed boy, and he stood before her, his head to one side half bashful-like, beaming with delight at his mother's praise. It was a beautiful moment in the play, exquisitely interpreted. It is such acting as this that inspires one to look on life, not as a thing of gloom, but joy-laden to the core if we care to see it so.

The industrious way she knitted as the strange old woman rambled on at the fireside, and the natural way she now and again questioned her husband, without allowing her busy fingers to cease for an instant, ceased to be acting and became nature. But I could enumerate delicate little bits of "nature's own image" all through her simple and eminently homely portrait of this true-hearted peasant mother that would fill pages; suffice it to say that she gave one the idea that she was not acting at all. . . .

The humours of the strange little comedy, *In the Shadow of the Glen*, by J. M. Synge were thoroughly appreciated and won nothing but applause. . . . After all, there is very little harm in this strangely conceived domestic scene set in peculiarly real, Irish everyday talk. . . .

Mr. W. B. Yeats was like a restless spirit of another world, wandering hither and thither in the gloom, now popping his head out from behind the curtains, and anon taking short spurts up and down the centre passage in the hall, ever restless, ever in evidence—but he did not make a speech so I forgive him.

Wednesday, November 11.   . . . A chat on the drama mostly occupied the evening at Cousins's, where Mr. and Mrs. W. J. Lawrence, Mr. and Miss Colum, Mr. George Nesbit, Mrs. and Miss Esposito, Miss Gillespie, and Mr. Conway were present. I asked Mr. Colum if they had found the missing second act of *Broken Soil* at Camden Street yet, and he told me I had been sitting on it all the time, to which I replied that it was not my custom to sit on a play until I had first seen it acted.

Friday, November 13.   Saw *The Hour Glass* and *Broken Soil* being rehearsed at Camden Street, where the comfort of a gas stove had been introduced since my last visit, and tea was served during the evening in quite a Bohemian way that reminded me forceably of the National Literary Society in the old days when the fifth story of a house in College Green was its home. The stove gave quite a homely air to the chaos around. For truly the Camden Street "Theatre" is a chaos with properties, scenery, etc., strewn higgledy-piggledy fashion over the place. The rehearsal of *The Hour Glass* went very well, but that of *Broken Soil* is yet very raggedy and wants pulling together badly especially in the last act. I was introduced to Mr. Synge, the author of *In the Shadow of the Glen*, and had a long chat with him. He is of opinion that the introduction of the "Mayor" etc. (the comic relief) in *On the King's Threshold* is a mistake, and arrests the interest: in which opinion I am inclined to agree with him. The night turned out awfully wet, but I was fortunate in getting home between two great big showers.

Friday, November 20.   . . . If care on the part of W. G. Fay will command a successful representation, then its success is secured, for no amount of pains is spared by him in making the stage players as perfect as possible in every detail. Making the actors repeat over and over again those lines which did not sound quite right on his ear, until he was thoroughly satisfied with every little intonation and shade of inflection. It is by such loving care and attention to details that finish and art become apparent in all that the Irish National Theatre Company undertake to present to the public, so that if the play on occasion fails to please everyone, the interpretation seldom if ever leaves anything to cavil at. . . .

They are more than amateurs, these players, for they work with the object of doing something that will be a credit to their native land and make people be prouder than ever of being of Irish birth. Each rehearsal I attend astonishes me more and more, and makes me marvel how all these young people, night after night, go there to rehearse after their hard day's work, instead of gadding about as most young people usually do. And the rehearsing is not all pleasure, I can assure you, but as it is a labour of love with them its labourious side is minimised almost to vanishing point. Labour is very light when liking accompanies it. Such is the case in an eminent degree with the Camden Street "Theatre" folk!

Thursday, December 3.   Again the performance of the Irish National Theatre Society attracted a very distinguished and highly interested gathering to the Molesworth Hall to renew the acquaintance of W. B. Yeats's beautifully expressed and interesting miniature morality play, *The Hour Glass*, and his merry farce, *A Pot of Broth*, and to see for the first time on any stage Padraic MacCormac Colum's play in three short acts, entitled *Broken Soil*. All three were followed with intense interest.

Mr. Colum has the knack of the dramatist, and though his play is more a series of slices from peasant life than drama in the ordinary sense of the word, the piece gripped the interest and held it right away to the end. The characters—five in number—are all clearly drawn, and the dialogue natural and eloquent. . . . The piece is very slender in plot, but strong in character, and quite Irish in sentiment.

It was admirably interpreted. F. J. Fay as the boastful old fiddler, whose pride in his fiddling almost blotted out his love for his child, looked and acted the part to perfection. Old "Con Hourican" with his fiddle under his coat might have stepped in off the road in any country town in Ireland, as presented by this clever actor. It was a character study of real merit. Miss Maire nic Shiubhlaigh, as his daughter "Maire," played with a pathos and sense of light and shade of unaffected emotionalism that touched the heart and made her study of this difficult character intensely interesting as well as dramatically effective. Her description of her parting with the neighbours in the last act was as naturally pathetic as anything could well be and touched the sympathetic chord in all breasts, to judge by the silence of dread that held the house. There was a lot of genuine human nature in her part, and the actress conveyed every grain of it in her unaffected, intensely womanly enactment of the part. She has the temperament of an artist and a fascinating personality that pervades all her stage work. . . .

The author was loudly called for at the end, and on complying with these requests surprised the audience by his extremely youthful appearance. Where he got his insight into the working of the human mind, displayed in *Broken Soil*, is beyond my comprehension. The play was extremely well received.

1904

Friday, January 7.   Despite a bad cold I attended a rehearsal of the I.N.T.S. at Camden Street. . . . Lady Gregory's *Twenty-Five* has been entirely re-written, and the sum played for is now reduced to £50 from £100; the play is shortened without, I fear, being made any more convincing than originally. . . . Mr. Synge was there, and I had a long chat with him. W. G. Fay was speaking to me quite seriously about getting a playhouse for the Company that would be their very own. He hinted that £5000 would be forthcoming if necessary.[1]

Thursday, January 14.   The National Theatre Society produced W. B. Yeats's weird, puzzling, melancholy, and depressingly gloomy dramatic poem, *The Shadowy Waters*, and the piece fairly mystified the audience by the uncanny monotony of its strange incomprehensibleness, until a peculiar, not wholly disagreeable dreariness filled the minds of all who listened to the strange music of the chanted words. What it was all about was hard to say, but the atmosphere of the poet was caught by the interpreters in a way that compelled attention, despite the depression conjured up by the poet's weird imaginings. . . . Had this dramatic poem any real dramatic life in it, it must have discovered itself under the living treatment given it by the players. That it possessed any would be drawing the long, long bow of fact to assert; but personally I am very pleased to have witnessed the experiment of presenting it

on the stage. It was strangely tiresome but very beautiful
and lovely all the same.

Friday, January 15.   F. J. Fay did not quite look the
ideal lover as "Forgael," [2] nor did he lend variety enough
to his delivery I thought. The headdress of "Dectora"
made her tower above him, and in the love duet their long
and short forms jarred a little on the poetic-steeped imagi-
nations of the audience. . . .

I again witnessed . . . *The Townland of Tamney*
(Seumas MacManus) which was so gagged and stretched
and over-done by business as to become quite tedious. Mr.
Synge remarked to me that if it were to be played another
night, it might last a month, the players were taking such
liberties with the text, and I agreed with him.

Saturday, January 16.   For the third and last time I
witnessed *The Shadowy Waters* and felt quite sad that
such a beautiful work of art should have failed owing to
the dense obscurity of the text. For I felt it was really a
beautiful thing that was thus spoiled, and the pity of its
failure oppressed me. Many present laughed outright at
the wealth of obscure imagery the characters indulged in,
as they could not make head or tail out of it. The jujube
speech, as I call the one in which mention is made of
"chrysolite, ruby" etc., caused much mirth, as did also
"Dectora's" calling "Forgael" her "little silver fish." Oh,
the pity of it, that such a precious thing should thus leave
itself open to ridicule!

Thursday, February 4.   Mr. F. J. Fay returned me my
paper on the Irish National Theatre Society, which I lent
him on last Sunday, with a letter full of interesting matter
by post. The letter is worth transcribing, so here goes.

> *Dear Mr. Holloway,*
> I return your paper which I have read with
> much interest. I am sorry you have not dealt with our
> later plays, but one can't do everything and doubtless a
> paper must be read within a limited time. If I might

make a suggestion it would be that you might mention that the brother was for a time on the professional stage. I think it gives people more confidence in an enterprise such as ours to know that the man at the helm knows his business. There is a very interesting contrast that could be made just now. Last year Stephen Gwynn wrote about "An Uncommercial Theatre" in the *Fortnightly* in which our work is described as the beginning of a National Theatre for Ireland. Archer's article on "Ibsen's Apprenticeship" in last month's *Fortnightly* describes the rise of the Norwegian National Theatre which is now an accomplished fact. It is very kind of you to take such an amount of trouble and the more friends the Society has, the greater the chance of its developing into something permanent. It is, as you know, curiously difficult to arouse Dubliners out of their lethargy to take a serious interest in the Arts. When Ole Bull was starting the Norwegian National Theatre in Bergen fifty years ago, the people were enthusiastic. Here the enthusiasts are in the minority, but you are helping to spread the light. The principal difficulty that I see ahead is to get strong modern plays and if possible plenty of comedy. The difficulty is all the more pronounced because of Shakespeare worship. People who write plays stick to old methods instead of taking to Ibsen and from him learning to express themselves in an up-to-date form. When it is not Shakespeare who is hurled at our heads, it is Boucicault who was a master of commonplace stagecraft with nothing to say. What we want is plays by people who have something to say in dramatic form. By the way, I don't know whether you know that only for the brother, *The Twisting of the Rope* could not have been given. He rehearsed and produced it at the Gaiety.

> *Yours sincerely,*
> *F. J. Fay*

Thursday, February 25.   Before a very distinguished audience the National Theatre Society presented J. M.

Synge's intensely sad sketch of fisher-life on an island off the West coast of Ireland, entitled *Riders to the Sea*, for the first time on any stage,[3] and revived George Russell's sadly-sweet telling of the old and ancient tragic love tale of "Deirdre" and "Naisi" . . . in the Molesworth Hall. . . .

Mr. Synge has given us an intensely sad—almost weirdly so—picture of the lives of the humble dwellers on an isle of the West . . . and, as it was interpreted with rare naturalness and sincerity, it held the interest of the audience in a marvellous way. This was a triumph of art, for the players as well as the dramatist, as the subject was one that the slightest error of judgment would have set the audience in a titter. But as the illusion was complete, no titter came, and a profound impression was created instead. The entrance of the keeners just a few moments too early was nearly proving fatal to the solemnity of the situation, but luckily did not. . . .

Miss Sara Allgood as "Cathleen" acted with a simplicity and sincerity that resembled nature so closely that it ceased to be acting to those who looked on, and Miss Vera Esposito made a very successful debut as "Nora," her sister, and played quite pathetically and unaffectedly, particularly in the final episodes of the play. Miss Honor Lavelle as the half-demented, wholly-distracted old "Maurya" gave an uncanny rendering of the part, much suggestive of "Cathleen ni Houlihan," and was most impressive in the scene with her dead son. . . . The author was called at the end and very heartily applauded.

Friday, February 26.   I have come to the conclusion that a more gruesome and harrowing play than *Riders to the Sea* has seldom, if ever, been staged before. The thoroughly in-earnest playing of the company made the terribly depressing wake episode so realistic and weirdly doleful that some of the audience could not stand the painful horror of the scene, and had to leave the hall during its progress. . . . The audience was so deeply moved by the tragic gloom of the terrible scene on which the curtains close in, that it could not applaud.

Tuesday, March 1.

> 12 ORMOND ROAD
> RATHMINES, DUBLIN
> 1 *March,* 1904

Dear Mr. Holloway,

Thanks for note and slip re *Dramatic Mirror.*
. . . I wish you could have analysed what disappointed
you in *Deirdre.* While I quite share your view as to
Digges (although I always thought him too sombre in
the first act), the only thing I ever admired in Miss
Quinn's "Deirdre" was the way in which her brains
made up for the lack of any depth of emotion. If, as I
have no doubt, the words you use about Miss Walker's
"Deirdre" accurately describe the impression it left on
you (and you know it is difficult to get one's real
impression accurately on paper), then I think you have
paid her a great compliment. But, all the same I was
not quite satisfied with her show of the part though
Russell was enthusiastic. I thought her too grave in the
first act. But she was very nervous and at present is not
in the best of health, all of which you know tells
against one in acting. Besides Kelly gave her no help in
the first act. He will insist on *acting,* instead of being,
in every part he plays outside of peasant plays and even
in them sometimes. If you have time, perhaps you
would write to me at length about *Deirdre.*

I am so glad you gave Miss Allgood a notice. I
thought her admirable and also Miss Esposito. The
fact is Miss Walker, Miss Garvey, Miss Allgood, and
Miss Esposito beat the men hollow. When Gwynn
wrote about us in the *Fortnightly,* he said the reverse
was the case, and he was right, but he would not be
right now. I look forward with hope to the future with
four girls like these in the company.

What is your opinion as to the smallness of our
audiences? Is it the sadness of the plays? Or are they
getting tired of always seeing the same people? Next
year I hope we shall have a historical play or two and
perhaps more comedy, and Synge's next two plays will

be devoid of corpses. When I went out on Sunday to see what prevented him from being present on Friday and Saturday nights, I found that he was in bed with a swollen face. What a time he must have put in with anxiety. I am glad to say that *Riders to the Sea*, despite its sadness, has pleased many. I think it is a masterpiece. And after all, just at present when people shirk facing the facts and sorrow of life and are always longing for the laugh that only hardens the heart, it is good that we should put on plays of this kind. Of course, I have every sympathy with the desire for laughter, if it is kindly, but there is so much laughter around that is hard and cynical and cowardly, that I am not sorry we do pieces like *Riders to the Sea*. The only difficulty is that people who drop in to see us for the first time may be frightened away. But I am hoping that next season will see us giving more robust work; that is, of course, provided it is to be had; but I am bound to think that so long as Ireland is in her present depressed state, her drama will *inevitably* mirror that state.

I hope Mrs. Holloway is quite recovered. Please remember me to her.

Yours sincerely,
F. J. Fay

Thursday, March 24. Having first seen the members of the Irish National Theatre Society off from Westland Row Railway Station to London where they are billed to appear at the Royalty Theatre on Saturday, March 26th (matinee and evening) in *The King's Threshold, A Pot of Broth, In the Shadow of the Glen, Broken Soil,* and *Riders to the Sea,* I went on to a meeting of the Literary, Dramatic and Musical Society at the XL Cafe, Grafton Street, parting with young Colum and a Miss O'Neill at the corner of Clare Street; they had also been to see the company off like myself. The two Fays, Kelly, Roberts, Ryan, Starkey, Wright, Misses Allgood, Walker, Garvey, and Annesley, and Mr. Walker formed the happy family party; the remainder of the company had gone over by the morning boat. They look upon me as their "Mascot" as I wished them every success on departing last year, and they wished me to do so again this year.

Wednesday, April 6.   Strolled over to Camden Street and found the company assembled there to hold a committee meeting re the expulsion of a member who had turned traitor to the company by joining those who were going to St. Louis to produce Irish plays at the Exhibition. I could see excitement ran high, and W. J. Fay was especially sore over the matter, seeing that Miss Horniman was coming over from England on Friday next to sign the contract to take over the Hibernian Theatre of Varieties, Abbey Street, and turn it into a first class little theatre for them at her own expense. As he says himself, "It is too bad, after all our trouble, that such a thing should have occurred at such an important time."

Mr. P. J. Kelly was the culprit whose firing out held the attention of the meeting. Seeing how the land lay, I immediately withdrew. The members present at the time I left were Messrs. G. Russell, P. Colum, Starkey, G. Roberts, Walker, Wright, Kelly, Ryan, W. G. and F. J. Fay, and Misses Walker, Allgood, and Garvey.

I see by the papers that Mr. Dudley Digges, Miss Maire Quinn, Miss Violet Mervyn are included in the company bound for St. Louis, and *Deirdre* and *Cathleen ni Houlihan* are chief among the plays to be performed. By the way, Miss Violet Mervyn was the original "Deirdre" when the second act was first tried in the back garden of Mr. George Coffey's house, Lower Leeson Street.[4]

Sunday, April 10.   Met Miss Horniman by appointment at her hotel (The Standard, Harcourt Street) and had a chat about turning the Mechanics' Institute and the Dublin City Morgue into a theatre chiefly for the Irish National Theatre Society.

Monday, April 11.   Met Miss Horniman and went through the Morgue with her, but the irate manager in

possession of the Mechanics' Institute Theatre indig-
nantly refused us permission to enter. Made appointment
to return at 3:30 o'clock in the hopes of gaining an
entrance, which we did. Mr. W. B. Yeats came with Miss
Horniman, and I was introduced to the poet who said he
had often heard of me. As we went over the building and
had just reached the stage, the manager came in by the
door at the back of the stage, and measuring us with a
withering look, exclaimed, "You've got a cheek!" And he
ordered us out without further ado, which we accomplished without delay amid a volley of "Land grabbers!"
etc., at them, and a wink of the eye, by way of a stage
aside, to me. His parting shot—"May you and your morgue have luck!"—was distinctly droll. I am just thinking
how I can face him to survey the place to-morrow or the
next day. Miss Horniman and Mr. Yeats then parted with
me to go into the Hibernian Academy.

Friday, April 15.   Called up with rough sketch plan of
the Abbey Street Theatre [The Mechanics] to Camden
Street "Theatre" to have a chat over it with Mr. W. G.
Fay. Found W. B. Yeats, Stephen Gwynn, and George
Russell present. The former conducted a rehearsal of *The
King's Threshold*. The new "King" was Mr. Starkey
(Seumas O'Sullivan). The great Yeats, by his interruptions every minute, proved himself an impossible man to
rehearse before, and if I were Starkey I would have been
inclined to tell him to go to the "old boy" more than
once.

Monday, April 18.   By luck or by accident, Edward
Martyn once wrote an interesting, actable Irish play, *The
Heather Field*, but try as he will he has never done
anything for the stage worth a brass farthing since, though
he has made two or three tries. His four-act play, *An
Enchanted Sea*, produced for the first time on any stage
by the Player's Club [5] to-night, under the auspices of the
N.L.S. at the Antient Concert Rooms, proved a dreary,
monotonous play full of daft ideas of the most improba-

ble kind. Many a "back drawing-room theatre" would disown such crude acting as the Player's Club put into this piece of Martyn's; but I doubt very much if its fate would have been otherwise were the cast filled by first-class professionals. W. G. Fay put it on for rehearsal at the Irish National Theatre Society and finding it impossible, withdrew it after the second rehearsal. It showed his good sense. Mr. Martyn, however, thought otherwise with the result above suggested.

Wednesday, June 8.   Dropped in for a chat at Cousins' where I stayed for a couple of hours. You are always sure to find some interesting people there. . . . Miss Cousins played a couple of beautiful pieces beautifully, and Mr. Joyce—a mysterious kind of youth with weird penetrating eyes (which he frequently shades with his hands) and a half-bashful, far-away, wistful expression on his face—sang some dainty ballads most artistically and pleasingly, some to his own accompaniment. As he sings, he sways his head from side to side to add to the soulfulness of his rendering. He is a strange boy; I cannot fathom him.

Friday, June 10.   Found a goodly gathering at the Camden Street "Theatre" where I saw *In the Shadow of the Glen* and *Riders to the Sea* rehearsed under the direction of W. Fay. Mr. Synge was present, and is said to have just completed a three-act play for the Society. Mr. Joyce also put in an appearance.

Friday, June 17.   I happened in on a big event at the Camden Street "Theatre" to-night. I allude to the reading of J. M. Synge's new three-act play, *The Well of the Saints* before the members. Mr. Frank Fay undertook the reading which lasted fully an hour and a half, and he read from the typewritten Ms. clearly and well. The members grouped round anyhow and listened with breathless attention the while the reader read. Mrs. and Miss Esposito sat on a long seat facing the stove, and Mr. W. G. Fay sat on the end of the same seat facing the reader with his arms over the back of the seat. Mr. Starkey, seated on a kingly throne, rested his arm on one of its [arms], while Miss Walker was contented with a "creepy" three-legged stool hard by, and on a long bench to the left of the reader and behind him sat in a row, à la schoolboys at lessons, Messrs. Roberts, Walker, Wright, George Russell, and the author nearest the door. Mr. Frank Fay sat by a table on the end of a short bench, I making balance at the other end.

Can't you fancy the scene in the midst of all the lumber of stage properties, etc., and a flickering gas pendant casting fantastic shadows around, as each sat as mute as a mouse, with only the voice of Frank Fay to break the silence? Occasionally a laugh broke out as something especially daring was given utterance to, and the author's voice chipped in with an elucidation of a knotty point in the dialogue here and there.

The play proved somewhat of an unpleasant surprise, as the subject chosen was scarcely a happy one, and the working out rather irreverent on the whole. Making a jeer at religion and a mock at chastity may be good fun, but it won't do for Irish drama. If there are two things ingrained in the Irish character above all else, they are their respect for all pertaining to their religious belief and their love of chastity, and these are the very subjects Mr. Synge has chosen to exercise his wit upon. . . .

Much of Mr. Synge's writing in this too long drawn out play is very coarsely and bluntly put, while the way the Holy Name is used frequently is almost blasphemous to my way of thinking. Of course, much of it is very clever and all that, but was it worth-while wasting so much genuine talent on such unpleasant matter? . . . To call it Irish is distinctly a libel on our race and country. Strange, before the reading of the play I had a long chat with Mr. Synge re F. H. O'Donnell's pamphlet amongst other things, and mentioned that very rightly Yeats had been attacked for his treatment of priests, the Catholic religion, and Irish peasants; and I expressed my condemnation of people meddling with subjects they knew little about—to afterwards find I had been speaking to one who had gone and done likewise in his latest dramatic effort. It was 11 o'clock when Mr. Fay concluded his reading, so I left hurriedly not having expressed an opinion to anyone — only to Mrs. and Miss Esposito who were home part of the way with me.

Saturday, August 20.   Mr. Campbell, K.C. (Solicitor-General) gave judgment on the application for patents by Miss A. E. F. Horniman on behalf of the Irish National Theatre Society in respect to the hall attached to the Mechanics' Institute.[6] . . . The following are the terms of the patent for the Irish National Theatre Society.

> The patent shall only empower the patentee to exhibit plays in the Irish and English languages, written by Irish writers on Irish subjects, or such dramatic works of foreign authors as would tend to interest the public in the higher works of dramatic art; all foregoing to be selected by the Irish National Theatre Society under the provisions of Part 6 of its rules now existing and subject to the restrictions therein contained, a clause to be inserted against the assignment of any person or persons other than the trustee for Miss Horniman, her executors or assigns, the patent to cease if the Irish National Theatre Society is dissolved. No enlargement of the theatre is to be made, so as to provide for a greater number of spectators than it is capable of holding at present. No excise license to be applied for or obtained.

Saturday, August 27.   In connection with the Irish Revival Industries Show being held this week in the Antient Concert Rooms a Concert was given to-night at which I was present. The attendance was good, but the management of the entertainment could not have been worse. . . . The substitute appointed as accompanist . . . was so incompetent that one of the vocalists, Mr. James A. Joyce,[7] had to sit down at the piano and accompany

himself in the song, "In Her Simplicity" from *Mignon*—
after she had made several unsuccessful attempts to strum
out the programmed item, "The Croppy Boy," over the
singer's name. . . . I do not yet give up hopes that some
day I may be present at a "grand concert" (Irish in
character) where things may go smoothly in their proper
order, the advertised time adhered to, the doors closed
during each item, and the audience conducting themselves with some semblance of good manners and not
demanding encores for every item or leaving noisily during
the items that do not please them.

Irish-Ireland audiences have little discrimination and
seldom display any artistic taste. A good shout is dearer to
them than all the artistic vocalism in the world, as witness
the enthusiastic reception of Mr. J. F. McCormack's vigorous rendering of "The Irish Emigrant" (a most crude
bit of abominable, inartistic vocalism to my mind). This
young vocalist is gifted by nature with a remarkably
strong, pleasing tenor voice, but as he has no idea how to
use it, nor a scrap of emotionalism in his rendering of any
ballad, the effect to me of his singing is very painful. But
who am I that I should object when large audiences go
wild with delight over his singing, and frequently double
encore his efforts, as they did to-night for his "robust"
version of "The Green Isle of Erin" and "Because I Love
Thee," giving as the third item "Annie Laurie." He also
sang "Believe Me" with all the vigour at his command. I
greatly fear his voice has been ruined past all redemption
by the blind folly of unthinking, popular audiences; and
what might have been a remarkable voice, if trained properly, will fizzle out into a cracked robust tenor of the pot-
house order of merit. . . .

Mr. James A. Joyce possesses a light tenor voice which
he is inclined to force on the high notes, and he sings with
artistic emotionalism. "Down by the Sally Gardens"
suited his method best of his selected items, and as an
encore he gave "My Love Was Born in the North Country"—a short and sweet item—tenderly. "In Her Simplicity" struck me as too high for him.

Wednesday, September 7.   Mr. Synge turned up at Camden Street to rehearse the second act of his play *The Well of the Saints*. He had been to Kerry since last I saw him and is going to the Aran Islands next week to spend a month there. The opening act of Lady Gregory's drama *Kincora* was gone through for the first time, the newcomers—Messrs. Butler, Justice, and Stuart—all having parts in it. It is likely to prove a very attractive dramatic work. Mr. George Russell also turned in, and when I asked him when his next drama would be ready, he replied that "There never will be a next." Another *Deirdre* would be a treat.

Monday, October 31.   Truly it was a strange coincidence that the merry little music-hall comedian Dan Leno should have shuffled off the mortal coil quite suddenly at his residence, Springfield, Clapham Park, from heart failure the same day that the Irish National Theatre Society held their first rehearsal on the stage of their new theatre in Abbey Street, where in the long ago Leno made his first separate appearance, when the hall was known as the Mechanics, and won his way into the favour of the Dublin public as an expert clog dancer. . . .

But to the rehearsal, which I hope is the start of a bright and glorious page in the history of drama in Dublin. A temporary supply of electric light had been got in during the day, and when I arrived at 8:20 I found most of the company had got there before me, and had wandered through the weird gloom of a candle-lighted vestibule, etc. The stage was the only place lighted by electricity. All seemed pleased with their new home, unfinished though it was and full of the debris of a building in the making. Lady Gregory and Mr. Quinn I found seated on the half-finished front pit seat, and W. B. Yeats wandering excitedly about among the planks and rubbish in momentary danger of coming a-cropper. Signor Esposito (to whom I was afterwards introduced) and Madam were also in front of the stage as I entered. I arranged with the Signor the position of the orchestra when necessary, and chatted with many of the company.

On Baile's Strand was gone through with the ever-restless W. B. Yeats at the helm, and I say without fear of contradiction that a more irritating play producer never directed a rehearsal. He's ever flitting about and interrupting the players in the middle of their speeches, showing them by illustration how he wishes it done, droningly reading the passage and that in monotonous preachy sing-song, or climbing up a ladder onto the stage and pacing the boards as he would have the players do. (I thought he would come to grief on the rickety ladder several times.) Anon he would rush on and erase or add a line or two to the text, but ever and always he was on the fidgets, and made each and all of the players inwardly pray backwards. Frank Fay, I thought, would explode with suppressed rage at his frequent interruptions during the final speeches he had to utter.

Mr. George Russell and Mr. J. M. Synge dropped in during the rehearsal of this piece, and Lady Gregory and Mr. Quinn changed their places to an old carpenter's bench, plaster laden, nearer the stage. A new comedy, *Spreading the News*, by Lady Gregory was afterwards read through under the direction of the dramatist, who was the very opposite to W. B. Yeats, in sitting quietly and giving directions in quiet, almost apologetic tones. I left at 10:30 with this piece in progress. *Kincora* is shelved for the time being to receive repairs. There is little likelihood of the theatre opening with it now.

Wednesday, November 16. I attended a rehearsal of the Irish National Theatre Company at the Abbey Theatre. The pieces selected for the opening performance were all gone through. A few minutes after eight o'clock found me a-tapping at the stage door in old Abbey Street for admittance, and on it being opened I stepped to the right and descending a few steps found myself on the stage. A fireproof curtain was up, and the auditorium looked dim and mysterious with its few temporary electric lights here and there, as electricians fixed the electroliers round the balcony. A temporary sky border of electric lights lit the stage, and the yet unutilised grille looked strange and weird with hangman-like ropes suspended ominously therefrom. The drum lofts looked busy with carpenters' work scattered about, and a beautiful, unfinished landscape hung suspended at the back of the stage, where the artist, Mr. Bryer, had left it on knocking off work. . . .

The fireproof curtain being lowered to shut out the sound of the workmen, and the stage cleared, Mr. W. G. Fay, the stage manager of the company, clapped his hands and exclaimed, "Now then!" And in a moment a rehearsal of *Cathleen ni Houlihan* was in progress, and Miss Allgood and Mr. W. G. Fay as "Bridget" and "Peter Gillan" hear the noise of the cheering, and Mr. Justice as "Patrick Gillan" goes to the window to investigate its cause. The piece progressed with many interruptions, and passages here and there were gone over again and again until the man at the helm . . . was satisfied.

Miss Mary Walker, the "Cathleen" of the coming revival of Yeats's popular play, just arrived in the nick of time to take up her part, and hastily taking off her hat drifted onto the stage as the strange old woman. . . . The sudden transformation from everyday manner into the weird, chanting personality of "Cathleen" was surprising. How Miss Walker as suddenly forgot herself and became the mimic role in a flash, to me, was almost incomprehensible. This young actress possesses just the temperament necessary to thoroughly realise such a part, and a big success is in store for her. . . . Mr. Frank Fay acted as prompter to this piece (he also looks after the elocutionary side of the actor's work on one or two evenings in the week).

No sooner had "Michael" followed "Cathleen," and "Patrick" declaimed that he had seen a young girl go down the path with the walk of a Queen, than "All ready for *On Baile's Strand!*" was called. . . . Mr. W. G. Fay during this rehearsal paced up and down in front of the performers close to the fireproof curtain as he puffed at his pipe fitfully and re-lighted it frequently, throwing the lighted matches away with a recklessness as to the consequences of where they would find haven. I felt quite nervous in watching him, I assure you. I hope the insurance company won't get to know of his habit. Every now and again he would pause in his walk and repeat the passage as he would like it said. This done to his satisfaction, he resumed his beat. . . .

Much time and great care and patience was bestowed on this poetic play of Yeats before the curtain was rung down—metaphorically speaking—and Lady Gregory's brand new farce *Spreading the News* was taken in hand. . . . The farce is amusing and is likely to prove interesting, as all taking part seem to enter into the spirit of the episodes, and Mr. W. G. Fay seemed in his element coaching them, breaking into little bits of exaggerated by-play and over-emphatic voice inflections in order to instill the true spirit and "go" of the thing into the company. One must over-emphasize in giving instructions, else youthful players will be inclined to under-act and let the piece down, so that the interest evaporates from an audience.

Thursday, November 24. An amusing incident—an echo of the past one might term it—occurred at the Abbey Theatre this afternoon during one of my professional visits. Hearing a ring at the stage door, I opened it as I was going out and found a man, accompanied by a little boy, there, who made this inquiry: "Is there an inquest going on here to-day?"

The inquiry took me aback at first, and then I explained to him that it was a theatre, not a dead house he was at, and he departed apologising. From this it would seem that its old fame clings to the transformed morgue still.

Thursday, December 8. All that is best in literary and artistic Dublin were present at Mr. George Moore's lecture on his "Personal Reminiscences of Modern Painters" at the Royal Hibernian Academy. Count Markievicz acted as Chairman and introduced the lecturer in French. The lecturer, surrounded as he was, by the fine collection of Modern Paintings, spoke most interestingly for fully an hour. His delivery is distinctly monotonous and rapid, as regards to rate of speed. He speaks in short sentences of some six words at a time without ever varying his inflections. The works of the French painter Manet seemed to be his pet hobby, and he almost raved over the unshaded arm of a lady in one of the artist's exhibits in the present exhibition, and over the feet of a little girl in another, and he plumped for French art, "in contrast with which the English Academy has fallen to the level of Madame Tussaud's." In the course of his remarks, he propounded many strange things such as "an artist should be almost unaware of any moral codes to succeed."

Mr. W. B. Yeats proposed the vote of thanks in his earnest, excitable way, and old Mr. Yeats was called upon to say something which he started doing hesitatingly in undertones until called upon by his son to speak up, and then he became eloquent on raising his voice. The vote was formally seconded and put to the meeting. Mr. Yeats in opening his remarks said that, "Mr. Moore and I are sometimes great friends and sometimes great enemies," and I may say myself I was astonished to see them on the same platform, because I thought they were at daggers drawn.

Friday, December 16.   On entering the stage door of the Abbey Theatre, I stepped down onto the stage and found it set for *On Baile's Strand* and with no one about —only the stage hands. The effect produced by the simple and novel setting, I thought, was very good and just the thing for rich costumed figures to disport themselves before.

Having viewed the scene from the front, I went up to the gentlemen's dressing room where I found all the actors in the confusion of dressing for their parts for the first time. The chaos of the whole thing was delightful to behold. I secured a corner out of the way and watched the transformation of the company into kings, warriors and beggars. One propped up a mirror against a barber's block as he built a whisker round his youthful face, transform-

ing it into an aged countenance of a king; another
wrestled with a tunic turning the wrong side forward;
while others amid a din of "Where's my wig?" or
"Where's my cloak?" or "Did anyone see my helmet?"
kept going hither and thither in the large dressing room
until things began to straighten themselves out and the
actors presented a truly strange sight in their gorgeous, if
strange, fantastical robes. Frequent tappings and inquiries
at the door during the enactment of this scene told that
the ladies in a neighbouring dressing room suffered the
same confusion. Such questions as, "Did you see the
Young King's cloaks?" etc., were frequently heard, on the
door being partly opened in answer to the gentle tapping
of Mrs. Esposito, who kindly acted as wardrobe mistress
to the company and played the part excellently.

The rehearsal proceeded smoothly, but many of the
costumes, especially those of the old kings and the long,
streaky hair worn by them, were found to border on the
grotesque or eccentric, and at the conclusion of the play
the entire company was recalled on the stage, and an
exciting and amusing exchange of difference of opinion
took place between author Yeats and designer Miss Horniman. He with his eye on the effect created as an author,
and she as the designer of the colour scheme of the
costumes. Yeats likened some of the kings to "extinguish-
ers," their robes were so long and sloped so from the
shoulders. Father Christmas was another of his compari-
sons. He wished the cloaks away, but the lady would have
none of his suggestions. Then commenced a lively scene
in which the actors played the part of lay figures, and
Yeats and Miss Horniman treated them as such in discussing the costumes. The red-robed kings were told to take
off their cloaks, which they did, and then the green-clad
ones followed. After much putting on and taking off, and
an abundance of plain speaking as to the figures or lack of
them among the players, a compromise was arrived at,
and the "grey-fur" on the green costumes was "made fly,"
and the red-clad kings were allowed to carry their cloaks
on their arms, though Miss Horniman was of opinion that

the red unrelieved, somewhat marred the colour scheme she had intended. . . . Candidly I thought some of the costumes trying, though all of them were exceedingly rich in material and archaeologically correct. "Hang archaeology!" said the great W. B. Yeats. "It's effect we want on the stage!" And that settled it!

After this review of the players and gentle "rift in the lute," we all retired to the dressing rooms where tea soothed ruffled feelings so that everything went smoothly with the rehearsal of *Spreading the News*. Mr. Frank Fay as the new magistrate cut a quaint figure in his "doublet and hose" of "Cuchullain." During this piece, Mr. J. B. Yeats sketched J. M. Synge in the dressing room. He sketched on the corner of a table, and Synge rested against the back of a chair. They chatted freely as the sketch progressed. After much chatting, "Home" suggested itself to all, and soon the company had dispersed, and the dress rehearsal had come to an end.

Thursday, December 27.   At the opening of the pretty little Abbey Theatre, the Messrs. Fay covered themselves with glory, both as the guiding spirits of the new theatre and as actors. The night was a memorable one, and the house was thronged and genuinely enthusiastic. The spirit of enthusiasm was in the air from the first, and everyone went away wishing for more. . . .

Two pieces were presented for the first time on any stage, and both proved successes. W. B. Yeats's legendary play, *On Baile's Strand*, . . . was most excellently played. The novel staging proved most effective; the figures of the players stood well out in relief against the amber coloured draperies of which the boxed-in set was composed. . . . A really fine poetic impersonation of "Cuchullain" was that of Frank J. Fay, the music of whose speech and the beauty of whose diction, together with the natural dramatic effectiveness of his acting, excited all to admiration. It was a performance any actor might be proud of, and one I shall long remember. . . .

Cathleen ni Houlihan which followed was exquisitely

enacted, and all present were thrilled by the weird beauty and intense pathos of Miss Maire nic Shiubhlaigh's embodiment of "Cathleen." Anything more strangely pathetic than her chanting as she leaves the cottage I have never heard. Her words sunk into one's very soul! A painful joy enveloped my senses and left me in an ecstasy of misery that was good to feel. Of all the "Cathleens" I have seen, this was the truest embodiment. The sorrows of centuries were on her brow and in her eye, and her words pierced the heart with grief at her woe! . . .

A merry, homely, little farce by Lady Gregory, *Spreading the News*, caught on at once. . . . Miss Allgood was admirably real. Her "giving-out-the-ay" on hearing of the news the neighbours were spreading about her "dacent quiet little man" was very convincingly conveyed, and as the dialogue was capitally true to life the effect was most amusing. Miss Allgood is an actress to her fingertips, and as "Mrs. Fallon" she reached a higher artistic level than heretofore even. . . .

All three plays were completely successful, and the audience dispersed delighted; and the opening night of the Abbey Theatre must be written down a great big success. Long life to it, and to the Society which gave it birth through the generous impulse of Miss Horniman!

Wednesday, December 28. Oh, what a falling off there was in the audience at the Abbey to-night. . . . Is it possible that there is not an audience with a love for the beautiful in Dublin sufficient to fill the little theatre for more than one night at a time?

. . . .

The opening of the Abbey Theatre was the most momentous event of the year in Dublin to my mind. History may come of it! Who can tell!

1905

Wednesday, January 18.   I saw *The Well of the Saints* rehearsed under the direction of the dramatist, without Miss Esposito being present to fill the important role of "Mary Doul." Lady Gregory came in when the second act was being gone through, having just arrived from Coole. She came up about her altered version of *Kincora* to see if it required further tinkering. She very kindly presented the Society with a huge barm-brack which she had brought from the country, and at the between-the-acts the amount that vanished showed how thoroughly her gift was appreciated. I sampled it and found it quite to my taste. She also got a number of kerchiefs at Athenry for the ladies to wear on their heads in Synge's play, which when tried on became them right well. . . .

I have written asking them to omit some of the expressions and soften down one or two of the situations, and got the reply that they intend to stick to their guns and speak the speeches as set down by the dramatist. . . . Maybe all will be well on the night, and time may tell me I have been unduly apprehensive over the piece. I hope so, for I have the welfare of the Irish theatre very much at heart.

Saturday, February 4.   As far as one could judge by applause, the first performance of J. M. Synge's three-act play, *The Well of the Saints*, at the Abbey Theatre was a success.

Tuesday, February 7.   Synge's play, *The Well of the Saints*, has failed to catch on at the Abbey Theatre as I always anticipated it would. No one, other than those connected with the theatre, has a good word to say for it, clever and all as it undoubtedly is, owing to its unsympathetic treatment and unnecessary loading with unpleasantly plain speech all through. Since I saw Synge's *In the Shadow of the Glen*, I always thought that Synge would be the rock on which the Society would come to grief, and that time has arrived I am sorry to say. Just think of it, when I arrived at the theatre sometime after the doors opened to see after the heating, on my way to the Orpheus Choral Society Concert, one solitary individual in the balcony was all the Dublin public that betrayed an anxiety to hear the play on its third representation. . . . On arriving at the Antient Concert Hall, I found the place full and my money refused, so I hastened back to the Abbey Theatre where I found some fifty people had come in in the meantime.

Saturday, February 11.   Probably the curtains have closed in on *The Well of the Saints*, Mr. Synge's harsh, irreverent, sensual representation of Irish peasant life, with its strange mixture of lyric and dirt, for the last time as far as Dublin is concerned . . . and I for one am not at all sorry. Only the inner circle gloried in its coarseness of language. The general public hearing the sort of piece it was remained elsewhere and showed their good sense in doing so. . . .

Mr. Synge has lived in Aran for some considerable time, and when asked by the leading comedian of the company [1] if he found the people down there like those he writes about, he answered, "No, I found them genial and loveable when amongst them, but when I write of them they turn out as you see!" That is to say that Mr. Synge converts them into creatures to suit his own warped, cynical bent of mind, and labels them Irish peasants to prove his generosity for the kindness shown him by the real article in the isles of the West. A nature soured by the world's neglect is a cruel foe to have, and I greatly fear such a one have the Irish in Mr. Synge. I have never witnessed a play that repelled me so much as this same *Well of the Saints* written by one who has as much sympathy for the humbler Irish and their Catholic faith as a Maxim gun with an Englishman at the side of it has for a lot of unarmed savages! It raised my gall every time I saw it.

Friday, March 24. The truth of the old saying "A thing of beauty is a joy forever" struck me forcibly on seeing a full dress rehearsal of *Kincora* at the Abbey Theatre to-night. The costumes and scenery harmonised like an exquisite piece of music. I heard Lady Gregory say with motherly pride that it was her son's part in the production that pleased her most, and I don't wonder at it. . . .

Mr. Yeats then told us a good story of George Moore, who was so annoyed by the repeated calls of an admirer of his work that he told the servant to say whenever the lady called again that he was in his bath. Next morning, while at breakfast, the lady called, as fresh as paint, and was told that he was in his bath. "Quite right," said Moore on hearing this. In the afternoon, the same person inquired again if he was in, and got the same answer from the maid: "He's in his bath." They don't speak now.

Wednesday, March 29. From the thinness of the audience at the Abbey Theatre, it is very evident that the general public has scarcely begun to nibble, much less bite with relish, at the wares presented by the Irish National Theatre Society. Even the tempting bite—an interesting historical drama written on purely Irish lines and laden with patriotic sentiment and served up most attractively— is failing to draw them.[2] . . .

I witnessed the drama to-night from the back of the balcony where every whisper on the stage is translated into ordinary conversational tones, and every declamatory passage seemed a ranting thunderstorm of sound, though in reality not over-loudly spoken; and the roughness of the speakers' voices came to one in all their hardness and provincialism of accent. It is a cruel place to judge the actors from as far as the spoken word is concerned, but it is an excellent position to see the continual panorama of lovely stage pictures created by them, and this company is strong in charming tableaux. . . .

As to the play itself, it loses much of its charm by repetition and has not the same witchery for me as say *Deirdre* had, for instance, after seeing it many times. However, many of the passages are really beautiful, and the second act and opening scene of Act III in particular are most dramatic, though Mr. F. J. Fay as "Brian" let down the final speech of the latter scene badly by underplaying to-night, and on the whole did not seem to have his heart in the work. For I noticed that in many passages he failed to give due light and shade to their meaning, and repeated them straight off, as it were, without his usual niceties of expression. . . .

Miss Maire nic Shiubhlaigh as "Gormleith" was splendid in the grand speech where she tells "Brian" the sort of woman she really is, and he refuses to take her life in Act III. Her acting here is memorably good. In some of the earlier passages, she was a trifle tame and inclined to "dream" her speeches too much, but ever and always she was lovely to behold and graceful of action. The lovely, deep, rich contralto voice in which Miss Allgood intoned the beautiful words put into the mouth of "Aoibhell," and the guardian spirit of "Brian's" house, was delicious to hear, and was in marked contrast to many of the other player's rough, discordant accents and tones. . . .

The more I see *Kincora*, the more interesting and beautiful do I find Miss ni Gharbhaigh's [Miss Garvey] lovely and unaffected realising of "Maire," the maid who travels all over Ireland richly clad and bejewelled and lone without being molested. After her "Sibby"[3] and "Mrs. Tarpey"[4] it was a revelation. She is an actress of wonderful versatility. The audience echoed the players in being out of sorts and applauded little.

Monday, April 24.   In the evening the fourth series of performances by the Irish National Theatre Society commenced at the Abbey Theatre with a revival of Lady

Gregory's *Kincora*, slightly altered and added to in places . . . but scarcely an improvement on the old. The holiday had the effect of decimating instead of increasing the audience in stalls and balcony, but the pit enticed a few holiday waifs and strays. . . .

I had a few words with Lady Gregory and her son, W. B. Yeats, F. J. Ryan, J. M. Synge, and the Fays in the Greenroom before the play commenced, and after the opening scene of the third act with D. J. O'Donoghue and William Boyle (to whom I was introduced) who sat in the second row of the stalls (much too near the stage to judge the effect of a play properly). Mr. Boyle said he was not moved by the acting as it was lacking in life and movement, and failed to impress him as being natural. The play itself, he thought a good skeleton to work on, but it wanted expanding and filling in or joining of the flats. Many passages were really fine, but much of it was commonplace. It badly wanted more full-blooded acting to make it convincing and as stirring as the nature of its theme demanded. The part of "Queen Gormleith" was a fine conception, but her actions were scarcely made clear enough in Act III, Scene 1. Miss Maire nic Shiubhlaigh, he thought, was too inanimate in the role when not speaking. In fact, all the actors only lit up when they were actually having their say.

This I explained was the method adopted by the company with pure "malice aforethought," and whether rightly or wrongly that was their system of interpreting the plays submitted to them. I walked home part of the way with them after the performance, and we discussed this and other kindred matters with perfect frankness.

I believe Mr. Boyle was present on Saturday last at part of the final rehearsal of his play, *The Building Fund*, or, as he expressed it, he "saw them walk through it, repeating the lines." Mr. Boyle is evidently not a believer, and when Yeats shook hands with him he made a joke about the interval choral noises with reference to the play—which drove Yeats away without saying a word. Yeats's play, *On the King's Threshold*, impressed him when he

saw it played in London, and he spoke highly of AE's
Deirdre.

Tuesday, April 25.   Every word spoken by the five characters that go to make up the cast in William Boyle's
comedy, *The Building Fund,* produced with every mark of
popular success for the first time on any stage at the
Abbey Theatre, fell on the ear with such a familiar ring
that there was no mistaking their truth to life. Touches of
nature followed each other so rapidly in the speech and
actions of those peasant-folk conceived by Mr. Boyle and
breathed into reality by the clever acting of those en-
trusted with the parts, that a slice of life itself seemed
lifted in its entirety from a Louth farmhouse kitchen and
transported in all its stern and cruelly sad actuality onto
the stage before us. Every word rang true, and though the
dramatist chose his types from most unsympathetic and
unloveable specimens of our fellow-countrymen, there was
no denying their truth to life. And though you might
wince under his lash as he laid bare the sordid natures,
without glossing over any of the little petty meannesses, of
the miserly old "Mrs. Grogan" and her more contempt-
ibly grasping son "Shan" who both begrudged a penny
piece to god or man, nevertheless no one could object to
his plain, unvarnished treatment of the precious pair. The
truth, so long as it is the plain, straight-forward, honest
truth, no matter how unpalatably it may be put before us
or rubbed into us, is never resented by Irish folk. It is
when men like J. M. Synge come along with a piece like
The Well of the Saints, with its strange, powerful, un-
Irish dialect and Irish folk evolved out of his own morbid
brain and alien alike to the sentiment and actuality of the
humble peasantry . . . that we then object. The great
literary quality of Mr. Synge's work cannot be denied, and
as literature must rank immeasurably above Mr. Boyle's
homely, real, flesh and blood talk; but, nevertheless, there
is no denying that much of his work rings so false to Irish
ears, that a red rag to a bull is the only way to describe its
effect. . . .

The company rose to the occasion. Miss Emma Vernon's portrait of old "Mrs. Grogan" could not be nearer to nature except it be nature itself—that is, unless it were "Mrs. Grogan" in the flesh. In make-up, speech, manner, and action, the miserly old woman whose sole anxiety in life was that she could not take her money with her when she died, lived for us. Her cough was a study in realistic mimicking, and her real way of saying the real words put into her mouth by the dramatist made the whole audience kin. Her first appearance was greeted by a round of applause, so perfect an old country-woman did the eye behold in her, and after each of her exits the applause was renewed with extra heartiness. For the young girl, it was truly a surprisingly clever character study, surpassing in completeness of detail even her fine study of old blind "Mary Doul" in *The Well of the Saints.*

Wednesday, April 26.[5] . . . At any rate, I think the "Murrough" and "Aoibhell" incident, though full of noble patriotic sentiment, ought to go. I had a chat with W. B. Yeats and Lady Gregory after the play on this matter, and they agreed that something was required to be done with those scenes, but what it was they had not as yet settled upon. . . .

Again Lady Gregory entertained most hospitably after the play, and Mr. Maurice Joy and I had a chat with W. B. Yeats in which he held forth most interestingly on drama, and said he had Charles Stewart Parnell in his mind when he wrote *On Baile's Strand.* "People who do aught for Ireland," he said, "ever and always have to fight with the waves in the end."

He called *On the King's Threshold* a processional play, commencing with the "King's" long tiresome introductory speech, and then going on from curiosity to climax, as drama always should, to the grand finale where "Seanchan" gains his point. Phase cannot meet phase at once; it must be led up to gradually, or the point aimed at will be lost. That is the essential and real meaning of drama. And he instanced the failure of some of the speeches in *On the King's Threshold* on that account.

Friday, April 28.[6]   . . . Tea followed the play and was presided over by Lady Gregory. I took George Sheridan round and introduced him to all the company and to Lady Gregory and to Mr. Yeats, with whom we chatted for some time on artistic matters in connection with the stage. Mention of Maeterlinck's play of *Pelleas and Melisande* cropped up, and Mr. Yeats said he never understood its meaning clearly until he saw Mrs. Patrick Campbell and Madame Bernhardt enact the roles of the lovers as if they were a pair of little children. Mr. Martin Harvey as "Pelleas" did not convey that idea to his mind, hence his non-appreciation of the play when he saw Harvey in it. Harvey presented a real grown-up lover; there lay his fault.

Mr. Yeats also mentioned he still keeps altering *On the King's Threshold* and hopes to get it to his liking in the end. A patched up affair is seldom a success. I shall never again get the same thrill from the play as I did the first time I saw it played at the Molesworth Hall, no matter how the poet labors at perfecting its dramatic significance. That night Mr. F. J. Fay's acting moved me as few actors had done before.

Sunday, April 30.   Met Mr. Boyle at O'Donoghue's and had a chat chiefly about the success of his play *The Building Fund*. He told me that Mr. Yeats wanted him to make "O'Callaghan" as bad as the rest of the characters, but he would not, for, he said, "there must always be one normal character in a piece to form a standard to judge how far the others had strayed from the right path by. Yeats, after he had seen the piece acted, agreed that Boyle was right. Boyle also said that Yeats in conversation told him to keep to *The Building Fund* style of play in which he was supreme. "For," added Yeats, "it is scarcely likely one could be supreme in more than one thing." Yeats nearly had a fit when Boyle told him he wrote poetry, but recovered somewhat when Boyle said it was only comic poetry.

Tuesday, June 6.   To see a farcical comedy more than once is like drinking stale champagne.

Friday, June 9.   A goodly crowd of patrons put in an appearance at the Abbey Theatre where Padraic Colum's three-act play, *The Land*, was produced for the first time on any stage, preceded by *The Hour Glass* by W. B. Yeats. I must say at once that the new piece was received with genuine enthusiasm. The actors were recalled after each act, and the author at the end of the play. He came forward and shyly bowed, returning hurriedly as if scared by the sight of the audience. Colum is a strange lad and always looks to me as if a good square meal would do him a world of good. A slight, fragile scrap of humanity with the look of a startled fawn ever hovering about his eyes. Loud and continued applause, intermingled with cries of "Speech, Speech!" brought him back again, and he shyly addressed a few words to the house having first thrown his cap aside nervously, and left the stage abruptly in what seemed to me the middle of a discourse. He had made a remark that was being applauded vigorously, and he remained motionless while the noise of the applause lasted, and then bolted unexpectedly. Truly a strange lad, but happily a clever one besides, as to-night's production proclaimed him beyond yea or nay.

The Land is seething with matter vital to the moment in Ireland, and the talk, especially between the two old farmers, is as natural as nature itself; and as spoken and acted by the Messrs. Fay it became the living actual thing . . . for us in front. . . . The whole play palpitates with life, but Acts i and iii are particularly fine; the second act was not quite as well acted as the others, and perhaps that might have made it appear weaker. Much of the acting was spasmodic and jerky, and not very convincing on that account. Miss Sara Allgood was the worst offender in this respect as "Sally," and used her arms with too monotonous regularity in the one gesture of lamentation; she also spoke too hurriedly frequently. There was too much rush and confusion about her acting to be wholly effective.[7]

Wednesday, September 27.   Met Miss Horniman at Abbey Theatre about plans of alterations to Annex, and afterwards saw a rehearsal of *The Land*. Miss Horniman told me she had purchased J. B. Yeats's sketch of the old Mechanics for the Abbey Theatre. . . . Miss Horniman has decided to pay the artists from this out. This is a move in the right direction. Miss Horniman is a wonder!

Wednesday, October 4.   Met Mr. Edward Martyn in the tramcar on my way down to the theatre, and we had a chat about the new plays at the Abbey Theatre. He thought both plays clever, but it was a big mistake of management to have two peasant plays on the one programme. He liked Colum's *Broken Soil* better than *The Land*. There were more ideas in it. "Peasant plays are over-done. One would imagine there was nothing else to write about in Ireland." He thought *The Laying of the Foundations*, as far as it went, very good and truthful, but it wanted to be expanded. Social plays were required. He liked the theatre very much and thought the acting improved all round. The ladies were much better. Miss Esposito he thought worthy of any stage.

Friday, October 13.   . . . After tea when the rehearsal was resumed, Synge, Yeats, and myself lingered and had a chat over plays. Yeats told me he had completely rewritten *Shadowy Waters*, and I up and told him that I disapproved of eternal chopping and changing of old work instead of putting all energy into new, and he remarked that he was gaining knowledge each day in dramatic work and could make an old work all right in a few weeks whereas a wholly new one might take him a year to write. Later on he might gain such knowledge that, when once done, his dramatic work might be considered complete; for instance, he had become master of the lyric form now, he considered, and never altered his latter lyrics. He incidentally told us that George Moore was now saying that no drama had been written since he wrote his last. Yeats claimed a good deal of credit for *The Bending of the Bough*, but gave the palm to Moore in the composition of light, bright dialogue after the style of the best French dramatists.

I asked him how *Shadowy Waters* was played in London, and he shrugged his shoulders in reply, and added he thought Gilbert Farquerson's "Forgael" disgusting. Miss Farr was better, but she always gets a very indifferent crowd to support her and cannot stage-manage. The scene used was a well defined galley and was effective. Mr. Synge thought the scene used at the Molesworth Hall too gloomy for anything, and Yeats agreed with him.

Wednesday, October 25.   . . . The company having assembled, we adjourned to the men's dressing room where a rehearsal of the first act and opening scene of Act II of *The White Cockade* [8] was carefully gone through, the authoress conducting the work. Mr. F. J. Fay was in one of his moods, and when Lady Gregory showed him, with great clearness and dramatic effectiveness (for the dramatic instinct is strongly developed in her), how she would like a certain passage . . . given, he turned crusty and sulked at it, saying, "It is out of the mood of the role," and adding that if she wished to make "Sarsfield" a comedy part he would play it as such. After much talk and explanation, Frank Fay went half-heartedly through the passage after the manner suggested by Lady Gregory. . . . Mr. Fay is like a bear with a sore head when out of temper.

Friday, November 10.   . . . Since the Society turned into a limited company some weeks ago, things have not gone so smoothly as heretofore, and a big change in the personnel of the players is likely to occur at any moment. F. J. Fay, Sara Allgood, and Mary Walker are now under salary, and have left their regular employment; and McDonnell [9] has been approached, but has not as yet decided to throw up his berth. Roberts and Frank Walker are not pleased with the new turn things have taken, and are most likely to secede. If they don't leave the company in the lurch for the coming London, Oxford, and Cambridge tour, all will be well. What the Society wants most is a person with business tact (having no connection with the

Society as actor or dramatist) to manage the commercial side of the theatre. The present people at the head of affairs are too stupidly independent and egotistical to cater to the interest of the public at home, and only look on Dublin as the training ground for London shows.

Saturday, December 9.   Lady Gregory's new three-act play entitled *The White Cockade* was produced for the first time on any stage at the Abbey Theatre by the National Theatre Society, and met with success. A goodly crop of the usual first-nighters to be seen at the Society's plays was present, but very few of the ordinary public put in an appearance. Yeats, as the mouthpiece of the Society, is forever saying in print that they don't want them, and certainly the public caters strictly to the Society's wish in the matter by remaining away. . . .

The end of the play tames off badly and is unsatisfying. When the curtains had finally shut out the stage, a gentleman behind me leaned forward and whispered questioningly in my ear, "Is it over now?" and he seemed surprised when I told him it was. Much applause followed, and Lady Gregory stood up in her place in the stalls, and facing the audience bowed to them most graciously. The play had taken over one hour and three quarters to unfold itself. It was very carefully staged and dressed, and the acting was uniformly good. Mr. Arthur Sinclair as the cowardly, lackadaisical "King James" was excellent, and Mr. F. J. Fay as "Patrick Sarsfield" especially in the second scene of Act II was very effective and impressive. Miss Maire nic Shiubhlaigh as "A Poor Lady," a follower of the Stuarts, suggested "Cathleen ni Houlihan" at almost every turn, and became quite weird in the final scene where she denies the king and laments him as dead. This was one of the most thrilling moments of the play and was finely played. . . .

The play interested but did not excite me. My niece and her little companion, however, thought it "the best of the long plays produced at the Abbey," and simply worshipped "Sarsfield." They had seen all the National Theatre Society's plays and were in a position to offer an opinion. The intervals were filled up by duets or the Irish pipes and fiddles played by Mr. and Mrs. Kenny. I cannot say that they enlivened the entertainment very much.

Tuesday, December 12.   Having first attended a council meeting of the Architectural Association of Ireland, I went to the Abbey where I saw Lady Gregory's charming play *The White Cockade* enacted for the second time in the presence of a meagre house. The piece was excellently gone through, and quite a series of beautiful historical pictures were exhibited to your gaze during its progress. The costumes and scenery had been designed by Robert Gregory with an eye to harmonious colouring, and the grouping of the various characters was arranged so as to realise to the full the colour scheme of the youthful artist. "Charm" is the only word to adequately sum up the result of this combination.

An experiment was tried at the end of Act II, when the Williamite officer enters the inn in search of the king. The candles were extinguished and the stage became pitch dark; on the candles being relighted, only their feeble rays illuminated the scene, the footlights not being turned on. The effect thus produced reminded one of a Dutch interior by some old master, and the figures silhouetted against the flickering tiny flames had a weird, creepy effect. . . . The Abbey Theatre is the place for such artistic experiments, and sometimes effects are obtained by the simplest means, that all the elaboration in the world could not surpass. Witness the mysterious sense of limitless expanse created by the dark blue back cloth with the pale limelight thrown on it from the front in Act III, and the formation of the speck of yellow introduced into the colouring from the lamp's flickering ray as it twinkles suspended from a beacon post, and you can quite ken what I mean.

This play is perhaps the most poetically staged of the entire period up to the present, and Robert Gregory is to be congratulated for his share in the result. Lady Gregory felt quite proud and justly so of her son's success, and in speaking to her afterwards of the pleasure the beauty and charm of the staging gave me, her faced glowed with motherly pride, and she pardonably waxed enthusiastic over her boy's artistic achievement.

Tuesday, December 19.   . . . Had a chat with Frank Walker, McDonnell, and Tunney on my way home. Walker told me that he intended severing his connection with the National Theatre Society, and we tried to persuade him not to. . . . I fear there will be a smashup of the company as at present arranged. . . . Eternal bickering and jealousies are the curse of any movement, artistic or otherwise, in this country.

1906

Wednesday, January 10.[1]   "Your play has several good qualities, a sort of strength or grit in the dialogue, humour and a sense of character. The central idea, however, is rather thin. The opening dialogue wanders a little, and it is a bad plan to introduce a character, 'Mrs. Seery,' merely for the sake of exposition and then to drop her out of the play. 'Matt's' scene (p. 7 end to 9 beginning) is quite useless and does not help the story in any way. The difficulty of your play as you have worked it is to keep up the interest — to increase the interest — while 'Winny' is out in the cow-house, and you have hardly managed to do so. To drop the interest about the second third of a one-act play is quite fatal to its success. Once or twice you use expressions like 'I was never any great shakes in a shindy,' which at least in *their associations* are not peasant dialect, and spoil the sort of distinction one can get always by keeping really close to the actual speech of the country people. On the whole, however, your dialect — is it not Kerry dialect? — is very good. If you write any more plays we would be glad to see them."

Friday, January 12.   . . . In the evening I went down to the Abbey Theatre where I had a chat with the two Fays and Synge. The latter told me his play *The Well of the Saints* was being played at Berlin to-night, and *In the Shadow of the Glen* would be performed in the National Theatre, Bohemia, towards the end of February.

The Greenroom looked quite lonely and strange in the
absence of so many old familiar faces and the presence of
new. Of the old crowd Messrs. Power, Wright, McDonnell
(Arthur Sinclair), and the Misses Allgood with the Fays
were present. The new members present were Mr. Ander-
son (from the North), Miss Hynes, Miss O'Dempsey,
and a younger sister of Miss Allgood. A sadness was over
the old room.

In chatting to Frank Fay, I casually mentioned the
breaking away of the old members of the company and
my personal regret that such was the case, and he told me
that it was so hard to keep a company like the National
Theatre Society together for any length of time as there
were so many contending elements against its success, and
petty jealousies were sure to arise, such as wanting his
brother not to stage manage, etc. All wanted to be bosses
and run the show, or, if not, they wanted to have their
own way and own no one as master, which comes to the
same thing in the end.

I did not enquire into the ins and outs of the dispute or
the differences which led to the rupture, but I fear the
members that left the company will fare the worse, as
without the guiding spirit of the Fays they are likely to
progress but slowly if at all. . . . When Frank Walker a
few weeks ago told me of his intention of leaving, I
strongly endeavoured to make him give up the idea, using
all the arguments I could think of to show him the folly
of his so doing. "With this company," I concluded my
remarks, "you are somebody—a young actor ever improv-
ing—out of it, nothing." Yet the next thing I heard of the
company was that the Walkers, Miss Garvey, George
Roberts, and Starkey had left, and to-night Frank Fay told
me that Colum, he thought, had also left, because the
company would not play to a sixpenny audience. He
wanted to appeal to a popular audience and much more in
the same strain.

Swelled head shows strongly in the mutineers' action.
Roberts was sore over his being ousted out of the role of
"King Concobar" in *On Baile's Strand* for the English

trip, and also Colum cast him for the role of "Matt" in *The Land*, and Yeats would not have it so. Miss Garvey followed Roberts as a matter of course, as they both are in the marrying stage of the world's progress. Frank Walker got the hump at being offered the paltry sum of 15/- a week, and of course his sister followed, and Starkey did the same, as Miss Walker and he are in the same stage of love's young dreams as Roberts and Miss Garvey. After the London season Miss Vera Esposito remained in London on the lookout for a "shop" in the profession, so she is lost to the company.

This is the second serious break the company has had in its career. The first was when Dudley Digges, Miss Quinn, and Kelly departed for the St. Louis Exhibition. It pulled itself together rapidly after that severe knockout, and I don't see why it won't do the same now. . . . After tea and rehearsal, I left with a sadness at heart for the absent members. Dissension is truly the curse of this country.

Saturday, January 13.   I met Frank Walker in College Green this afternoon, and had a long chat over the break with the National Theatre Society. . . . Mr. Walker told me they (who looked upon themselves as the Irish National Theatre Society) did not intend joining any other company, but of starting out on their own, and including Gaelic plays in their programmes. George Russell and Padraic Colum are on their side. When Miss Horniman heard of the latter's severance, she wrote to him that she was sorry he intended to imperil his artistic career for nationality. I believe the Society wanted him to sign an agreement only to write for them for the next five years, which he refused, adding that he did not belong to them at all.

Having gossipped in the rain for a considerable time, we bade each other goodbye with complimentary wishes for the New Year, and his parting shot was "Don't listen to any stories of what has been said of you by the Abbey Street folk which you are sure to hear from *kind* friends. Beware of tale bearers; they thrive on destroying." One of

Mr. Walker's remarks to me was that "All the unpopular people remain on at the Abbey—Synge, Yeats."

"But," I interposed, "you must remember that only for Yeats the theatre would not exist."

"That is so, but is it an unmixed blessing?" queried Walker. Ah, there's the rub!

Saturday, January 20.   In watching the programme of the National Theatre Society at the Abbey to-night, I was forcibly reminded of the saying, "We'd none of us be missed," from *The Mikado*. . . . The acting on the whole was a trifle too subdued, but the wake episode was admirably realised. . . . It was only by comparison it seemed to have lost a little of its tragic sorrow for me. The intense silence of the house when it was being played was a true test of the grip it had on those in front.

All gloom was soon dispelled as soon as William Boyle's new three-act satirical comedy *The Eloquent Dempsy* got under way, and the house took to its humour as kindly as a duck takes to water, from the start. It is a splendid satire on a type of hedging politician not un-known in Irish politics. . . . The piece is full of good things, and the house rocked with laughter over some of them and keenly enjoyed most of the others. The author was called at the end of the comedy, and bowed his acknowledgement of their kindly reception of his work, amid genuine enthusiasm.

W. G. Fay as "Dempsy" (made up extremely like C. S. Parnell before he let his beard grow) gave a vivid if rather broadly farcical portrayal of the ambitious village politi-cian with a turn for high-falutin' talk. Let him loose on a speech, and away he went as if wound up. Occasionally his face-play might have been more expressive. . . . A little more rehearsing might not have been any harm, as the acting showed a little roughness here and there, and a few slips in the text let the piece down occasionally. . . .

Among those present I noticed Stephen Gwynn, Ed-ward Martyn, William Boyle, J. M. Synge, Padraic Colum, Maurice Joy, Kettle, Arthur Griffith, J. [D. P.]

Moran of *The Leader,* the Miss Yeats, Lady Gregory and her son, and Hugh Lane.

Friday, February 23.   . . . Lady Gregory's extremely amusing farce of country-town life, entitled *Hyacinth Halvey* (played for the first time on any stage on Monday last) went like wildfire from first to last. If anything, it is funnier than *Spreading the News.*

Tuesday, April 17.   Having business down at the Abbey, I visited it at about 12 o'clock and found *In the Shadow of the Glen* being rehearsed under the author's guidance —who, seated at the footlights with his back against the proscenium pilaster, followed the players closely, offering a suggestion here and there. W. G. Fay also had his eye to details though taking the part of "The Tramp," and was very particular as to how "Michael Dara" should count the notes "Nora Burke" had in her possession. At first, Arthur Sinclair crumpled them up carelessly and put them on the table, and instantly was hauled up by the Chief, who explained that "You should have done so with loving care and folded them carefully as if they were all the world to you, before laying them down." It is by such care to detail that the National Players have made their reputation.

Meeting W. B. Yeats just outside the Greenroom, he asked me how I liked Molière's farce,[2] and I told him, "Well." He was loud in his praise of W. G. Fay, whom he thought richer in his humour than ever as "Sgnarelle." He was tickled at the idea of the audience wanting the author out at the end of the farce, and thought Lady Gregory's translation the finest he had ever seen of any of Molière's plays, and dilated on how easily the works of Latin countries could be translated into racily Irish surroundings, such as Lady Gregory had done in *The Doctor in Spite of Himself.* Catholic peoples could always enjoy fun for its own sake, whereas people like the English, who had more moral than religious sense, always wanted their comedy with a sting in it before they could appreciate it to the full.

I asked him if he had had any opinion expressed to him re the new version of his play *On Baile's Strand,* and he said he had from Colum and others, and they were favourable. I frankly told him I did not care for it nearly as much as the original version, and thought it less clearly worked out, instancing that a person whom I had with me, who saw the play for the first time could not follow it. He thereon spouted something about a poetic play needing to be seen more than once before it could be understood. So that settled that point.

Speaking of the poor playing of Sinclair and Power as "Concobar" and "Fintain," he did not agree with me; he thought them very good, and we parted agreeing to differ on many points in our short conversation. . . .

Mr. Padraic Colum called in Sunday afternoon to ask me if I had any press critiques of his play *The Land.* . . . He certainly is a strange boy with all the manners of a little child. When he gets sense, what will be the result? Ah, what!

*Wednesday, April 18.*³   . . . F. J. Fay's musical voice and fine declamation delighted the ear as "Cuchullain." He speaks beautiful verse beautifully. It was only towards the close . . . that he became unduly dramatic and unconvincing; and his prolonged musical laugh before making his final exit is a thing to be avoided in future. It was out of the picture and illusion shattering. Art made Garrick, who was a man of small stature, appear six-foot tall we are told, and it certainly does not take from Mr. Fay's height, but, nevertheless, one cannot help thinking that if he were taller he would be more physically suited to heroic characters of the "Cuchullain" type.

Wednesday, May 9.   Mr. D. J. O'Donoghue in a chat about Synge said he did not think he had much initiative or invention, and wrote very slowly and laboriously, going over and over his work again and again until he could recite it all. I noticed this trait when he conducts a rehearsal, that he has his lines off by heart and can give

the cue when the actors require a word, without the aid
of a prompt book.

*Friday, May 11.*⁴   . . . Mr. Synge has completed a new
play, but has sent it elsewhere for production as it
wouldn't suit the Abbey company.

Saturday, October 20.   Has the era of success dawned at
last for the National Theatre Society? To judge by the
crowded house to-night at the Abbey, one would be inclined to say so! A rainstorm flooded Dublin all the afternoon and evening, and yet the stalls were better attended
than any night save the opening ones of the theatre. The
new sixpenny seats were crowded to overflowing, and
some who sought shilling seats had to be accommodated
in the balcony. This was all very refreshing to those who
have followed the fortunes of the little company through
thick and thin, and Mr. Henderson, the new secretary,
must feel very proud that his untiring exertions met with
such instant success.

The theatre was alive with notabilities—Madame Maud
Gonne MacBride amonst the number. Edward Martyn
hobnobbed with George Russell—the latter looking quite
remarkable with his long untidy hair and reddish beard.
"He looks like one of those strange beings who always
hang round a literary theatre," said Sergeant Dodd, K.C.,
who sat behind me, to his lady friends. W. B. Yeats, of
course, was present in his velvet coat, butterfly tie, and
pronounced stray lock on forehead. He wandered about as
usual; "the perpetual-motion poet of the Abbey" would be
a good name for him. Lady Gregory and her handsome
son Robert also were to be seen. Old J. B. Yeats was
sketching as I entered, and Jack B. Yeats with notebook in
hand soon arrived with his wife. . . . In fact, artistic and
literary Dublin were present. . . .

Everything worked admirably, and the two new pieces
proved successes. The audience was attentive, alert, and
enthusiastic. During the progress of *The Mineral Workers,* one of the occupants of the back seats forgot that he

was not in the "Old Mechanics," and grew indignant with "Dan Fogarty" (W. G. Fay) when he tried to oppose "Stephen J. O'Reilly" (F. J. Fay) in his endeavour to materially improve the country's prospects. His exclamations threatened to annoy the house during the second act, and he wound up by sending "Dan" to the lower regions in four letters.

Lady Gregory's tragic incident *The Gaol Gate* impressed by the excellence of the playing rather than by the excellence of its dramatic quality. . . . Miss Sara Allgood as "Mary Cahel" the mother and Miss Maire O'Neill as "Mary Cushin" the wife entered the spirit of the terrible situation, and made the intense grief of the women appear almost real to us. The caoine sung by "Mary Cushin" composed by Arthur Darley was effectively rendered. The figure of "The Gate-Keeper" (F. J. Fay) in the gloom of the open gate with the faint light from the lantern which he carried cast upward on him, was most impressive, and the actor hit off just the right tone to keep the unmoved, matter-of-fact official in the picture. The grouping of the three figures at the point when he hands out the clothes was very fine and worthy of a great artist's brush. The lighting of the gloomy gate and the high repellent wall just suited the scene enacted and added to the pathetic grandeur of the tragedy of humble life. Rounds of applause followed, and the actors took these calls in artistic attitudes in keeping with what had gone before. . . .

Mr. Boyle's new play *The Mineral Workers* caught on from the first, and the applause increased after each act until on the final fall of the curtain the whole house became enthusiastic, and calls for "Author!" were heard from all parts of the house. The actors having taken their calls, Mr. W. G. Fay stepped in front of the curtain and thanked those in front for their kindly appreciation of the work and for their reception of the play. "The author," he added, "is unfortunately laid up in bed in London. I telegraphed him after Act II how his play was going and will be happy to now telegraph again the warm reception it has had at your hands, as a whole." It is a clever play, full of natural touches, strongly marked character, and telling dialogue. It is admirably constructed and carries the interest right on to the end.

Saturday, November 10.   W. A. Henderson is truly a magician. It is little over a month since he became officially connected with the Abbey Theatre, and he has piloted the thought-to-be sinking ship into the smooth waters of success and hopefulness for its future seaworthiness. It was only he could do it. To see the audience pouring in in a continual stream, filling up pit, balcony, and stalls was a sight to behold and rejoice in. When one looks back at the fine performances given at this theatre during the past couple of years, sometimes to a mere handful of spectators, and the brave way the gallant little company played up to such dispiriting audiences, one is all the more pleased to see that reward has come at long last to their labours of love.

Friday, November 16.[5]   . . . Shortly after I was seated, Miss Sara Allgood and Mr. Kerrigan passed in, and also W. B. Yeats and Lady Gregory, and the rehearsal was under way. The Miss Allgoods as "Singing Women" open the play. W. B. Yeats, takes up his stand at the footlights with his back to the auditorium. His attitudes during rehearsal were a sight to see, as he kept posing unconsciously all the time. The Miss Allgoods spoke in the measured tones dear to the heart of Yeats, and . . . Mr. Kerrigan, as the king, possesses a big voice which he uses too monotonously, and Mr. Arthur Sinclair declaims so loudly at times as to be quite out of the picture. A Yeats play is like a symphony in which the voices are the instruments employed, and if one or more is harsh or overloudly employed the harmony is slain. . . .

Yeat's attitudes during rehearsal would have made a fortune for a comic artist had he been there to note them down. He is a strange, odd fish with little or no idea of acting, and the way he stares at the players from within a yard or two of them, as they act, would distract most

people. You would think he had a subject under a micro-
scope he stares so intently at them.

Friday, November 23.[6]   . . . After the rehearsal, Yeats
came over to where we sat and chatted about the piece.
He seemed not to be quite satisfied with the important
position "Fergus" took, as he dwarfed "Naisi" somewhat.
In dramatic work he had great trouble in keeping the
unities of the drama in proper proportion, and it was only
by constant emendations that he arrived at any satisfac-
tory result. A short drama was the most difficult of all art
forms to perfect.

Saturday, November 24.   . . . Another great night at
the Abbey. . . . The curtains were drawn aside on
Yeats's new one-act play of *Deirde*. The setting . . . was
very effective, and the costumes beautifully harmonized in
the colour scheme designed by Robert Gregory. The play
is a thing of beauty, ending in tragedy, and for a one-act
piece unusually long. . . . Yeats's play was followed with
rare attention and was keenly appreciated to judge by the
applause. . . . Miss Darragh's "Deirdre" was consistent
and beautiful, with an undercurrent of intense subdued
emotionalism underlying her outwardly seeming calm.
Her acting was always skillful, artistic, and dramatically
effective (she is an artist to her fingertips), but lacking in
the exquisite poetic touch that made the "Deirdre" of
Miss Walker a being remote from this world—in fact, a
legendary heroine! Miss Darragh's realisation of the part
had too much of the flesh and too little of the *spirituelle*
in its composition. Some of her moments were delicious—
her description of how she would set out the body of her
dead lover I thought particularly so. Here her gestures
were exquisitely appropriate. The way she extended her
two hands in front of her with entwined thumbs to express the laying out of her lover's feet was perfectly lovely
in conception. . . . "Deirdre" is a fine acting part, and
Miss Darragh realised it excellently and artistically. The
way she led up to the final climax, husbanding her re-

sources, showed the trained actress that she is. Her mannerism of constantly closing her eyes to express strong, suppressed emotion is not effective and took greatly from my aesthetic enjoyment of her acting. When the eyes are closed and the face contorted, nothing is conveyed to my mind except a meaningless grimace.[7] . . .

F. J. Fay's "Naisi" was vigorous in the dramatic moments and impressively subdued when occasion required. He spoke his lines with due reverence to the metre, and were it not for his lack of inches . . . he would have filled the eye as well as the mind. . . . He sings his words too much on occasion, recalling Benson to my mind whenever he did so.

Arthur Sinclair as "Fergus" struck twelve o'clock too quickly in his acting and began to rant and fume almost from the first, instead of gently and gradually leading up to . . . his rage at the king's treachery. J. M. Kerrigan made a most promising debut as the love-tormented "King Concobar," and spoke his lines well and musically, if in a trifle too measured and monotonous voice. For a baffled lover, he struck me as too calm in manner and statuesque in deportment. A really beautiful impersonation was the "First Musician" of Miss Sara Allgood; her beautiful voice was a joy to the ear, and her singing of the various snatches of songs was thrilling in its purity of tone and pathetic significance.

Thursday, November 29. A violent storm accompanied by rain swept over the city during the evening and night, preventing many from leaving their homes, I have no doubt. Be it from that or other causes, I found but a handful at the Abbey, and Henderson quite disconsolate in the vestibule. Yeats, having so much space to wander about it, kept continually on the move. Lady Gregory also looked gloomy, and after *Deirdre* asked me, "What has become of the audience?" I could only say that, "Perhaps they don't like verse plays." And she said, "Then we must teach them to like them!"

I then spoke of the regard people had for AE's *Deirdre*,

and she wondered if they were so fond of it that the
Theatre of Ireland people did not play it; there was nothing to prevent them doing so. I showed her the post card I
had received re the first performance of the Theatre of
Ireland at the Molesworth Hall next week, and she said
she was sorry they were not producing anything new, as
everything new in the dramatic way helped the movement
along. . . .

I saw Yeats's *Deirdre* played for the second time to-night
and must confess that I thought it tame and lifeless. . . .
Sensuality is over the entire play, and nightly-decreasing
audiences testify to the lack of interest taken in such-like
work. Miss Darragh's "Deirdre" does not improve on
acquaintance; it lacks sincerity and charm.

Friday, December 7.   The Theatre of Ireland made a
good start at the Molesworth Hall.[8] Most of the literary,
artistic, and dramatic people who have followed the artistic awakening of Ireland during the past few years were
present to stretch out a hand of friendship and welcome
to the new offshoot of the prolific dramatic tree of the
Irish literary movement. Personally I should like to see the
branches lopped off, and all the sap restored to the parent
tree. . . . George Moore, Douglas Hyde, Lady Gregory,
J. H. Cousins, Padraic Colum were present. I was home
part of the way with Dr. Sigerson, and he was saying,
"George Moore is getting fat since he changed his religion
and eats meat on Friday."

Saturday, December 8.   Another very large and eager
audience was present at the Abbey to see Yeats's new
acting edition of his verse play *The Shadowy Waters* and
Lady Gregory's postponed new three-act play *The Canavans*. That the bill of fare proved very palatable it would
not be safe to say. . . . Lady Gregory's comedy was nothing more or less than an extravaganza of the type popular
in the days of my youth, without the enlivening music—a
piece written round the realising of a picture of Queen
Elizabeth, from an engraving by William Rogers (kindly

included in the programme to show how near the copy the stage presentation was). There was nothing convincing about it. It reminded me of children playing at make-believe with their elder's gowns. The piece was simply too childish for grown-ups.

Monday, December 10.   Mr. Padraic Colum enticed a great number to the National Literary Society rooms by the bait of a lecture on "National Drama," only to disappoint them by speaking on "Lyric Poetry," in a sort of mosaic of quotations from continental philosophers without any reference to the subject they had come to hear. . . . Every now and then, I was inclined to tell him to cut the cackle and come to the point, but he sat down before he arrived at the subject as advertised; in fact, he never, or hardly ever, travelled on the road to it. . . .

The after-speakers were non-plussed at first, and Mr. Maurice Joy who proposed the vote of thanks and myself who was called on to second it scarcely knew what to say. Mr. Joy tried to speak to the paper as it was, but I refused to say anything about lyric poetry as it was of national drama I came to hear and speak about. I merely formally seconded the vote.

Mr. F. Ryan, who followed, boldly plunged into the subject the members had turned up to hear, and from that out wigs were freely scattered over the green. He attacked right, left, and centre the mystic style of drama and the making of plays out of our mythical heroes. Nor did he think the movement was assisted by amateur attempts at the production of more or less immature plays in backyard halls. The gauntlet was down, but unfortunately he had thrown it ere W. B. Yeats entered, having been detained in witnessing his play *The Shadowy Waters* at the Abbey ("For," as he said himself, "I am always changing my dramatic work, and the only way one can do so advantageously is by watching the performance of the work").

But Mr. W. J. Lawrence soon gave Yeats plenty to think about in a slashing, intemperate speech in which he canonized the poet by styling him "St. Yeats" ("The

Abbey was run according to the Gospel of Saint Yeats"). He attacked Miss Darragh's style of acting as "watered-down Bernhardt," objected to the low-necked costume she wore in *Deirdre* (considering she had just dropped in from Scotland), and also the velvet material she wore, as being before date. He spoke of *The Canavans* as "the first pantomime of the season," and generally speaking he ran amok about the Irish Theatre.

Mr. F. Sheehy-Skeffington followed in a clever speech, in which he said the last batch of seceders broke away from the National Theatre Society "through pique," which was very near the mark.

Then Yeats in a fine, well-reasoned reply in defence of the policy of the National Theatre movement, wiped the floor with the detractors, and said that the limitation to Irish subject matter in their plays was necessary for the present. So long as plays dealt with Ireland, they had a chance of getting them better acted than they could be acted anywhere else. The end, if they succeeded, would be the creation of a theatre in Dublin like the municipal theatres in Germany where all plays could be produced.

Dr. Sigerson in putting the vote had much that was interesting to say, and Colum responded to the vote in his usual enthusiastic and interesting way, in which none of his literary friends, the ancient Greeks, were neglected.

Saturday, December 15. . . . I hope Synge's presence tonight means *The Playboy* soon.[9] Heard he had been ordered away and his playwriting stopped for the time being. Perhaps it was only a rumour.

1907

Saturday, Matinee and Evening, January 12. The Elo-
quent Dempsy wooed back to the Abbey large audiences
at both performances, and Henderson beamed on all patrons as they entered the vestibule. He is like a barometer
—bad house, he is gloomy and down in the mouth; good
house, and a summer day is not more bright and cheerful.
. . . The matinee was very well attended, and everyone
seemed profoundly impressed with the weird, strange sorrow created by Synge's gem of sadness *Riders to the
Sea.* . . . Few things finer than Sara Allgood's portrait of
the old mother have been seen on the stage. It was a
masterpiece of acting, quite flawless in every detail. To see
her return with the bit of bread the girls had sent her with
after "Bartley," and totteringly reach the chair by the fire
with a look of dread on her face that was thrilling, was to
witness as fine a moment of realistic acting as could be
desired. . . . *Riders to the Sea* was superbly acted in the
evening, and I overheard the author say to D. J. O'Donoghue who sat behind me that he had never seen it better
played. When an author thinks the child of his brain
realised on the stage, the audience very well may be satisfied.

By the way, a trifle light as air spoiled this almost
perfect performance for me, and it was nothing more or
less than a label bearing the legend, "National Theatre
Co." pasted on the side of the shaft of the stretcher on
which the body of "Bartley" was borne into the cottage.

Thursday, January 24. . . . Yeats, before he left for England, told F. J. Fay he did not like his teaching of poetic speaking, and Frank had given up doing so in disgust since.[1] There is great dissatisfaction in the camp.

Saturday, January 26. The Abbey was thronged in the evening to witness the first performance of Synge's three-act comedy *The Playboy of the Western World*, which ended in fiasco owing to the coarseness of the dialogue. The audience bore with it for two and a half acts and even laughed with the dramatist at times, but an unusually brutally coarse remark [2] put into the mouth of "Christopher Mahon," the playboy of the title, set the house off into hooting and hissing amid counter applause, and the din was kept up till the curtain closed in.

On coming out, Lady Gregory asked me, "What was the cause of the disturbance?"

And my monosyllabic answer was, "Blackguardism!"

To which she queried, "On which side?"

"The stage!" came from me pat, and then I passed on, and the incident was closed. . . .

"This is not Irish life!" said one of the voices from the pit, and despite the fact that Synge in a note on the programme says, "I have used one or two words only that I have not heard among the country people of Ireland, or spoken in my own nursery before I could read the newspapers," I maintain that his play of *The Playboy* is not a truthful or just picture of the Irish peasants, but simply the outpouring of a morbid, unhealthy mind ever seeking on the dunghill of life for the nastiness that lies concealed there. . . . Synge is the evil genius of the Abbey and Yeats his able lieutenant. Both dabble in the unhealthy. Lady Gregory, though she backs them up when they transgress good taste and cast decency to the winds, keeps clean in her plays, and William Boyle is ever and always wholesome. . . .

W. G. Fay as "Christopher Mahon," the hero, was inimitable in a very disagreeable role. Miss Maire O'Neill as "Margaret Flaherty," the publican's daughter who sets her cap at "Mahon" and gives the cold shoulder to "Shawn Keogh" (F. J. Fay), a sheepish admirer of her (played after the fashion of "Hyacinth Halvey" by Fay) was excellent, and Sara Allgood as "Widow Quin" who had designs on "Mahon" was also good. Two more undesirable specimens of Irish womankind could not be found in this isle I be thinking. A. Power, repulsively got-up, played "Old Mahon" with some effect. Arthur Sinclair as the drunken bar-keeper, and J. M. Kerrigan as "Jimmy Farrell," a small farmer, interpreted the characters . . . carefully. I only pitied the actors and actresses for having to give utterance to such gross sentiments and only wonder they did not refuse to speak some of the lines.

Sunday, January 27.   Met W. G. Fay and Mrs. Fay together with Frank on Pembroke Road while out for a walk, and we chatted about last night's fiasco, and the feeling of the actors during and leading up to the scene. The players had expected the piece's downfall sooner, and W. G. Fay expressed it that "Had I not cut out a lot of the matter, the audience would not have stood an act of it." I praised the acting and said it was a fine audience to play to. It frankly did not like the play and frankly expressed itself on the matter, having patiently listened to it until the fatal phrase came and proved the last straw. Frank excused Synge on the score that he has had no joy in his life, and until he has had some you may expect drab plays from him. . . . The influence of the Elizabethan dramatists was on Synge, and he loved vigorous speech. Frank partly defended him on this score. He told me Lawrence came round after the comedy and was in a terrible state about the piece. Both brothers wondered what would be the result of last night's scene, and I said, "Bad houses next week, but a return when the right stuff would be forthcoming again."

Monday, January 28.   . . . Henderson and I went down to the Abbey . . . and on our way spoke of Synge's nasty mind—to store those crude, coarse sayings from childhood and now present them in a play. The influence of Gorki must be upon him. Henderson also told me that the new English manager had arrived, and he was thinking of retiring before being dismissed. The new man was to get £5 a week; he was only getting 30/-.[3]

By this time we arrived at the Abbey. Two stalwart police at the vestibule suggested trouble, and we found plenty and to spare when we went in. The performance was just concluding amid a terrific uproar (the piece had not been listened to, we were told). The curtains were drawn aside, and W. G. Fay stood forward amid the din. After some minutes, in a lull, he said, "You who have hissed to-night will go away saying you have heard the play, but you haven't."

"We heard it on Saturday!" came from the back of the pit, and the hissing and hooting were renewed.

The scene which followed was indescribable. Those in the pit howled for the author, and he with Lady Gregory and others held animated conversation in the stalls. Denis O'Sullivan made himself very conspicuous railing against the noise producers, and Signor Esposito gesticulated abundantly. Small knots of people argued the situation out anything but calmly, and after about a quarter of an hour's clamour, the audience dispersed hoarse. "Heblon,"[4] in a half-tight state, blackguarded the Irish people and upheld the dramatist, and George Roberts said, "The play is the finest ever written if you had only the wit to see it!" I wished him joy of the dungheap of a mind he must possess to arrive at that conclusion, and Lawrence and I departed.

Tuesday, January 29. . . . Arrived at the Abbey when *Riders to the Sea* was half through. D. J. O'Donoghue was going in at the same time. We waited in the side passage near the radiator until it was over. A number of youths were dimly seen in the stalls. The piece was well received. We joined W. J. Lawrence in the back row of the stalls during the interval. I noticed that the youths in the stalls were mostly under the influence of drink (and learned that the management had allowed them in for nothing to back up the play that the crowded pit had come there to howl down). This precious gang of noisy boys hailed from Trinity, and soon after *The Playboy* commenced one of their number (Mr. Moorhead) made himself objectionable and was forcibly removed by Synge and others, after a free fight amongst the instruments of the orchestra.

W. B. Yeats came before the curtain after *Riders to the Sea*, and made a speech "inviting a free discussion on the play on Monday night next in the theatre." Shortly after the commencement of the police-protected play, a remark from the pit set the college boys to their feet, and for a moment they looked like going for those in the pit, but didn't. The uproar was deafening, and it was here Moorhead got put out. One of the theatre's bullies removed by the people who wanted him in struck me as a funny sight. This set the noise in motion, and W. B. Yeats again came on the scene and with raised hand secured silence. He referred to the removal of one drunken man and hoped all that were sober would listen to the play. The noise continued, and shortly after a body of police led on by W. B. marched out of the side door from the scene dock and ranged along the walls of the pit. Hugh Lane now made himself very conspicuous by pointing out some men in the pit and demanding their arrest as disturbers of the peace. Yeats also was busy just now as a spy aiding the police in picking out persons disapproving of the glorification of murder on the stage. . . . A gent [5] addressed the audience from the stalls, and the students with Hugh Lane in their midst behaved themselves like the drunken cads they were. At the end chaos seemed to have entered the Abbey, and the college youths clambered onto the seats and began the English national anthem, while those in the body of the hall sang something else of home growth. I felt very sad while the scene continued. The college boys had ultimately to be forcibly ejected by the police, and they marched off in a body singing, police-protected, to the college. One of them was arrested for beating the

police and fined £5. Two of those who were ejected from
the pit were fined 40/- each, W. B. Yeats prosecuting.

Despite all, *The Playboy* was not heard!

Wednesday, January 30.   I sauntered down about 7:45
to Abbey Street, and saw an immense crowd awaiting the
pit-door to be opened, and police everywhere. Met Sinclair in the crowd and had a chat about the turn things
had taken. He was hopeful that the success of scandal
would be the makings of the theatre, and said Miss
Horniman had telegraphed over her delight at the turn
things had taken. . . .

A loud-voiced, glorified music-hall patron took up his
seat in front of me after *Riders to the Sea* had been
perfectly played and enthusiastically received, and commenced shouting in grating, piercing tones, "Shut up!"
making more noise than all the house put together. He
was a distinctly vulgar type and began to call the play
"rotten" during Act III. The house listened to the piece in
patches to-night. Every time Synge would appear, he was
hissed. Over fifty police were in the theatre, and uproar
was frequent; nevertheless, a few were ejected from the
pit. W. B. Yeats was eager to get people charged. . . .

The theatre was full to-night to witness a row, and was
very disappointed that they did not get value for their
money. Several I spoke to thought the play a poor one—
the first act having some slight merit, but the others none
whatever, and as to the plot it was too absurd for words.
All the very nasty bits have vanished. Mr. Short is of
opinion that the excitement will do the theatre good. I
have my doubts. Outside the theatre in Abbey Street, the
place was thronged with people and police, but I did not
wait developments. Did I ever think I would see the
Abbey protected from an Irish audience by the police!

Thursday, January 31.   The police-protected drama by
the dramatist of the dungheap . . . got a fair hearing to-
night, and was voted by those around me very poor, dull,
dramatic stuff indeed. After the first act all interest of any

kind ceases, and were it not for the claque imported into the stalls very little applause would be forthcoming. A Free Theatre is a droll cry where police line the walls and block the passages . . . ready to pounce on anyone who dares say "boo" to the filth and libels of the Irish peasant girl on the stage. "Free" indeed! The theatre is forever damned in the eyes of all right-thinking Irishmen. One sack, one sample. Yeats, Synge, and Gregory are all degenerates of the worst type; the former pair indulge in sensuality in their later work, and the latter condones with them. . . .

Over two hundred police guarded the Abbey to-night, with the only result of two arrests for leaving the theatre before the programme was ended. The prestige of the theatre has fled, and Henderson's work of creating an audience frustrated.

Friday, February 1. William Boyle has publicly withdrawn his plays from the Abbey. As an Irish Theatre, the Abbey's knell is rung. This was the biggest blow to the National Theatre Society received since it became a police-protected society.

Saturday, February 2. . . . After dinner I went to the matinee at the Abbey, and found the police in large numbers around the building. The first act had concluded as I went in. Everything was quiet and matinee-like inside, except the number of police lining the walls and blocking up the passages. The audience was not very large and mostly ladies. W. B. Yeats came and had a few words with me about the arrest last night, and I told him what I thought of it and others, and also of the drunken Trinity students of Tuesday night.

He replied, "There were plenty of drunken men in the pit, and I prefer drunken men who applaud on in the right than drunken men who hiss in the wrong." A beautiful sentiment quite worthy of his pal Synge, I thought.

When I pressed him further about the freedom of every man to judge for himself, and yet if a man hissed or left the theatre before the play was over he was likely to be taken, he fled. He would not work in the art-for-art's-sake theory into an answer to that question, and so his flowers of speech did not blossom on the subject. "Humbug," thy name is Yeats.

Sunday, February 10. . . . Copy of a letter from William Boyle to W. B. Yeats:

> 90 BUSHEY HILL ROAD
> CAMBERWELL, S. E.
> *31st January, 1907*

Dear Mr. Yeats,

I regret to be obliged to write to withdraw my three plays—*The Building Fund, The Eloquent Dempsy,* and *The Mineral Workers*—from the repertoire of the National Theatre, Ltd., as a protest against your action in attempting to force a play—at the risk of a riot—upon the Dublin public contrary to their protests of its being a gross misrepresentation of the character of our Western peasantry.

> *I remain,*
> *Yours truly,*
> *William Boyle*

Copy of a letter from William Boyle to D. J. O'Donoghue:

> 90 BUSHEY HILL ROAD
> CAMBERWELL, S. E.
> *13 / 2 / 07*

My dear O'Donoghue,

. . . People here in the theatrical world know nothing about the Dublin row at all. It has surprised me that Miss Horniman's name has been kept out of the discussion. As a matter of fact, she is at the back of it. Her hatred of the Irish people almost amounts to lunacy. She wouldn't allow a word of patriotic sentiment to be brought out in what she calls her theatre! As I gathered this on several occasions at her own dinner table, I can't say it openly, but I know it and know that Yeats has not a free hand as he pretends. Every word I put in of a soft or kindly nature was ruthlessly cut out. This I should not have endured I feel now. I was overborne by the argument that it was "bad art." You don't know how I have been boiling for some time; I assume you my design was not hasty. I should have spoken out sooner. My comfort is I could not have spoken more opportunely. . . .

Yours,
W. Boyle

Saturday, February 23.   . . . I found Lady Gregory's new comedy in one act, entitled *The Jackdaw*, in progress, and the audience enjoying it very much. . . . To me the whole appeared a mad, merry farce frankly played in a farcical spirit by the company, but Lady Gregory styles it a comedy, and there you are. As one of the Directors of the company, she calls the tune, and you have to dance to it, or police will be called in.

Saturday, March 9.   After dinner I went down to the matinee at the Abbey and was in time to witness *Hyacinth Halvey*—the hero in spite of himself—and Lady Gregory's little patriotic incident, entitled *The Rising of the Moon* (which was played for the first time). I found a fairly good audience present, though the weather was anything but inviting outside. Lady Gregory was to the fore (she invariably is when her plays are being performed), and I also saw Mr. Payne making himself busy bustling about. . . .

After an unusually long delay, *The Rising of the Moon* was presented, and from the start had the spectators interested. . . . It is a splendidly written little piece, and was acted to perfection by W. G. Fay as the escaping prisoner and Arthur Sinclair as the soft-hearted policeman. Such acting of Irish characters is rarely seen and never outside the National Theatre Society.

Friday, March 15.   As I came home in the tram in the afternoon between 2 and 3 o'clock, I saw W. B. Yeats looking intently into Browne & Nolan's window at artist's materials, and afterwards dodge along until he came to Lawlor's tobacconist's shop where he again loitered for a few moments. He looked very dreamy and near-sighted as he walked along with head erect. He is a strange, odd fish to see mooning along the streets in his soft hat and big astrakhan-collared overcoat in which his spare figure seems to have gone astray.

In a chat with P. J. O'Reilly in the evening, he mentioned having purchased *The Abbey Row*, and noticed that the artist, R. C. Orpen, gave W. B. Yeats an immense brain box in his sketch—"the very thing," he added, "the poet is lacking in."

Saturday, March 16.   . . . Yeats came up to speak with D. J. O'Donoghue, who sat beside me, after Maeterlinck's play to ask his opinion.[6] "Impressive," was the word O'Donoghue used in describing it, but added that he thought it would read better than act. Yeats said they had got two strong plays that would create as much dissension as *The Playboy* when they were produced, but D. J. O'Donoghue declined to argue the point with him, and Yeats sloped away to talk to someone else. He is ever restless. . . .

"Everyone in Dublin writes plays nowadays," is what Colum says, and I am inclined to agree with him. Miss Letts, a Wicklow name, is the authoress of one of the two plays which Yeats referred to when he spoke of the two strong plays the company had in pickle for Abbeyites.

Sunday, March 17.   . . . I met Maurice Joy on O'Connell Bridge, and he stopped me and told me of poor John O'Leary's death which occurred last night. It was at Dr. Sigerson's some months ago that I last met him. He was then very feeble and worn almost to a shadow, but, nevertheless, his piercing eyes lit up his fine outline of face with vitality; and his scorn of me, because I took no wine at dinner, was amusing to see. His query, "are you one of those dreadful people called teetotalers?" was mingled with pity in its contempt for my temperate habit. A few weeks after this, a wet Sunday evening, he got into the tram at the corner of Lower Mount Street on his way to Dr. Sigerson's where he dined every Sunday as long as he was able to go out. He did not hear the conductor call out Clare Street, so he was taken on to Kildare Street corner before he became aware of the fact that he was being taken too far. Poor old man, he was greatly put out when he found out his mistake, and his feebly alighting in the rain and storm to pace back towards Clare Street was the last I saw of him.

He was born in the town of Tipperary in 1830, and in 1857 became a Fenian. He got twenty years on the charge of treason felony in 1865, was released from prison in December, 1870, on condition that he went into exile for the remaining fifteen years. He returned to Ireland in 1885, and a few years after I became acquainted with him at the National Literary Society. In his latter years, he was an ideal bookworm, ever prowling about second-hand book shops. As I knew him, he was a gentle old man with a noble head. RIP

Friday, March 22. . . . Henderson said Yeats said to Fitzmaurice that they would require 200 police when they produced his play, seeing that 150 were required during the run of Synge's *Playboy*. We shall see all in good time.

Saturday, March 30. I have not enjoyed myself so much at a theatre for a very long time as at the Abbey to-night in witnessing the first performance in Dublin of the Ulster Literary Theatre. What struck me most was the fine physique of the players when compared with all in the N.T.S. The lovers and heroic characters were fine fellows to look upon and not like puppets of a pigmy race. What the company lacks is finish; the players have talent and plenty to spare. At times their playing is delightfully fresh and natural. They have a quiet and effective way of speaking, but when they went to come on or off they invariably did so in a jerky manner that smacks of the stage and rarely convinces. . . .

Both pieces were full of humour which the comedians brought out with infectious merriment. The performance commenced with Lewis Purcell's (Parkhill) two-act comedy *The Pagan.* I noticed that the setting and dressing were most artistic. The Morrow brothers were responsible for the designing of both. The darkening of the stage at the end of each act before the curtain descends, I think, is an affectation better avoided. . . . Rutherford Mayne's (Waddell) Ulster folk play in two scenes and an epilogue, *The Turn of the Road,* was full of human nature and clever telling dialogue. The struggle of an artistic soul amongst uncongenial surroundings is set forth convincingly by the dramatist. . . . Mr. Waddell, the author of the play, was capital as . . . "Samuel James," who coveted his brother's share of the property. . . . This play was splendidly received, and the author bowed his thanks to the enthusiastic audience, which was the largest I have seen at the Abbey since *The Playboy* row.

Monday, April 1.   The National Theatre Society opened a week at the Abbey with a new play (or rather, incident) in one act by a new dramatist, Miss W. M. Letts, entitled *The Eyes of the Blind.* The piece is slight but impressive. . . . Miss Letts has the sense of the theatre, and her dialogue is strong and effective. Her ideas are weak at present, but I believe she is very young, so they will develop all right in time, no doubt. . . .

A revised version of W. B. Yeats's *Deirdre* was next tried with Mona Limerick (Mrs. Payne) in the title role. The acting all round lacked sincerity, and the audience felt it. I found the performance very wearying and tiresome. Yeats's tinkering with the text has not improved matters a bit. The new "Deirdre" is a high-strung, hysterical actress, with a monotonous, wail-like voice and a restless manner. A sort of Mrs. Benson run to seed. This cheap, hysterical style of playing likes me not. . . . In fact, "Deirdre" as presented by Mona Limerick (what a name, ye Gods!), was a very uncomfortable personage for poor "Naisi" to have been exiled with for seven long years. "Concobar" was lucky to have escaped her.

Saturday, April 13.   A terribly wet morning and afternoon left the Abbey deserted for the matinee. . . . The
air of "swan song" is all over the place. The only stir
about the theatre is the English manager Payne's frequent
flights from front to rear and from rear to front again.
They are quite as distracting as Yeats's restlessness and
affectation, and much less entertaining. Payne is like a
hen on a hot griddle when a piece is in progress. He
enters, and is no sooner seated than up he starts, and out
he rushes again. A few minutes after, the doors open again,
and in glides the ever-restless manager, to disappear again
before you can say "Jack Robinson." Why he doesn't take
this violent exercise during the intervals (they are long
enough, goodness knows,[7] . . . is a mystery to me.

Thursday, April 25.   W. J. Lawrence was in and left me
two copies of the *New York Dramatic Mirror*. He told me
he met Synge in the street and stopped him and had it out
with him in a friendly chat. Lawrence told him he had no
enmity towards him personally, but a principle was involved in refusing the rights of an audience, which he
strongly objected to. Synge said that the Abbey was a
subsidised theatre in which the audience had no rights.
Lawrence answered back that he thought they were trying
to build up a National Theatre and get an audience to
support it, but if they only wanted to have a hole and
corner sort of show, then no more need be said on the
matter. They parted with a friendly shake of the
hands. . . .

Willie [8] and I had a long chat over things in general
and the acting of poetic drama in particular. He had a six-
month agreement to produce peasant plays for the company. After that he did not know what he would do,
hadn't considered it as yet. Things could not go on as they
were was what they all felt. . . . Willie thought that a
National Theatre Society managed by an English manager was too funny for anything. The idea was farcical.
Yeats teaching people to speak blank verse and he not
knowing how to do so himself was bad enough, but a

person who brought out all the bad qualities of the players
was worse.

Monday, July 12.   Met Henderson in O'Connell Street
and had a long chat with him. He left the Abbey on
Saturday for good.[9] . . . Synge, he told me, was very
thick with young Miss Allgood, and they were likely to
strike a match. It would be a good thing for him, Henderson thought, as she is a bright, merry girl. Colum had
given *The Land* back to the company on terms of a pound
a week for every week it is performed. The company is
anxious to get Boyle's plays back into their repertoire and
would give him a pound a week for the permission. Henderson promised to ask O'Donoghue to approach Boyle
with a view to that end.

Saturday, August 31.   . . . The other day I wrote asking
D. J. O'Donoghue for a loan of William Boyle's letter.
. . . "My dear O'Donoghue," he writes:

> The "Abbey" folk are amusing. Of course, I won't
> have any more to do with them under any condition.
> But the suggested payment! It's on a par with Roberts
> 5/-. They must be fools pure and simple to take me
> for a fool of such magnitude. Still I'm glad you didn't
> give them a direct answer as I'd like to have the pleas-
> ure of giving a direct refusal and have the proof in my
> hands that they did make me an offer. I thought Hen-
> derson had left them. Did he seem to think a guinea
> for a week or two would make me eat my words? I'd
> pay it to smash up such a crew of imposters. If they had
> any ability I'd forgive them a lot, but their little vein is
> worked out, and they have nothing to hope for but
> someone's skirts to cling to now. They have grown to
> hate Ireland with an Orangeman's hatred—for meaner,
> personal reasons too. I wish there was some sort of
> stage on which I could show them up, for the charac-
> ters are funnier than those in *Patience.* . . .

Thursday, October 3.   No troops required, not even a policeman, at the Abbey to-night when George Fitzmaurice's three-act comedy of life in North Kerry, entitled *The Country Dressmaker,* was presented for the first time on the stage. Yeats is a false prophet where Irish character is concerned. This is not the first instance of that truth that has occurred at the Abbey. Irish people can stand any amount of hard things being said of them if there is truth at the back of them, but what they won't stand for a moment is libellous falsehoods such as those contained in *The Playboy* and such-like foreign tainted stuff that makes them out sensual blackguards, cruel monsters, and irreligious brutes. Now, the new dramatist, George Fitzmaurice . . . hits hard enough at times, and his "Clohesy" family is anything but a lovable lot; nevertheless, their faults are human and Irish. . . .

A large, fashionable, and most appreciative audience assembled to do the new playwright justice, and give his first staged work an attentive and unprejudiced hearing. The comedy was not long on its way when it was easy to see that Fitzmaurice had a grip of his subject and that his dialogue was the real article and his men and women those one might meet with any day down in Kerry. Two natives from Kerry sat before me and assured me that the turn of phrase of the Kerry people was aptly copied, and that the types were perfect specimens of the ordinary folk to be met with down there. "Even the very names of the characters are Kerry to the backbone." This opinion from those on the spot, as it were, was very flattering to the dramatist; and, as he clothed the simple story . . . with humour and tenderness in easy, natural dialogue, he won over the audience completely and romped home, a successful dramatic writer.

Applause followed each act, and repeated calls for author at the end had to be acceded to before the audience would be satisfied. Quite a young man modestly bowed his thanks in acknowledgement of the applause. The large audience dispersed delighted with the comedy. "There was nothing *Shadowy Waters* about it. . . . It was fine.

. . . We could understand it," is how I heard approval expressed.

There was an absence of curtains about the comedy; each act ended somewhat tamely I thought, and the second act was not nearly so well constructed nor real to us in front as the first and last acts. . . . The Abbey woke from its slumbers in wide-awake fashion. May it long continue to keep awake now!

Friday, October 11.   . . . I was introduced to young Fitzmaurice, the writer of *The Country Dressmaker,* and found him a nice, unassuming fellow with, I am sorry to say, a hankering after Synge and his methods of presenting the Irish character on the boards. We had a long argument over the matter, but he was of the same opinion at the end, I fear. He thinks hardly of the Irish peasant, but agreed that the stage was a place for selection, and everything one saw or heard should not be crudely noted down and served up for townsfolk's consumption. Much of the peasant's ways would seem hard and coarse and be misunderstood by audiences in the Abbey, for instance. I like Fitzmaurice and hope he won't be spoiled by the cult. He was surprised when I told him I thought his play would have never been accepted, only Boyle withdrew his work, and the company was in a hole.

Saturday, October 26.[10]   . . . Synge personally is such a nice, unassuming, silent fellow in private life. One has to draw him out to get talk from him at all. Frank Fay . . . took a walk one day up the mountains with Synge and hardly a word passed their lips for hours. To meet Synge and not know the nature of his work beforehand, you would never suspect him of such a strange output. He is mildness itself, and never a coarse or suggestive word passes his lips. He was a dark, silent boy, I've been told. He is the same as a man.

Thursday, October 31.   First nights at the Abbey are pretty frequent. We had another to-night in Lady Greg-

ory's one-act tragedy *Dervorgilla*. It is a one-part piece
which would read infinitely better, I feel sure, then it acts.
It is quite poetic in composition—a poem in fact, but
scarcely a play. . . . There was little life or reality about
the incident, owing to the lifeless, inanimate lay figures
that surround the stately old lady. Their wooden mannerisms took away all sense of reality from the scene. They
seemed only to exist to supply the central figure with
questions to hang long soliloquies on. . . . Sara Allgood's
. . . beautiful elocution charmed the ear, and, as I said
before, on occasion thrilled, but from a dramatic standpoint her "Dervorgilla" scarcely convinced.

Thursday, November 21.   "Where there is nothing,
there is God"—that's the sum total of the knowledge
picked up by "Martin Hearne" in his adventures in the
Land of Trance in W. B. Yeats's and Lady Gregory's
strange and dramatically ineffective three-act play *The
Unicorn from the Stars*, produced at the Abbey to-night.
. . . It is a mystical and unsatisfying piece of dramatic
work . . . presented before a thin house (mostly of
friends of the dramatists), and greeted with laughter in
the wrong places. The audience was mystified during the
first act as nothing was explained to them. They got an
inkling in Act II, but it was not until Act III that any real
interest was taken in the piece. . . . Yeats and Gregory
are too violent when taken in one draught, however palatable either may be when taken neat.

Saturday, November 23.   Visited the Abbey in the
morning on business and saw Willie and Frank Fay and
also Ernest Vaughan in the Manager's Room. . . . They
are all quite sick of the Yeats-Lady Gregory management.
Willie Fay thinks them both off their heads. They seemed
quite satisfied with the play, he said, although the receipts
for the first night were only £6 and dropped to £2 last
night. What a falling off from the opening night of
Deirdre last year when over £36 was taken. *The Unicorn*
was a shade worse than *The Canavans*. "Sometimes after

the last act of the latter I was in a fever heat," Willie added, "from trying to keep the piece going." . . . He is sick of the whole thing.

Saturday, November 30.   D. J. O'Donoghue invited me as his guest . . . to the Contemporary Club, as the discussion was to be on the preface to *John Bull's Other Island*. . . . During the debate I mentioned something about the introduction of the sixty policemen on the first night of *John Bull's Other Island* at the Royal, and W. B. Yeats was drawn at once, and up in arms against me. . . . I was jumped upon whenever I made a remark. Yeats said with great sarcasm that "The architect of the theatre is very fond of the police." I always thought it was he that was, but didn't say so. What was the use? To the artist, the Philistine is impossible, and vice-versa. "The unclean is artistic; the pure commonplace"—such is the opinion of the times.

Saturday, December 14.   A very large but distracting audience filled the Abbey for the second and last performance of *Deirdre* and *The Matchmakers*.[11] Fits of coughing frequently drowned the words being spoken by the players, and an undesirable levity manifested itself, especially on the appearance of the "Messenger" in the last act and ruined the solemnity of the final tragic episodes of the play. . . . Of course, the actors laid themselves open to ridicule by the crudeness of their method and awkwardness of their gestures often, but it would have been more seemly for a sympathetic audience to bear with them for the sake of the author whom they were playing old Harry with occasionally. . . .

The over-earnestness of the Countess Markievicz as the Druidess "Lavarcam" sometimes failed to be effective. An artist can be too intense and in earnest sometimes and appear ridiculous to those in front. The thing is to act the emotion you wish to convey . . . rather than to feel the actual emotion. This is where the real art of the stage comes in, for nature and art are quite different. For in many cases to be natural on the stage is to appear quite the contrary from the front. Now I am sure the Countess felt all she said, but it did not come naturally across to us who listened; hence her acting appeared over-wrought and unnaturally exaggerated at times. She looked a strange weird figure in her black robes and gold breast ornaments, but she failed to impress one with the awe that was in her.

Friday, December 20.   Had a long talk with W. G. Fay at the Abbey this afternoon re the impossibility of working the Abbey into a success with Yeats, Lady Gregory, and Synge at the helm. He was for chucking the whole thing, and I advised him not to until he saw his way clearly ahead. We talked the matter over seated in the balcony for close on half an hour. He was most despondent; he had trained several companies and had arrived at the age of thirty-five and had made nothing. Had he worked fourteen hours for over five years in America, he would be a rich man today and not a poor fellow without a copper. Even the company is getting out of his control, and come and go when they like.

Thursday, December 26.   From a play-goer's point of view, the past year has been one of the best we have had in Dublin for a long time. Most of the best-known actors and actresses paid us a visit during the year,[12] and our own theatrical output was very considerable. *The Playboy* rows at the Abbey will long be remembered as the most exciting events in our theatrical annals for many years.

1908

Monday, January 13.   W. G. Fay told me he had given a month's warning, together with Mrs. Fay and his brother Frank, to leave the National Theatre Company on Friday evening last. . . . He thinks the public don't want a company of Irish players or at least for not more than three months in the year. . . . I sincerely hope that the theatre won't come smash over the present crisis. Dublin without its Abbey would be a very dull place indeed for me!

Friday, January 17.   It may be of interest to jot down the following list of authors amongst others whose plays have been rejected by the National Theatre Society from time to time, viz. —Rosamund Langbridge, James H. Cousins, Stephen Gwynn, Arnold Graves, T. O'Neill Russell, John Guinan, Edward McNulty, George Bernard Shaw, W. P. French, Edward Martyn, Kingsley Tarpley, Padraic Colum, Seumas MacManus, Anthony P. Wharton, George Fitzmaurice, etc., etc. AE's *Deirdre* was shelved as childish and insipid for W. B. Yeats's unsavoury rendering of the same theme. The fact of the matter is that the present management of the Abbey is impossible.

Saturday, January 25.   I met Mr. Sheehan at the Abbey Annex to arrange about an estimate for electric lighting. On ringing at the stage door to get to the dressing rooms upstairs, W. B. Yeats opened the door with a curt "Good morning" when he saw who was there. As I passed across the stage, he said he wished a word with me, which I granted. It was to explain about his writing to Miss Horniman about the heating of the theatre, as he heard I was annoyed about it, and he, having no quarrel with me, did not mean to discredit me in the eyes of the lady. I accepted his explanation for what it was worth, and said I had no quarrel with him but differed with him on many matters re the plays, etc., and expressed myself freely on all occasions, though never in print since I became connected with the theatre. As I was speaking to him, he attended to a ring, and Mr. Norreys Connell entered, followed by Sinclair and other members of the company. I then left to transact my business.

Thursday, February 6.   . . . Received the following letter from William Boyle, dated 5th February:

> *My dear Holloway,*
> This is great business. Fay is engaged by Frohman at £40 a week to play *The Pot of Broth* in America. He has been staying with me since last Thursday and he, his wife, and Frank Fay (if he can be got over in time) sail for New York on Saturday next. He was first engaged to play the piece at the Duke of York's in front of Barrie's *Admirable Crichton*, but Frohman changed his mind suddenly, doubled the money, and offered Fay America at which the wee man jumped. It seems the quarrel was more between the other members of the Abbey Company and Fay, than between the latter and the directors. The proof of this is that the actor is anxious to work only the three directors' plays off on Frohman. He never mentioned my things to the great man at all, and when I asked him to hand a copy of *Dempsy* to Frohman today he very reluctantly took the book from my hand without saying a word, and told me when he came back this afternoon that he found no opportunity of handing in the work. So you

see it is the same old game transferred to a new field. No matter! The "sketches" of the three will soon run dry and then—we shall see.

The introduction was worked by Yeats through Shaw through Barrie. Barrie saw Fay in the *Pot* and liked him, and so the *Pot's* to go on, and *The Rising of the Moon* and *Riders to the Sea* are to follow.

When Fay found himself here a week ago without funds, he was glad to come to me and brought his wife here after, but day by day as his prospects improved he cooled off, and now with money in his pocket he is quite a bantam cock, and I and my wife are treated like a pair of lodging-house keepers—without rent. We keep our temper, however, as we feel certain that in spite of themselves they are making the running for me as they did before.

There's a lot of unwritten history about the Abbey. I said to Fay the other evening, "Suppose they don't let you have their plays, what'll you do?"

He answered, "I'll go back to Dublin and blow the whole gaff on them!" Whatever that may mean. You see, I am telling you exactly how things are. You may show this to our friend, D. J. O'Donoghue, *but to no one else*. Let Fay tell his own story as he likes.

One thing to bear in mind is that the Fays can do the sketches by themselves without outside aid, and they were prepared to try the Halls if Frohman proved obdurate. So has ART fallen!

Yours in haste,
W. *Boyle*

I know I can depend on you and D. J. not to give me away! I think I owe it to you both to take you into my confidence.

Monday, February 10.   After business with W. B. Yeats, he had a few words with me about the Fays and the theatre. Things were going smoother, since Willie Fay left, with the general management of the theatre. Fay should never have been anything but stage manager and actor. The other duties irritated him. It was unfortunate that he fell out with the company. . . . Yeats spoke of Frohman and said that the Fays were an experiment. If they succeeded, he was in treaty to send the rest of the company over. He was arranging with the Fays by tele-gram before they left for America, and was now in com-munication direct with Frohman. . . . O'Rourke was in readiness to leave at any moment for America. Fay asked for him instead of Sinclair which he thought strange. No one could replace Sinclair as the "Sergeant." . . . I merely said to all this that it was a pity to be always building up to knock down and build up again, as the company at the Abbey had been doing almost from the beginning. I was sorry that the Fays had left as I would miss their fine acting very much.

Thursday, February 13.   There was actually a buzz of excitement at the re-opening of the Abbey to-night. Every-one interested in the dramatic movement in Dublin was to be seen there. . . . The vestibule was in a hum of excitement as we arrived, and there to my surprise was Henderson all beaming welcoming his guests as of old.[1] . . . All the literary cranks came pouring in, and Yeats was beaming in evening dress and boiled shirt front. Lady Gregory was conspicuous by her absence, but Synge was present. . . .

I may say at once that the acting was more individual and less artistic than under Fay's stage management. Indi-vidual actors shone at the expense of the ensemble, and some of the actors occasionally were out of the picture. This refers to *The Man Who Missed the Tide* only. The way all the actors shouted in *The Piper*, save and except Sara Allgood as the half-witted "Piper," put them out of count from an artistic point of view. It was not acting at all; it was simply lung power, forcing itself above a cease-less din.

The darkening of the theatre some minutes before the curtains divided on this extraordinary grotesque almost wrecked its chance of success before it commenced.

Sounds of kissing, cats mewing, and other playful sounds were heard, and the scene disclosed itself amid laughter and annoyance. *The Piper* was barely tolerated during performance, and boohed and claqued at the end; most of the audience, however, treated it with the silent contempt it deserved. The what-you-may-call-it (the author names it "An Unended Argument in One Act") is a strange, weird, fantastical, nightmarish, unreal sort of thing with hideous, loud-voiced demons in the shape of *Punch*'s Irish peasants splitting the ears of stall-ites and groundlings alike with their eternal parrot-like cries of "We are bet," and "No, we are not bet," seasoned plentifully with oaths and wishes for the priest to have a nice "bloody end.". . . Contempt is the only thing the play deserves. There wasn't a moment of reality from start to finish.

There were two or three great acting successes in *The Man Who Missed the Tide*, and, despite the crudeness and uncertainty of construction, the play was genuinely well received. There was drama and interest in the piece. . . . The big fault of the piece was that up to the final scene the audience was kept in the dark as to who was the man who missed the tide. A too plentiful supply of bad language did not add to the strength of the dialogue.

Friday, February 14.   Had a chat with Yeats at the Abbey, and he walked with me across O'Connell Bridge talking of last night's performance. He asked me what I thought of Casey's play, and I told him I like it though crudely constructed, and that notable acting crowned its success. He said it was very promising for one so young. Mr. Casey is only twenty-five. The play was picked out of rubbish thrown aside. Mr. Casey hid himself in one of the presses while his play was going on. They found him and said he must take his call.

As to *The Piper*, I said it was not worth considering, and he said, "Strange, the Arts Club people liked it and were divided about the other; they had seen it before." I said it was just like the Arts Club; strange people like strange fare.

Yeats told me the author meant *The Piper* for a satire

about Parnell. How or why I could not tell. They intended opening up the company more, he told me, and regretted the Fays' loss. I said there was great fear that the so-called Irish school of acting would now vanish, and more individuality take its place—the ordinary everyday style of acting one sees on the regular stage. Yeats owned up that there was a fear of that happening. . . .

The Piper has proved another *Playboy of the Western World*. It was played for the second time to-night at the Abbey and was listened to with highstrung patience almost to the end when the pit rose against it, and one man was so carried away by resentment that he had to stand up and address the house: "It's a shame to produce such a piece! And they call this the National Theatre!"

Cries of "Sit down!" from the stalls.

"No, I'll not sit down! Woe betide the company if they produce such a play in America. I've a perfect right to express my opinion, and I will!"

"Hear, hear!" and applause from the pit. . . .

"That's not Irish!" and "Queen's Theatre!" were remarks passed on various incidents, and hissing was instantly suppressed by the pit at "Black Mike's" blasphemies, so the piece got a fair hearing and was condemned.

Amid the clatter of disapproval, the curtains divided, and the author stepped before them. He said, "As the author who has so offended you to-night, I wish to say a word. As you wanted to express your disapproval to the end of the play, I take all the blame on myself, and have to thank you very much for your treatment of the players." Then amid excited talking, the audience dispersed.

Saturday, February 15.   . . . Had a word with Henderson as I passed into the theatre. He said Yeats was telling them of a chat he had with me, and what I said of the acting, and of what a good judge of acting I was.

Friday, February 21.   Received the following letter from William Boyle:

> *My Dear Holloway,*
> So the latest pose of that really comic person

W. B. Yeats is as a Sinn Feiner. Parliamentarism talk sickens him. One day he tells you art must preach nothing—it must tootle "as the linnets sing." The next day that the futility of talk must be taught the Irish people. "It's the author of *Cathleen ni Houlihan* appeals to you. . . . When I wrote *Cathleen ni Houlihan* I did not write to make rebels." The odd thing is that Fay told me Lady Gregory wrote the whole of it except the part of "Cathleen." [2] The fellow is quite shameless. Did I tell you that he asked Fay to press Frohman to take the whole company? "I don't mind trying you," Frohman said, "but I won't have stuff forced on me." "Is Yeats the long, black fellow who was passing continually between the audience and the footlights?" Frohman enquired. Clearly, the American has formed his own opinion of the author of *Cathleen ni Houlihan*. . . .

You will see by the enclosed clipping where Synge lifted *The Well of the Saints* from.[3] It seems that Lady Gregory is the only one has an original idea among them. . . .

Yours,

W. *Boyle*

D. J. O'Donoghue and W. J. Lawrence were in in the evening. . . . I showed both William Boyle's letter, and O'Donoghue remembered Richard Best (who was with Synge in Paris) telling him that Synge had got the suggestion of the plot of *The Well of the Saints* from a French play (probably the one referred to in "Gossip from the Gay City" in *The Referee*). . . . Synge wasn't a play-goer in his Paris days, and used as a rule only to come out in the day to take a stroll in the Luxembourg Gardens. Probably he saw a notice of the play in the papers, and thus captured the plot.[4]

Sunday, March 8.   D. J. O'Donoghue . . . lent me a promised letter of W. B. Yeats re production of his play of *The Land of Heart's Desire* at the Avenue Theatre, March 29, 1894, which I now copy.[5]

THE IRISH LITERARY SOCIETY, LONDON
BLOOMSBURY MANSIONS
HART STREET, W. C.

Dear Mr. O'Leary,

My play comes on tomorrow, and I am over head and ears in work at rehearsals, etc. But for this I should have written before or at more length now. You will have since you wrote heard more I doubt not of the . . . .⁶ The proposed list of contents—as it at present stands—was made out by Johnson and myself a couple of weeks ago and sent to Barry O'Brien. It is, I think, good but will I have no doubt be greatly modified in practice. I shall cross over with Johnson when he goes to lecture unless these plays keep me. Should we have a success, and I am not very hopeful, I shall put on another and longer play—also Irish—I mean if Miss Farr finds she can keep the theatre open. She is desirous of doing my next play as it is a wild mystical thing carefully arranged to be an insult to the regular theatre-goer who is hated by both of us. All the plays she is arranging for are studied insults. Next year she might go to Dublin as all her playwrights of a curious chance are Irish. . . .

Yours,
W. B. Yeats

Your letter to *Independent* and the Ryan interview very good.

Thursday, March 19.   The Abbey scored two half-successes and one dead failure in the new triple bill presented for the first time to-night before a discouragingly small audience. Where are all the Abbey first-nighters? I have come to the conclusion that short plays—no matter how good—are not a draw. . . .

A beautiful love episode near the end of Sudermann's play *Teja*, beautifully enacted by J. M. Kerrigan as "Teja" and Miss Maire O'Neill as his newly-made bride "Bathilda," steered the little piece into the haven of success. Lady Gregory's translation into English was very happily done, and a double call followed the fall of the curtain. . . .

The Pie-Dish,[7] George Fitzmaurice's peasant comedy, was "a studied insult to play-goers" that failed to come off. "A lot of gabble strung together," was Lawrence's summing up. Truly, it was a piece smothered up in blather. The so-called comedy fell to pieces owing to the lack of sympathy of the author with his characters, and the whole seemed false and, what is more, was false to the life it depicted. . . . after a little more unreal cackle the curtains close in, and a few handclaps from Synge & Co. and a great big "Boo!" from Lawrence marked their fall. The rest of the house treated Fitzmaurice's second dramatic effort with the silent contempt it richly deserved. Why do people touch subjects they don't know how to handle? As a disciple of Synge, this young dramatist has proved himself a dead failure. . . .

W. B. Yeats's heroic farce *The Golden Helmet* was effectively played. It is a fantastic legend about a strange "Red Man" who came out of the sea. . . . Ambrose Power was quite impressive as the "Red Man" and spoke his lines with excellent effect. J. M. Kerrigan's "Cuchulain" was also excellent in its way. The talkative group of chattering men and women who filled the stage was confused and unpicturesquely disposed. The dressing of the stage was sadly needed again. The author was called at the end, and bowed with the actors as they took their call. . . .

W. A. Henderson gave me a letter he had received from F. J. Fay. . . . Post mark bears the date "New York, March 5."

240 WEST 34th STREET
NEW YORK

My dear Henderson,

I learn this morning thro' a letter which Lady Gregory has sent to my brother that, *mirabili dictu,* you are back in the Abbey Theatre. This is indeed a victory for you, but isn't it irritating that the conceited infants at the head of affairs could not have seen the error of their ways—assuming that they now see them—without causing disruption? It will interest you to know that Yeats and Lady Gregory's agent here (John Quinn) wants £10 a week for *A pot of Broth* and £10 a week for *The Rising of the Moon!* Not bad remuneration for two snippets that have not been and never will be successes here. The magnanimous Yeats, who shed crocodile tears over our leaving, has evidently his eyes to business. Frohman's man here says *A Pot of Broth* is not worth forty cents! . . .

Yeats is evidently anxious to get the Abbey Theatre Company out here. Well, I doubt they'll be successful if they come. This place takes not the smallest interest in Irish life or peasant dialect. They don't mince matters about outsiders who come here. Mrs. Pat has gone back, and Olga Nethersole has been riddled by the critics. A little plain-speaking will do some of the Abbey Theatre people a lot of good, and for that reason it may be for the betterment of their souls that Frohman takes them. . . .

The people here are all right, but the city is a noisy, dirty, dusty, unfinished wilderness. The roads are lamentable and veritable lakes on wet days, and when snow falls, as it has done twice since we came, they leave it at the roadsides, and you have to plunge into three inches of slush if you want to cross from one side of the street to the other. In the night the city is very pretty, all the shows having various coloured electric-lighted signs. There are immense buildings here as high as Nelson's Pillar, and they keep the sun off the streets and make the streets icy cold. There are no fires in the houses, nor chimneys. Everything is steam-heated. . . .

I saw by *Evening Telegraph* report that Holloway said we left Ireland for lack of public support. Why does he say things like that? The public had nothing to do with it, and *he knows that well*. The public would have given us support if they had been let. . . . Every good wish,

Yours sincerely,
F. J. Fay

Thursday, April 9. I wrote as follows to Miss Horniman. "I could not let the opening of the Gaiety Theatre under your guidance pass without sincerely wishing your new venture every success. Your enthusiasm in the cause of artistic drama cannot be over-estimated. Would that I could be there on Saturday next to see Mr. Poel's Elizabethan stage ideas realised in *Measure for Measure*. I sincerely hope your kindly appreciation of Miss Allgood's artistic work may find an echo in the press and with the public. She has worked very hard to attain the position her beautiful speech and graceful method of playing justly entitle her to. She must feel very proud that you have so kindly given her the opportunity of taking a leading part in the first production under your management at the Gaiety. May she prove equal to the occasion. You have been the Fairy Godmother to so many artistic ventures that the novelty has somewhat worn off ere this, but, nevertheless, the present undertaking over-capping all the others must give you extra pleasure in launching. Manchester play-goers can never forget you. . . . The company you sent to Dublin in Shaw's plays was superb, and admirably managed by Mr. Payne whose "Lickcheese" was a revelation to those who had met him while at the Abbey. . . ."

Had a long chat with Henderson at the Abbey in the morning. . . . W. G. Fay's quarrel with Miss Horniman did much to damp her enthusiasm for the Abbey. He gave her dog's abuse and deserved to be kicked for his pains. . . . Yeats took a delight in the Abbey. Henderson had told him he was wasting his time there rehearsing, etc., instead of writing deathless lyrics, but his heart was in the place. He loved it. It had become a part of himself. He was happy in it.

Monday, April 20.   . . . This is a copy of Frank Fay's letter.[8]

. . . I have a rather apologetic letter from Henderson telling me how Yeats converted the *bourgeoisie* to worshippers at the shrine of Norreys Connell, and describing it as "wonderful." *Nothing that the compulsive jelly-like Dublin crowd does surprises me.* They were always telling us what a bad lot Yeats was, but they are evidently quite happy to swallow the dose. . . .

I see *Sinn Fein* devotes two columns to *Teja, The Pie-Dish* and *The Golden Helmet,* and talks of the need for more competent stage management. There is none at present, as Yeats is worse than useless. His stage management would be a bad imitation of what he sees on the regular stage. I see it also charges the company with monotony. The latter is, I think, probably due to the course of "training" Yeats has given them lately as well, of course, as to Lady Gregory's ballad-metre dialect. Only my brother can keep that crowd right. They are all so uneducated and in need of constant watching that they are bound to go wrong in one or more ways. *Sinn Fein* I see complains of bad making-up and "unnatural" movement and speech on the part of the small characters. This, tho probably *Sinn Fein* spite, is what I mean. The slovenly movement and speech of the class of Dublin man and girl out of whom the company was and must be formed requires always in front someone with eyes and ears. Now Yeats is seemingly physically incapable of standing or moving like a human being, so you can guess how capable he is of correcting these important things. . . .

April 10⁹—The oracle has spoken. We received our suspension yesterday. "At a meeting of THE IRISH NATIONAL THEATRE SOCIETY held March 18th, 1908, present Messrs. W. B. Yeats, U. Wright, J. M. Synge, you were suspended from membership of the Society for breach of and under Rule V (R). Your breach of this rule might under different circumstances have been merely technical, but recent misrepresentations have made the step necessary in the interest of the Society. J. M. Synge (Sec.).". . .

Thursday, April 30.   During a visit to the Abbey, Henderson told me Synge was very bad and was going into hospital to-morrow to undergo a painful operation on account of some stomach trouble.

Saturday, May 9.   D. J. O'Donoghue dropped in for a chat. He told me Synge underwent an operation on Tuesday last at Elpis (the Greek for "Hope"), Lower Mount Street. Stephen MacKenna has returned to Dublin and is anxious to settle down in Dublin again and get on the papers again if possible. . . . Oliver Gogarty has passed his medical exams and is showing great promise as a throat specialist. He has taken Deane's house in Ely Place [10] and sports a motor.

Thursday, May 14.   . . . On going to the Abbey, I found a meagre audience had turned up to witness the revival of Synge's strange, weird play (with plot borrowed from the French), *The Well of the Saints*. . . . The unsensual acting of the company threw a glamour over the play that was wholly absent from the original performances. . . . The wild beast nature of "Martin Doul" was artistically kept in check, and it made him a far more agreeable personage. W. G. Fay made him a very repulsive old man overwhelmed in sensuality. Arthur Sinclair made him more of a dreamer with a longing for the beautiful. . . . In fact, the play was lifted out of reality into the realm of fancy where it should have been from the first. . . .

Yeats came to me after Act 1 with, "Here you are again! You never miss one of Synge's plays!" In a tone of voice as if he meant, "You hypocrite, although you rail against them!" I ignored his insinuation and told him I enjoyed the acting which was much milder and less offensive than the first production, and that I liked the scenery, though somehow or other it reminded me of Siberia in character. Yeats then told me that the designer [11] had the idea of desolation in mind when he designed it; that being so, he succeeded admirably.

Friday, May 22.   . . . Honestly I must confess that it was a tedious, dreary, and thoroughly depressing performance that the Theatre of Ireland company gave at the Abbey to-night in the presence of a very good audience. When I, who am looked upon as theatre mad, say I would not willingly sit it out again, the quality of the performance may be judged as below par. No footlights were used, casting all the characters into gloomy silhouettes. Padraic Colum's play *The Miracle of the Corn* was tried for the first time on the stage, but as it was taken in such a minor key by those taking part the dialogue failed to reach us in the pit, and, consequently, was not understood. The first essential of acting is to be heard. Fail in this and you fail in all. . . .

Edward Martyn's strange, unconvincing, two-act "psychological drama" *Maeve* also was a depressing affair. Maire nic Shiubhlaigh made a brave effort to make the mind-troubled heroine convincing, but the task was too Herculean even for her out-of-the-world style. . . . Some of his dialogue provokes laughter in the wrong places frequently because its author had no sense of humour to see such a result inevitable. . . .

The Theatre of Ireland has as yet to give a successful performance . . . and they don't seem to improve as they go along, which is the most depressing feature. Artistically they cannot hold a candle to the National Theatre Company whom they are in hopes of driving out of the field.

Friday, May 29.   Truly it was a night to enthuse over at the Abbey. The acting reached such a high level of excellence all round. The reception accorded Sara Allgood after the fall of the curtains on *Dervorgilla* was quite embarrassing to the young artist. . . . Her acting was always impressive and on occasion extremely beautiful. The little tragedy written by Lady Gregory is practically a monologue for the central character and gives great scope for acting of the noblest kind. . . .

W. B. Yeats came over to us before the performance and shook me by the hand and asked Lawrence all about Sheridan's farce.[12] (Lawrence afterwards said, "The poet of Ireland came and shook Holloway by the hand before the whole theatre—what do you think of that for an honour?") After the first curtain of the farce, he came again to us, and Lawrence and I impressed upon him the necessity of using flats as of old for the farce, and so keeping the interest going right away to the end. Breaking it up into patches robbed it of all interest, as every scene had to re-create interest in the characters' doings, and was over before the attention of the audience was thoroughly gripped anew. Yeats was in thorough agreement with us over the matter. As to the acting, we had nothing but praise, and Yeats beamed as we so expressed ourselves.

Saturday, May 30. "Mr. Holloway, I am sure you feel sorry that this is the last performance of the season," said Lady Gregory after me as I passed out of the theatre with D. J. O'Donoghue to-night.

I answered back, "I am, but everyone has enjoyed the evening I think."

Now those two remarks sum up my feelings over the matter and leave me longing for more till the Summer lives its course into the Fall, when the curtains will ring up again on the National Theatre Company.

Strange that the news should come of the Fays' return from America on the very day that the company wound up their season. The players deserve all credit for getting out of the tight place into which the leaving of the Fays placed them for the time being. Their work during the past five months has been prodigious, and their accomplishment truly great. . . . So excellent have become their performances that the Fays' absence from the cast is in no way felt by the audiences. In many instances, the players have found themselves for the first time, and a freer performance with more go and genuine fire in it often results. . . . Actors may come, actors may go, and dramatists and patrons do likewise, but the dramatic movement goes on.

Sunday, June 21. Lawrence called in, and I went for a walk towards the Poolbeg Lighthouse. . . . We spoke of

the acting of the Abbey Company since the Fays left and
of Frank not believing him that it was so good. . . . This
brought us on to speaking of acting generally, and the
aptitude of the Irish for acting. Their temperament just
suited it. They were all actors if trained. Some of the
ablest professors of acting were of opinion that the less
educated the pupil was, the better the chance of making
an actor of him or her. Those that had some defect to
conquer were the greatest actors in the past—such as
Garrick, Kean, Irving, etc. Spranger Barry had everything
in his favour and did not rise to great things, and Mrs.
Pritchard was a great "Lady Macbeth," although it is said
she did not know what the play was about. The brainy
seldom make good actors. It is the heart and not the head
that plays a part. For instance, McDonnell at the Abbey is
not of the brainy order, and yet he seldom makes a
mistake as an actor. He reminds me of the old players who
simply learned their own parts and cues, and knew nothing more of the pieces they played in. Thoughtful actors
like Frank Fay seldom did great things on the stage.
Acting is a matter of temperament more than profound
study.

Tuesday, July 28.   Visited the Abbey and saw Henderson. Sara Allgood and O'Rourke were with him at the
time. We spoke of Poel and his method, and she told me
they were nearly dead from trying to carry out his instructions as to voice production.[13] Their throats were all in a
bad way. He wanted them to arrive at simplicity of speech
and delivery by artificial means—to grunt and groan out
many passages, as it were. I styled it the "menagerie
delivery," and Miss Allgood said that was a capital name
for it. A stage call took both away.

Kerrigan soon joined us, and we got talking on the same
subject. He said Donovan said, "Maybe a seed might
spring out of all Poel's teaching, after all." They were not
at all impressed by his style of teaching. It might do for
the English, but not for them. He wanted them to go up
and down a scale . . . and when Kerrigan burlesqued a

little child's idea of reading to try to produce a sound something like what Poel intended to convey, all on the stage were astonished to hear Poel exclaim, "That's it! That's very good. It's what I want."

Thursday, October 1.   Mr. W. F. Casey scored another bull's eye with his mild three-act satire on Rathmines Society, entitled *The Suburban Groove,* at the Abbey to-night. There was a splendid audience, and they took kindly to the comedy almost from the first, hearty applause following each act, and loud and prolonged calls for author at the end. He responded and bowed shyly and awkwardly the while the curtains were drawn aside. The piece is one of dialogue rather than incident, and though the construction is much better than in *The Man Who Missed the Tide* I think the latter the more interesting work of the two. . . .

W. B. Yeats came to me before the play and asked could I see him during the evening as he wanted to chat with me. I appointed after Casey's play and met him in the Greenroom, and he took me up to the Manager's office where we chatted for a few minutes before Henderson and the man with the pit checks came in, and we moved our quarters to the rehearsal room. William Boyle was the subject of our conversation, and his plays and the recent unsuccessful negotiations of the theatre with his agent to secure them was gone over by Yeats. I could learn from all he said that he was in fear and trembling that the Theatre of Ireland would secure them, and the Abbey wanted them solely to prevent that happening. . . .

When he had spoken a long while and I saw his object was to get me to approach Boyle, I told him I had recently seen Mr. Boyle, and he told me he had placed his plays in the hands of a new agent (Mr. Mayer) and signed an agreement for ten years with him to place his plays at a certain percentage, and that the opportunity of securing them on reasonable terms had slipped by forever. He seemed greatly surprised. He said he was sorry he did not know I was going to London so that I might have conveyed his explanation to Boyle. The letter Boyle had written could not be answered. "You know what an angry Irishman can say when he is vexed," said Yeats. Such was Boyle's last letter to them. Yeats longed for the time when all dramatists at the Abbey would be paid; that time had not arrived yet.

Friday, October 2. . . . In the evening the theatre was well attended; many distinguished people were present including George Bernard Shaw whom W. B. Yeats captured and held in conversation.

Thursday, October 8. S. L. Robinson's tragedy in one act, *The Clancy Name,* produced for the first time at the Abbey to-night, was not a success. It might be called a tragedy in a lightning's flash, so abruptly and rapidly did it all take place. The dramatic idea was good, if gruesome, but unnaturally worked out, so that the little tragic snippet . . . seemed unnecessarily crude. Many times a laugh was heard in the wrong place, and this was fatal to the grim and tragic import of the piece. . . .

The acting of the company was not up to their high standard either; they seemed nervous and fluffy in their roles. Sinclair was distinctly off in the character of the son —the last of the Clancy name on whom "Mrs. Clancy" has centred all her hopes. He was cast for the role of a conscience-stricken poor wretch who kills a man in a dispute and is haunted by the deed ever after. The actor became gloomy too soon, and his gloom was mistaken by the audience for food for laughter in consequence. He played better after his initial mistake, though on the whole his portrait of the poor fellow was much too highly coloured to seem natural. It is not everyone who can play a "Mathias" [14] so as to give the proper thrill. . . . Sinclair is not built for the proper portrayal of a man haunted by a guilty conscience. He acted instead of lived the role. The illusion was not there. The melodramatic villain of a Queen's sensational shocker took nature's place. . . . Slight applause followed the fall of the curtain, but there was no call for author. The audience was thoroughly disappointed.

Friday, October 9.   . . . All was different today when the acting was all right. The little play went well and without a jarring note. . . . A long, thin, lanky-looking youth with glasses, who kept hopping acrobatically over the backs of the seats in the stalls last night whenever he wanted to vacate his seat, turned out to be the author of *The Clancy Name.* He is a wriggling fidget of a youth. Henderson introduced me to him as I came out with, "Allow me to introduce you to Mr. Holloway, the best critic in Dublin."

"I hope you won't be too hard on my little play," was all Mr. Robinson said to me.

Friday, October 16.   Was present at the second performance of Thomas MacDonagh's tragedy in three acts, *When the Dawn Is Come,* a peep into the future fifty years hence, when Ireland is having another dash for liberty with better success than in '98. . . . I found Mac-Donagh's play both dull and very talky.

Thursday, October 22.   . . . The mention of Aran suggested Synge's name to us both, and McEgan told me he saw him a short time ago, and he looking terribly badly and moving about by the aid of a stick. He looked like one who wouldn't live long.

COOLE PARK [15]
GORT, CO. GALWAY
August 28 (1908)

Dear Mr. Guinan,
    Your play is very disappointing if it is new work, but if it is old work as I think it must be, you have come on. The play you have just sent is impossible. I had made up my mind to recommend for production anything of yours that was possible at all, or could be made so by alteration. This play is like very early work, there is a soliloquy in the middle entirely out of place

in work of the kind, and at the end where there should
be dramatic crisis there is description. You don't even
keep to the dialect, but constantly drift into a very old
fashioned kind of poetic diction. I am sorry to be so
severe. If you like you can send the play to Synge. I
shall not write to him about it so you can get a quite
independent opinion. I don't think you have any clear
idea as to what the subject matter of a work of art
should be. Your work, to use a term common with writers, does not rise out of the anecdote into the region of
idea. No serious writer thinks it any part of his business
to make a couple of uninteresting young lovers happy
or unhappy, or to tell any story that does not reveal
some discovery in human nature. One must always
either display a character or define, in a way personal to
oneself, passion and motive. I am writing in this way to
you because you have showed in previous work power
of character-drawing and dialogue-making, which you
have never known how to use. Your last long play
contained one genuine invention of character, the eld-
erly old man, but he was almost in the background. If
he had filled the scene as, let us say, Boyle's eloquent
"Dempsy" filled it, or if the other characters were as
much creatures as he, the play would have been excellent. You should always make up your mind what your
subject is, always remembering that a work of art can
only have one subject and having decided what it is,
give up the entire scene to its expression either direct or
by contrast. I think you have been misled by reading
Irish novels, the worst in the world, and by living in a
country where no story is considered to be quite safe if
it contains an idea. Give yourself six months of Balzac
before you write another line.

Yours,

W. B. *Yeats*

Thursday, November 5.   . . . I called in at the Abbey
in the morning and found the stage being set for *Deirdre,*
and Mrs. Campbell and Yeats chatting amid the boxes,

etc., in the scene dock. Lady Gregory and some of the players were in the Greenroom. I met Sinclair and Kerrigan at the foot of the stairs leading to the dressing rooms, and we got speaking of *Electra*. They thought Mrs. Campbell fine and Miss Florence Farr quite farcical.[16] They laughed over the Punch-and-Judy show death of "Aegisthus" and thought the company weak in the play. On Lady Gregory coming out, I said, "Wasn't Mrs. Campbell's 'Electra' fine?" And she said it was, but Mrs. Campbell would be much finer in the smaller theatre where she could get all her voice tones heard to perfection as "Deirdre." Lady Gregory was thoroughly disappointed with Miss Farr's voice and acting, and asked her why she spoke so at supper afterwards, and she said it was to depict old age. Her performance was a terrible failure at all events. . . .

As I was passing the open door leading from the scene dock to the auditorium of the theatre on my way out, I heard Miss Sara Allgood singing her opening ballad in *Deirdre*, and I listened a minute. I then went on to the stalls and remained awhile to watch the rehearsal. Sinclair came up and sat beside me. Yeats and Lady Gregory sat in the front. Yeats kept busily walking up and down in front of the stage, and his gesticulation occasionally sent Mrs. Campbell off in a laugh until she finally had to tell him to sit down. She was quite nice to the players and made many suggestions in an almost apologetic way. She chaffed Kerrigan for not looking at her at all. "You mustn't like me," she said. Kerrigan is cast for "Naisi," and is much too small in stature for Mrs. Campbell's build. She has to bend down whenever she comes near him. . . .

Mrs. Campbell was going through her part in intense, suppressed, emotional way, going over and over again some passages which she hadn't as yet quite committed to memory. . . . I notice that Mrs. Campbell has no hesitation even in facing an audience with her back. Modern acting introduced this habit to the stage. Sinclair said Frank Fay was greatly missed in such parts as "Naisi."

Tuesday, November 10. . . . The excellent orchestra attached to the theatre played delightfully on the fall of the curtains, and then the weird figure of Arthur Darley was seen to emerge from between the act drop with his beloved instrument in hand. As he put his fiddle to his shoulder and raised the bow, the house became as death, and the wail of a beautiful lament full of sorrow and mystery soon filled the theatre with thrills of sadness. . . .

This tear-drenched air was a fitting prelude to Yeats's tragic love story of the fate of "Deirdre" and her lover "Naisi.". . . Most of the audience had been attracted to the theatre to see Mrs. Campbell fill the role of "Deirdre," and a hush passed over the house as the play commenced, and never was broken until the scene was shut out again from all our eyes. Such a highly-wrought audience is seldom seen inside a theatre. It must have been a pleasure to have played to such a one. All the players seemed inspired by its rare attention, and played as they have seldom played before.

The beautiful speech, exquisite posing, and delicious chanting of Sara Allgood as the "First Musician" led up to the coming of the ill-fated pair of lovers in truly poetic way. The atmosphere was perfectly created by this unusually talented young player so that when "Deirdre" in the person of Mrs. Campbell appeared, the way had been perfectly paved for her great, well-won success.

At first her mannered style of delivery and somewhat stooping form did not attract me much, but as the piece progressed one forgot her strongly marked mannerisms, and only saw the baffled woman's fight for death by the side of her loved one, slain by the order of the treacherous king who coveted her body. Her cajoling "Concobar" into allowing her to attend to the dead body of her beloved "Naisi" was a supreme piece of dramatic art, full of subtlety and intense emotionalism. Her savage outburst on his refusing her first request was superb in its tigerish savagery; the baffled woman let loose the floodgates of her wrath on the loveless old man who waded through crime to attain her, and annihilated him into submission. . . .

Mrs. Campbell's "Deirdre" grew on one until it quite captured by its sheer intensity. When the actress is moved by emotion or passion, her whole body moves in jerk-like wriggles that punctuate her every word. This eternal lack of repose in her acting, to my mind, militates against "perfect" being applied to her creation in poetic work, where the dignity and repose of tragic grandeur is the coping stone of all classical art.

Now Sara Allgood has this repose and grandeur of style, so that her every turn and word engrave themselves on the mind. . . . Personally, I long for the day when she shall live the stage life of Yeats's "Deirdre." Of the three impersonators of the role, Mrs. Campbell was by far the most perfect, but I have yet to see the truly beautiful "Deirdre" of my dreams realised, and I think Sara Allgood capable of realising my dreams in the part. . . . When Miss Darragh and Miss Mona Limerick filled the title role, they were out of harmony with the company who supported them. It was not so with Mrs. Campbell's rendering. It fitted in perfectly with her surroundings, and a perfectly harmonious whole resulted. She is too great an artist to let herself get outside the picture for a moment. The audience was deeply moved and applauded enthusiastically when all was over. . . . I had a word with Dr. Douglas Hyde on the stairs leading to the vestibule. It was the greatest bit of tragic acting he had ever seen. . . . Oliver Sheppard, the sculptor, came over to speak to me. . . . He was pleased when he heard I was going to the supper for Mrs. Campbell at the Gresham Hotel and walked up with me. . . . At supper I sat next one of the Miss Yeats. She who looks after the printing at Cuala Industries. We spoke on many things during the evening, or rather morning. She said the Theatre of Ireland intended playing MacDonagh's play *The Dawn Is Near*, as the Abbey people made a mess of it, both in staging and acting. She spoke of what a nice boy young Robinson, who wrote *The Clancy Name*, was. Quite boyish and gentle. He visited the Cuala Industries and was so nice to everyone there as he was shown around. He is the son of a clergyman and was inspired to write drama by seeing *Cathleen ni Houlihan* played in Cork. Up to that he had only been once to a theatre. He was writing another drama. . . .

After supper Judge Ross proposed a vote of thanks to Mrs. Campbell. The passage in which he eulogised her "Electra" was a really fine bit of oratory. . . . Mrs. Campbell responded in a few brief words which she had noted down on the back of a menu card, and said she had grown to love all the Abbey Company, and ended with an amusing attempt to express herself in Gaelic which set the table in a roar. . . .

Yeats commenced by saying that for once in his life he had nothing to say, and then went on to say it at some length.

1909

Thursday, January 21. I have come to the conclusion that Lady Gregory's translation of Molière's comedies into Irish idiom is a big mistake, as it robs them of all atmosphere, and makes the characters appear like a lot of peasants masquerading in fine clothes. . . . To-night, Molière's *L'Avare* (*The Miser*) so treated was presented at the Abbey for the first time before a meagre audience. . . . Be it said at once that Messrs. Sinclair, Kerrigan, Gorman, and Boyd, and Misses O'Doherty and O'Neill tried their very best to take the destroying sting of Irish dialect out of it, and to speak it in a refined way more in keeping with the dramatist's idea. Unfortunately, Sara Allgood thought it well to frankly impersonate "Frosine" as a good-humoured Irish matchmaker, brogue and all, and instantly became out of focus with the others. . . . This is the third Gregoryised Molière play that has been staged at the Abbey; let us hope it will be the last. If they want to play Molière, let them honestly translate him into English and do so, but for God's sake don't murder his work by turning it into peasant plays and retaining the French surroundings, dress, and scenes. The thing is too hopelessly absurd and offends me to the soul.

Saturday, January 23. . . . W. B. Yeats . . . drew me aside to speak to me about William Boyle and the misunderstanding about his plays, etc. Ultimately we had a long chat over the matter in the wardrobe room, resulting in I suggesting a meeting with Boyle to thrash out differences, as no doubt they have arisen. Yeats did not know whether Boyle would refuse to meet him if he wrote suggesting such a course, and I promised to write sounding him on the point. This met with Yeats's approval, and we parted.

Tuesday, January 26.   I received the following reply from William Boyle:

> 90 BUSHEY HILL ROAD
> CAMBERWELL, S. C.
> 25 / 1 / 09

My dear Holloway,
    . . . As to the poet's scheme of meeting me in the dark—I don't like the security. As far as I'm concerned there's no misunderstanding. If Mr. Yeats is afraid of committing his proposals to paper, I draw my own conclusion. He wants to make a trace horse of me. When I drag one of his burdens up the hill, I'm sent back for another. I don't like to drag up Playboys and such ugly loads. Let him drag them up himself or leave them. . . .

> *Yours,*
> *W. Boyle*

Wednesday, March 10.   Eileen[1] told me that Synge was in the next room to Kitty Clinch at the Elpis and that Maire O'Neill visited him each day. There is little hope for his recovery as the poor fellow is suffering from internal causes.

Wednesday, March 24.   About twenty to three, Lawrence called in to tell me Synge died this morning. . . . The production of Robinson's play is put off in consequence of the death. Eileen said the last time she saw him alive was in the passage of the Elpis on her way to see Miss Clinch on Thursday week. He was in a dressing gown and was looking very thin and pale. She would not have known him for the person I pointed out as Synge to her in the Abbey, did he not go into the room she knew he occupied. Poor Synge, he was a gentle and lovable man personally and not at all like his works. . . . The last time I saw Synge alive was at the Abbey during Mrs. Patrick Campbell's *Deirdre* performances. I expressed my pleasure at seeing him so well, and he thanked me for making so many kind enquiries while he was in hospital. "I feel much better," he said.

Friday, March 26.   . . . The prayers having been said, the clergyman left with some others, and the grave was filled in. Tears started to the eyes of Henderson as he silently watched the earth being shovelled in on the mortal remains of poor Synge, and all seemed genuinely sorry for the poor fellow departed. When the grave was filled and the mound of earth built up, many lovingly laid the wreaths on the grave and lingered around the place for some time, as if loath to depart.[2] It struck me so lonely that attempt at a prayer at parting is made in this cemetery. We left Yeats wandering about the tombs that surrounded the recently filled grave.

Monday, March 29.   Miss Clinch told me that the nurse who attended Mr. Synge was a Roman Catholic, and Synge knew she was, and when she went to Mass he always asked her on her return, "Well, have you been to Mass? And said a prayer for me?"

"Oh, yes," she would answer, "but you ought to say one for yourself sometimes."

On hearing which, he used always to smile.

Thursday, April 1.   A hit, a palpable hit, has been made at the Abbey by S. L. Robinson's play in a prologue and two acts, entitled *The Cross Roads*, when it was produced for the first time to-night before a critical but thoroughly appreciative audience. It is a play that sinks deep into the heart as you follow it with breathless attention, and the last act is the saddest tragedy I have ever witnessed; the stillness of the audience during its enactment was the greatest tribute that could be paid to the wonderful enactment of a thrillingly dramatic scene. The stillness could be felt, so intense was its quality. . . .

Sara Allgood has done many memorable things in other plays, but never did she play as she did to-night in the final appallingly sad and realistic incidents of this powerful play. Her picture of a woman with all the spirit gone out of her—a human wreck, a tired and weary being trying to battle against ill luck—was not acting; it was reality. . . .

Robinson is a mere lanky boy at present, but he has the dramatic instinct strongly developed already. What he will do when he developes is no knowing. The promise of his little play *The Clancy Name* is more than borne out in his strong dramatic work in *The Cross Roads*. The applause after each act was sincere and hearty.

Thursday, April 15.   . . . I hastened down to the Abbey where *The Heather Field* was being revived for the first time by the Abbey Company. . . . Yeats and Lady Gregory also came in, and I hoped her Ladyship was better; it was the first time she had been to the theatre since her illness. She said she was. Yeats looked every way but towards me. It is a funny little way he has got. He certainly is very droll.

Saturday, April 17.   Mr. Norreys Connell was appointed Director of the Abbey in place of the late J. M. Synge. He had been acting as manager for the past three weeks.

Thursday, April 29.   In the evening the Theatre of Ireland presented two new pieces for the first time on any stage at the Large Concert Hall, Rotunda, before a very distinguished audience. They have a fine following, have the Theatre of Ireland Company; therefore, it is a great big pity that they do not more carefully prepare their plays for public representation. The effect towards the end of *The Shuiler's* ³ *Child* by Seumas O'Kelly was completely spoiled by the actors not having off their lines and fluffing badly. No play could stand this treatment, and

Seumas O'Kelly has no reason to be proud of his interpreters in this, his most ambitious stage effort.

As a dramatist, his work wants condensation; he mean-
ders too much and goes over the one thing till you get tired
of hearing it. . . . There is much cleverness in his new
play, and from its subject ought to have got a stronger
hold on the audience. Observation of life there is plenty,
and strong sense of character is also apparent, and yet the
dramatic touch is somehow missing. . . .

Up to a certain point, Miss Mary Walker realised the
role of the poor, hunted vagrant woman to perfection, but
towards the end the prompter's voice altered all that, and
her splendid conception was completely marred, and the
grip her acting had secured on the audience slipped
away. . . .

Rutherford Mayne's farcical incident which followed,
entitled *The Gomeril*, proved an amusing North of Ireland sketch, but in no way to be compared with either of
his three-act comedies, *The Drone* or *The Turn of the
Road*.

Friday, April 30.   . . . Norreys Connell . . . has complete control over everything and everyone at the Abbey
now. . . . Henderson and the company are of opinion he
is a great big mistake in the position he now occupies.[4]

Tuesday, July 6.   Miss Kitty Clinch, on looking over a
copy of *The Sphere* for last week, came across a likeness of
J. M. Synge, and it set her speaking of his life in Elpis just
before his death. Poor fellow, he kept murmuring, "God
have mercy on me, God forgive me," in his delirium just
before death. His favourite nurse was a Catholic and used
to make him say his prayers each morning and night. She
used to pray for him, and he thanked God he had someone to pray for such a sinner. He called her his "tidy"
nurse because she was always in apple pie order when
attending on him. He liked her, and she liked him and did
everything she could to make his last hours happy. Before
he lost consciousness, she sprinkled holy water over him,

and he opened his eyes and asked was she baptising him, and then added, "Perhaps it is best so."

Not being sure of Heaven, he used to say he'd like to remain as long as he could on earth. The day before he died, he longed to be changed to another room where the sun could shine in and got his wish. He entered his new room saying, "Now I will see the sun shine," but, alas, he never did, for he died that night. He was told by Sir Robert Ball the Sunday before he died, that he would not recover, and he begged of the doctor to do something for him like he did before, but the doctor only shook his head in answer to his piteous appeal. He suffered great pain and used to walk up and down the corridor outside his room to get a little relief. Mrs. Huxley, the matron, used to have long chats with him each day; he invariably was writing when she went in, and she would say, "There you are, tiring yourself again," and he would say, "Stay and talk with me, and I won't write any more."

The nurse who attended him all through his illness thought him the best and gentlest of creatures. Sometimes he was full of fun and called Dr. Parson's attention to her, and said he never heard the doctor praise her for her tidiness (this was said in the spirit of mischief to tease her).

His people used to call to enquire, but never went up to see him. Every day he used to ask were any of his *affectionate* relatives there that day.

It was a terribly sad sight to see Miss O'Neill (to whom he was engaged) enter the room in the morning at eight and find him whom she loved dead. When he was dead, his relatives removed him to their home from which his funeral went—though in life they cared not to see him, poor fellow. . . . He read a portion of the Bible each day, but did not care to see minister or priest. Mrs. Huxley actually sent for a minister some days before his death, and he came, and Synge chatted with him about the weather and such-like topics. In his chats with Mrs. Huxley, he often spoke on Woman's Suffrage and such up-to-date matters. Nurse was of opinion that he had much more religion than many who pretended far more. He was very contrite and docile in his last hours. May God have heard his prayers. At times during his illness he was in great good spirits and would chat on for hours at a time. He was greatly liked by all in the Elpis.

Saturday, August 14.   Saw by the papers that Mr. J. M. Synge left personal estate valued at £2632. By his will he left £80 per year during her spinsterhood to Miss Mary Allgood, whose stage name is Maire O'Neill, a sister of Miss Sara Allgood. In the event of her marrying, the bequest to be reduced to £1 a week for life. Synge and Miss Allgood were engaged to be married at the time of the former's death.

Monday, August 23.   D. J. O'Donoghue called in in the afternoon and had a chat. Amongst other things he told me that James Joyce had translated Synge's *Riders to the Sea* into Italian, and was about to have it played in that language in Italy. . . . Joyce has an admiration for Synge's work, but does not like *The Playboy;* he thinks the last act taken from *The Master Builder.* He likes "Pegeen Mike."

Tuesday, August 24.   All the fuss that is being made over the production of Shaw's play on tomorrow night drew a big house to-night to the re-opening of the Abbey with *The Playboy* and *The Rising of the Moon.*[5] . . . I had a chat with James Joyce who had been out of town for five years and had never been to the Abbey before. He told me he had a letter that morning from Synge's brother re the dramatic rights of *Riders to the Sea* which he had just translated into Italian. I again had a few words with him after Act 1 of *The Playboy,* which he said he liked in the acting. He thought O'Donovan's "Christy Mahon" the true type intended by the author, but I told him W. G. Fay's was a much more repulsive and realistic type, and the latter was rehearsed under the dramatist's own direction and, therefore, his idea of the part. He asked me

how Colum's *The Land* acted, and I told him very well indeed when the Fays were in it. It was not performed at the
Abbey now owing to some little differences of opinion
among the original members of the company, and Colum
sided with the seceders. He had heard all that.

Wednesday, August 25.   . . . Excitement was intense
when the curtains were drawn aside, and the town hall in
a territory of the United States of America was disclosed
to view. All held their breath and listened with all their
ears; an event of a lifetime was taking place. The drama
was followed with intense interest right up to the end, and
heartily applauded. The stirring events leading up to the
conversion of "Posnet" were like a page torn out of Bret
Harte and brought to life on the stage. . . . The scene
Shaw has conjured up is lurid and strong—melodrama
made tolerable by the genius of the author, but the drama
will never compare with Shaw at his best. . . . The bab-
ble of voices expressing wonder at the Censor's verdict on
the play was a thing to hear and remember.

Wednesday, September 8.   Sinclair had just opened the
stage door for a messenger as I came up to the door. I
crossed the stage with him as there was no rehearsal on at
the time. . . . James Joyce was then announced . . .
and came in with an Italian paper with his critique of *The
Shewing-up of Blanco Posnet* in it. He hoped to make the
Italians interested in the Irish theatrical movement. He
did not give Henderson the copy of the paper, but said he
would send him one on.[6] He leaves Dublin tomorrow.
Every day he stays here means a loss of money to him.[7] He
had translated Synge's play *Riders to the Sea* for the love
of the thing, and handed his Ms. over to the manager
about to produce it; therefore, he told Henderson to com-
municate direct with the manager as he did not want to
be personally troubled about it further. I asked him how
he liked the acting of the company, and he said, "Well."
He got a few postcards of scenes in *Riders to the Sea*, and,
leaving his address, left himself also. He told us he chiefly

remained in Dublin so long in connection with a book of short stories he intended bringing out through Maunsel & Co.[8] . . .

D. J. O'Donoghue came in for a chat in the afternoon. He told me he had met James Joyce who showed him his article in the Italian paper, *Piccolo Della Sera,* and he managed to read it. . . . Joyce spent last evening with Tom Kettle, M.P., who was married this morning to one of the Miss Sheehys. . . . James Joyce is younger by years than Tom Kettle though he went to school at Clongowes years before him. He was only six when sent there— younger than boys are usually taken there. He was a precocious youth and learned to sneer young.

Sunday, October 17.   I received the following from William Boyle.

> 56 CRESCENT LANE
> CLAPHAM, S. W.
> 16 Oct. '9
>
> I received Lady Gregory's re-addressed letter by same post as yours this morning. I am quite agreeable to the terms offered and wish no more restraint put on their arrangements than that they should not put up a piece of mine *along with The Playboy.* . . . I thank you and all my Dublin friends for your allegiance to me while I was sulking in my tent. If Dublin wants plays from me, I promise you I can let it have plenty. I have at least a dozen in my head, but felt it waste of time to write them.
>
> *Yours in haste,*
> W. *Boyle*

Saturday, November 13.   . . . *The Image* [9] went right well and was received with great mirth from start to finish; the dialogue is studded with good things, and the actors spoke them excellently. Lady Gregory has tried to put a slice of Galway life on the stage, and I think succeeded in doing so, but made the fatal mistake for stage purposes of not selecting her material, but giving it in its natural state. . . . Lady Gregory fell into the error of giving us too much talk with too little action. She gave us nature instead of illusion. It was surprising how well the comedy took to-night despite its defects. The acting was superb in its simplicity and semblance to nature. . . . Of all the players, perhaps Kerrigan and Maire O'Neill's character studies were the most perfect. Where all were so good, it is hard to say. . . . Having seen the play played twice from start to finish, I must say, with all its defects, it is the cleverest long piece Lady Gregory has as yet written.

Saturday, December 11.   As I was looking over the papers in Eason's this afternoon, I saw James Stephens doing the same. He is a strange looking little fellow with a head much too large for his burly, bandy frame, and set almost neckless on his body. Major MacBride, meek of look and fair of hair, came in to have a look round at the papers also. . . . I saw George Russell looking into Naylor's old curiosity shop in Nassau Street. His overcoat hung carelessly unbuttoned about him, and a big pipe struggled through his ample straggling beard and moustaches from his well-concealed mouth. He wore a soft felt hat perched on his long unkempt hair—a strange mixture of the dreamer and businessman.

Thursday, December 23.   . . . Henderson told me the Abbey refused Shaw's *Press Cuttings* when he sent it on to the theatre after the production of *Blanco*.

Friday, December 24.   I was surprised to come across James Joyce with a lady and gentleman in Fleet Street this afternoon. I thought him away in Trieste on the borders of Italy. I think he had forgotten me; he looked so dazed and blank when I took off my hat as I passed.

1910

Thursday, January 13. . . . There was an air of life about the Abbey vestibule as O'Donoghue and I entered close on 8:15. . . . All or nearly all literary Dublin was present. Yeats was as restless as ever, and Lady Gregory anxious looking. George Moore (who, by the way, when asked what he thought of *The Image,* replied, "A bog slide!"), Magee, James Starkey, P. Colum, Arnold Graves . . . and dozens of other well known people. . . . There was a stir of first night expectation about the house that was very noticeable, and Larchet's specially written prelude put us in the proper frame of mind to follow the play sympathetically. Of course, there was a sadness over all in the thought that Synge died ere he completed the work to his own satisfaction.

I suppose it was in the natural order of things that Synge should have followed the example of Ferguson, Rolleston, George Russell, Yeats, Father O'Kelly, etc., and taken the story of Deirdre as his theme. . . . His idea seems to have been to wrest the legend from its exalted plane and breathe the commonplaces of everyday life into it — in fact, to vulgarise the beautiful legend. That he succeeded in doing this is only too true. His characters of "Lavarcham" . . . , of "Owen" a half-witted servant, and of an "Old Woman" might have stepped out of any of his latter-day peasant plays; the ruck of muck was in their speech. As a stage play, I fear Synge's *Deirdre of the Sorrows* is of little worth. Up to a certain point, the last act is dramatic, but there it is allowed to fizzle out drearily in ineffective anti-climaxes, and the final curtain comes as a relief to all in front, even to Synge's most ardent worshippers. As a drama it is not to be compared with either AE's or Father O'Kelly's versions, and the taint of the author that runs through all his work save *Riders to the Sea* was again distinctly noticeable in his last work.

When the play was over and done, Seumas O'Sullivan said, as many of us chattered in the vestibule, that "There was nothing incomplete about it. The people in the play were human beings at all events and not merely inanimate Kings and Queens!" I grant that the loftiness of the theme was trailed in the mud if that's what he meant by "human beings," but the treatment took the grandeur and poetry out of the tale. . . .

Maire O'Neill was a distinct success as "Deirdre," and in the final act her costume in distinct contrast to the background of the tent created many memorably beautiful pictures. Her acting was always sincere and restrained, and lent interest to the play where it would otherwise have proved excessively dreary were it not for her dainty and lovely creation. Her "Deirdre of the Sorrows" was an exquisite embodiment of the simple child of nature as conceived by Synge. . . .

All seemed afraid to express themselves freely or candidly on the play when it was over, but that the general impression was not favourable could easily be felt. Were the play an undoubted success, nothing could keep back the hymns of praise. It is only when failure is close at hand that silence holds thoughts in check.

Sunday, February 27.   Received the following from Frank Fay: [1] ". . . I think you rather exaggerate the merits of the Abbey Company. Sinclair never was and never will be 'great'; he is a born actor, without brains or taste. They all need the test of bigger and more complicated plays. Their heads have been unduly swelled by excessive praise. . . . The more I see of Shakespeare and the more I play in him, the more I see the futility of Yeats's plays in verse. The verse play is not a modern form. . . ."

Thursday, March 3.   I received the following letter from Edward Martyn.[2] ". . . I have to thank you for the copy of *The Evening Telegraph* . . . containing the report of your very interesting lecture on the acting of the Irish players. I have, as you know, a very great admiration for their work. If some of the members of the company are flying away from Dublin that is perhaps a matter for congratulations as well as for regrets; and I only hope they may be making comfortable nests for themselves elsewhere, and that the English stage may benefit by their example and their influence. Indeed, I have suggested in more quarters than one that certain ladies and gentlemen of the company should be offered engagements in London. . . ."

Saturday, March 5.   MacDonagh mentioned that Robinson was about to be appointed stage manager to the Abbey Company, and he did not know how it would turn out; he had his doubts if it would be well.

Friday, April 1.   I met Sinclair with Fred Jeffs and another as I left the Abbey after the revival of *The Eloquent Dempsy,* and Sinclair said, "It was a great victory for you . . . and Boyle." There never was such a Friday night's audience before at the Abbey. I mildly but sarcastically said, "Perhaps it was *The Glittering Gate* attracted them," and my remark raised smiles in the group.

The Eloquent Dempsy had proved a huge success, and there was no denying the fact. Yeats might look glum, Dunsany bored, and "Ethel" Robinson startled, but the audience overflowed the pit and balcony and almost filled the stalls, to laugh themselves almost sick. . . . The various shades of discontent on the face of Yeats were a study worthy of any face contortionist. The director of a theatre usually is in high glee when he sees the theatre . . . full. However, it is not so with Yeats; when he sees it so and his work not on the stage. Egotism is king of his soul!

Thursday, May 5.   Padraic Colum's new play *Thomas Muskerry* was played for the first time at the Abbey before a large and very distinguished audience. It is a play full of unrelieved gloom, and I fear were it not for the really excellent interpretation given it by the Abbey Company it would have been generally voted very dull and depressing indeed. The play is full of crude, under-developed ideas that worry the spectator in trying to piece them out to their logical ends. Colum leaves too much to the imagination; as a dramatist he seldom "joins his flats," as they used to say in the theatre long ago. . . .

I also noticed with regret that the author's style had been coarsened by the influence of some of the modern writers for the stage, and it did not sit lightly on his work. . . . He has an irritatingly abrupt way of getting his characters on and off the stage, and his dialogue is frequently unsatisfyingly skimpy.[3]

Saturday, May 7.   . . . Sinclair speaking of the confusion behind the scenes at the Abbey when the curtains were down said he couldn't think how anything came ever right. The confusion was so great, with everyone rushing here and there, and telling everyone else to mind his own business. . . .

The Queen's, the Gaiety, the Cinematograph Theatre in O'Connell Street closed on account of the King's death,[4] and also the Tivoli, Empire, James's, Samuel's, and the Volta. The Abbey was alone in its glory in opening its door to the public, and a big house resulted. Henderson told me he had received Lady Gregory's telegram too late to act upon it. Robinson was all for notoriety and opening. Had Henderson been in his place, the theatre would not have opened.

I had a chat with Miss Allgood who felt the opening very much—thought it was a shame not to show a little respect. From what she said the company have no great love for Robinson. What does he know, having been only six weeks in London?[5] When she first read the script of *Thomas Muskerry*, Robinson told her to put more emotion into it. Fancy telling her such a thing at first reading when she was merely feeling out the meaning of the part.

She simply told him she couldn't, and that he did not know what he was talking about. . . . Robinson knew nothing about directing a play; the company felt the loss of Frank Fay in this particular; he knew, and took great pains to be perfect. . . .

Edward Martyn was seated in the vestibule waiting for Yeats's farce [6] to be over. I had a chat with him. I opened by saying Colum's play was gloomy, and he said he did not mind that so long as the piece gave him "sensations" and set him thinking. *The Land* he thought commonplace, but *The Fiddler's House* was full of imagination and poetry of thought. Boyle's plays were vulgar and commonplace and without a scrap of imagination. The peasant as peasant did not appeal to Martyn at all. Boyle . . . just like Pinero wrote plays that attracted the common herd of playgoers; they were no better than Dion Boucicault's dramas which he detested. They were merely mechanical essays at drama without imagination or ideas —meant to please the unthinking herd.

I ventured to say I preferred "Shaun the Post" [7] to the dirty tramps that replaced him on the Abbey stage. He despised my ideas and said a tramp when poetically treated, as he was in some of the plays he had seen at the Abbey, was a glorious fellow.

If Martyn's thoughts were not set going by the play, he considered it as nothing. Hundreds wrote drama for the multitude like Boyle, but few could write drama for the intellect. He was sorry they wanted Boyle back, and when I said, "But he draws as no other Abbey playwright does," he said, "I know that, and it is for the simple reason that his work is devoid of anything but the commonplace." I insisted that Boyle knew how to write plays and mentioned the "Grogans" [8] as admirable character studies, but he would not own that they were aught but commonplace and idea-less.

In fact, I came to the conclusion that Edward Martyn was a crank of the worst kind, and did not want a play to be a play at all, but a frame to hang fancies and dreams upon.

Thursday, May 12.   I saw in the evening papers that Miss Horniman threatened to withdraw her subsidy to the National Theatre Society for opening the Abbey on last Saturday unless proper regret is shown in the press by the directors. Following Miss Horniman's letter came the Directors' regret and explanation of the why and wherefore of the said keeping open when all other places of amusement were closed. "The Directors regret that owing to accident the theatre remained open on Saturday last."

Thursday, May 19.   The afternoon and evening turned out very wet and gloomy. Nevertheless, a goodly crowd attended the Abbey to see the first performance of S. L. Robinson's new three-act play, *Harvest.* The new play shows a vast improvement on the young dramatist's previous essays in drama, and despite its gloom, strong language, and nastiness of material held the audience to the end. The plays at the Abbey are getting more and more gloomy. . . . When will Irish dramatists treat of something bright, clean, and healthful in the lives of our people? They surely are not all rotten at the core, as Synge and Robinson would have us believe.

Saturday, June 11.   Frank Fay and Mrs. Fay were in to tea. We chatted theatres for over three hours. . . . I happened to mention *In the Shadow of the Glen* in connection with the wake scene in *The Shaughraun,* and Fay was of opinion that Synge never heard of the play or its author before he wrote his little piece.[9] . . . He afterwards saw James O'Brien in *The Shaughraun* and was delighted with him. . . .

The Abbey company had fallen into indistinctness of utterance and gabbled the text frequently; this was an unpardonable fault, he thought. He complained that Shakespeare as a rule was spoken too slowly on the stage. In his opinion much of it was written to be spoken rapidly, but never indistinctly. Synge could not be spoken quickly. The Abbey folk in *Deirdre of the Sorrows* made

the grave mistake in thinking it could, and became indistinct. . . .

The St. Patrick's Club at Oxford held its annual dinner
and entertained Lord MacDonnell and Mr. W. B. Yeats.
"Lord MacDonnell's speech was received with great enthusiasm," while Mr. Yeats's is described by the correspondent of the *Pall Mall Gazette* as "a perfect work of
art, yet, at the same time, natural, sincere, and
unaffected." This is the first time Yeats was ever accused
of being sincere or unaffected.

Monday, June 13.   I received the following letter from
William Boyle.

> 56 CRESCENT LANE
> CLAPHAM, S. W.
> *Saturday*

Dear Holloway,

Dempsy has got through the ordeal.[10] All the
papers note it amusing—some brilliantly so—one or
two think it rather thin—which is not news to me—but
none abuse it. The other Abbey plays have received
mixed receptions. The majority condemn *Harvest*,
though some gush over it, and the same may be said of
Thomas Muskerry. . . . On the whole, I have little
hope of the future of the Abbey. The visit has depressed me. I don't think I'll send them my new play
which is now well on towards completion. In truth, I
don't think they want it. The first two days Yeats
passed me by without speaking, but after Thursday's
(*Dempsy*) having filled the house—the only full house
they have had so far—he changed, and came and spoke
to me in a friendly manner. Robinson does not notice
me. Her Ladyship I haven't seen at all. If it wasn't for
poor Henderson, who has shown me every courtesy,
and the actors, whom I cordially admire, I'd have no
more to do with the performances. . . .

> Yours,
> W. Boyle

Thursday, June 16.   I received the following letter from Edward Martyn.

5 RUSSELL MANSIONS
RUSSELL SQUARE, W. C.
15 / 6 / 10

My dear Sir,

I have to thank you for your very kind and interesting letter. It gratifies me to find myself in accord with one who has evidently so much sympathy with the work of the theatre and so clear an understanding of it as you have. It is my firm belief that ninety-nine people in a hundred cannot tell good acting from bad and, being used to the bad, acquire a taste for it, as they do for indifferent wives. You and I, my dear sir, are epicures in the theatre.

Sincerely yours,
Edward Martyn

Thursday, July 14.   Met W. B. Yeats at the Abbey about lowering of stage to level of footlights, and also discussed the Gordon Craig scheme for reducing the size of stage pictures by an arrangement that expands or contracts from sides and top automatically. But somehow to Mr. Barlow and me it did not seem very practical on a small stage like the Abbey. While waiting for the builder to come, Yeats spoke of Gordon Craig being so sensitive, and he foresaw the amount of correspondence he would draw down on his head if he could not carry out Craig's scheme intact.

A poster on the wall of the manager's room set him off speaking on collector's fads. He knew one man who collected addresses presented to public men, and another who collected hotel door keys and had his walls decorated with them and the name of each hotel from which he made the capture attached to each. On the whole, he thought the fad of collecting a very poor pastime. I did not agree with him, and said, "Every collection of no matter what becomes more valuable the more complete it becomes. Without collections many perishable things like playbills would be lost completely; they are trifles easily destroyed or forgotten by most people."

Monday, August 1.   . . . Mrs. Dudley Digges was speaking to Henderson in the vestibule as I entered, and Mr. Digges soon joined us. The people came pouring in all the while we spoke in most encouraging way. *The Eloquent Dempsy* is a magnet that draws even in a deluge. The Digges told me they had been all through the theatre the other day and found it splendidly appointed in every way; the dressing rooms were particularly well fitted up and convenient.

A stout-built block of a fellow in a bowler hat came in, and Mrs. Digges recognised him as Mr. Connolly,[11] a socialist, anarchist, and she did not know what, whom she met in America. He had just come over to preach his gospel in Ireland a few days ago. She went over to speak to him and then brought him over to introduce him to me. We spoke for a few moments. He said he had been told Boyle's play was a good thing, and also that the theatre was over a morgue. . . . There was a good deal of the Irish-American about him, and he looked a determined bit of goods.

Thursday, September 29.   . . . I was bound for the Abbey to see the first production of R. J. Ray's new peasant play in three acts, entitled *The Casting-Out of Martin Whelan.* . . . Mr. Ray has made a great advance in his new play on his first attempt, *The White Feather*.[12] The chief faults with the new work are that it is too talky, rather loosely constructed, and the characters are too fond of explaining themselves to each other, rather than through their actions. . . .[13]

Kerrigan made quite a hit as old "Peter Barton," an ignorant old farmer with an educated daughter whom he could not make head or tail of and with a drunken sot of a

son who was not above setting a grabber's hay rick on fire
on occasion. It was a fine character study. An actor new to
the Abbey—Brinsley MacNamara—was excellent as
"Denis Barton," and got a round of applause on his exit
in Act 1 and a call at the end of the act.

Monday, October 3.   Antient Concert Rooms. Lecture
on "The Poor Law and Destitution in Ireland" by George
Bernard Shaw. . . . Shaw arose clad in a dark suit, with
short square-cut double-breasted coat that gave him the
appearance of a hardy yachtsman. He went to business at
once, and kept at it without pause for over an hour and
twenty minutes, stating facts straight in the face and
stating them clearly and with stinging humour. It was a
wonderfully brilliant talk containing a wonderful amount
of food for thought. He was hissed for a slighting reference to the Gaelic, and Dr. McWalter contradicted his
assertion that the Irish girls have bad teeth. Shaw deplored the time and energy wasted on the denunciation of
Synge's *The Playboy* when it could have been given to
some other more useful cause. He made his uninviting
subject extremely interesting, and put his hearers into the
dock, as it were, before he concluded his remarks, and
they all felt condemned criminals ere he had done with
them. Shaw uses few gestures and "speaks right on without pause, just as he writes," as Magee (John Eglinton)
said to me after the lecture. Everyone felt he had heard an
unusually brilliant discourse by an astoundingly clever
man, and all said they would not have missed it for
anything. . . . In the course of his remarks, Shaw said he
never argued; you could take or leave the statements he
made. He saw facts and stated them as plainly as he
could. The obvious was always startlingly original. . . . I
felt as I left the hall that I had been through one of those
great exciting events of one's life, that come so seldom
and stand out so clearly in one's memory afterwards.

Wednesday, October 12.   I received the following from
William Boyle.

56 CRESCENT LANE
CLAPHAM, S. W.
11 Oct. '10

Dear Holloway,

What's the good of saying you want another play from me when everything makes it clear that the Abbey Directors don't? Since they have taken up the role of reviling Irish characters—apparently for political purposes—I must remain out of it. I am not and don't intend becoming a party hack. The Abbey Directors' censorship is worse than that of Russia. Only one side of life must be presented on their stage and that the side against Ireland. Art, beauty, truth—everything is ignored so long as one political faction can be helped. Surely everyone by this time sees this. . . .

Yours,

W. Boyle

If I knew a new play of mine would be produced, I'd send it quick enough.

Thursday, October 13.   Called in at the Abbey and had a chat. I went up to Henderson and showed him both Boyle's and Frank Fay's letters. He told me Maire Walker was coming back next month. He never thought much of her; Annie Walker is just as good now as ever she was. I agreed to differ with him, and said she could play some parts as no other actress could play them. Sara Allgood still suffers from tonsilated sore throat and intends having them cut out. Maire O'Neill does not intend playing any more old woman characters—a style of role in which she excels. She is also good in winsome young girl parts, but strong emotion is out of her line. Sara Allgood excels in strong emotional work or character roles like "Mrs. Grogan." Sinclair says she does not like to be told so. Few of us know what we are really good at. Even Sinclair himself thinks he excels in serious work and gets riled if you hint you do not think so. Henderson thinks the coming of Maire Walker will break up the company.

Thursday, October 27. I may say at once that T. C. Murray scored with his lurid melodrama *Birthright* at the Abbey on its first production, and was loudly and unanimously called before the curtain at the end of the play. . . . As the curtains divided, Mr. Murray bowed hurriedly and fled. He held a programme in his hand. He is a young man with boyish expression of face, and in speaking shows his gums and teeth abundantly. . . .

Of late, the Abbey has earned for itself "the house of the drama of bad language," and *Birthright* caps all previous efforts in this direction; it was studded with oaths. Mr. Murray got the straight tip of how to get his play through at the Abbey. Mr. Guinan would not take Mr. Fitzmaurice's advice when he wrote *The Cuckoo's Nest* and sent it in to the Abbey. Fitz said, "It will never do as it stands; pepper the dialogue with oaths, and they will swallow it at the Abbey." His words came true, and the play was returned. . . . *Birthright* is a very strong, promising play, but it was nearly damned by damns. . . .

The acting was admirable—superb in some cases. Eileen O'Doherty [14] as the mother, full of kindness and motherly love, made the hit of her life and was wholly admirable from start to finish. She got thoroughly into the skin of the tactful woman and created quite an impression. . . . Sinclair looked more like a cowboy of the Far West than a farm hand on a farm in County Cork.

Friday, October 28 At the professional matinee at the Abbey, I met Mr. Murray, the author of *Birthright,* in the vestibule and congratulated him on his success and afterwards got into conversation with him. He was not pleased with the dressing of his play; they dress as well as himself on a Sunday in the part of Cork in which his plot was laid. He also wrote to Robinson to omit firing the last shot —leaving the ending to the imagination. He had a letter from Robinson about other things and with a footnote: "We must fire the last shot." All the critics say that last shot spoils the play. "It won't be fired to-night," said Mr. Murray.

He also objected to O'Donovan being so drunk and stammering in his father's presence. Morgan he thought fine and Miss Walker perfect as the mother; she thoroughly realised the part as he conceived it. . . .

Lady Gregory sat behind Mr. Murray last night, but did not know him, and he overheard many remarks about what she called "the realistic school of Cork dramatists," and spoke slightingly of them. Many complimented her on her own work. Mr. Murray thought there was far too much of Lady Gregory's work on the Abbey programmes. He thought it weak of the Directors to beg for money when they could make money by playing the right plays. Boyle was their chief asset if they were clearsighted enough to see it. *The Playboy* ought to be stopped. It was in no sense characteristic of the people. . . .

Mr. Murray wrote a farce for the Cork theatre, his weakest thing. When in rehearsal he noticed some "bloodys" in the text and said they had better be omitted to him who was producing the play, the other replied that to be like the country speech such a word would want to be in every sentence. Now Mr. Murray found on hearing his own play last night that he had fallen into the same error and used much bad language which he did not discover until he heard it spoken on the stage—a lot of which he has omitted. . . .

We parted at the end of the performance, and I left him speaking to Yeats under the verandah as I hurried away. Mr. Murray was speaking to George Moore who told him "not to alter a word of it," meaning the play, of course.

Tuesday, November 10.   The limit was reached surely in Lady Gregory's new comedy *The Full Moon* at the Abbey to-night before a good house. One would imagine that Lady Gregory considered her audience a pack of lunatics to put before them such a hopelessly inane production. Oh, the pity of it all, to see fine actors and actresses having to make such fools of themselves just to please the whims of a conceited old lady who happens to be the boss of the show and who must be obeyed. Such undramatic rot it has never been my misfortune to see before. It led nowhere. All the characters talked and talked, and every now and again behaved like people in a pantomime rally.

Thursday, November 24.   Maire nic Shiubhlaigh made a triumphant re-entry on the Abbey stage as "Moll Woods," the stroller and ballad singer in O'Kelly's gloomy yet powerful two-act play *The Shuiler's Child*, before a large and enthusiastic audience who welcomed her back by a round of applause on her first entry and by repeated enthusiastic calls at the end of Act 1 and at the end of the play. Hers is a truly pathetic figure of the strange wild creature of the roads, hungering for the child she once deserted. And the strange, weird, woe-begone picture she presented just suited the part. There was something in her manner and voice that thrilled through me and made me pity the poor wretch from the bottom of my heart. Towards the end of the second act where she sings in a sort of frenzied madness a snatch of one of her street ballads . . . the picture presented was one of thrilling pathos, and the audience followed it with the stillness of death.

Tuesday, November 29.   . . . I called in at the Abbey and saw the stagehands setting Gordon Craig's new ideas of scenery—a series of square box-like pillars saffron-hued, with saffron background, wings, sky pieces, and everything. The entire setting struck me as like as peas, only on a big scale, of the blocks I as a child built houses of. As Yeats never played with blocks in his youth, Gordon Craig's childish ideas give him keen delight now. . . .

Miss A. E. F. Horniman, whose generosity nursed the Irish school of drama and acting into success, relinquishes her hold on it today on the expiration of the six-year patent granted to her for the Abbey Theatre. . . . To-morrow Lady Gregory takes up the reins as patentee for its renewed lease of life for twenty-one years to come.

Friday, December 2.   Received the following letter from Miss Horniman:

H 1 MONTAGUE MANSIONS
PORTMAN SQUARE W.
LONDON
Dec. 1/10

Dear Mr. Holloway,

Courtesy from Dublin is so very rare that I must write at once to thank you for sending me yesterday's *Evening Telegraph.* You are just a little wrong about the sum spent—£10,350 has been spent by me at the Abbey. This does *not* include the losses made on tours in England; the profits made there were always handed to the Directors. As to the £1,000 to be returned to me —the shop and house in Abbey Street (now let) and a stable behind the Abbey cost £1,428, but the Directors would not give me the latter sum which I asked for originally, although I am giving them the whole of the contents of the buildings as they stand. I should like you to know that I offered to come over to aid in the application for the patent, but my presence was not considered necessary. My initial mistake was simple—it took me a long time to learn that there was no room for an educated middle-class woman who loves the Arts in Dublin. Commercial Manchester is a very different city.

Mr. Robert Gregory was solely responsible for the dressing and staging of *Kincora.* I should not wish to take any credit from him.

With kind regards,
Yours sincerely,
A. E. F. Horniman

1911

Thursday, January 12.   With a great flourish of egotistical trumpets on the part of the management and Yeats in dress clothes with crush opera hat in hand, the Gordon Craig freak scenery and lighting were tried at the Abbey in Lady Gregory's Hiberno-Egyptian one-act tragic comedy *The Deliverer,* and also in Yeats's morality *The Hour Glass.* And while most voted the innovation an affected failure with possibilities for effective stage pictures, none considered it in any way an improvement on the old methods. . . . The dresses designed or carried out from sketches supplied by Craig were most unsightly and ungainly, especially in *The Deliverer.* The ladies wore a sort of short hobble skirt that reached a little below the knees and brought to mind to Mr. Hughes *The Playboy's* description of "the twelve eastern maidens in their shifts.". . .

The Deliverer as a piece of dramatic writing is beneath contempt. "Tripe" was the name applied to it by Miss Allgood when referring to it the other night at the National Literary Society. . . . The audience looked on in wonder during the progress of *The Deliverer,* all wondering what it was about and why all the Egyptians spoke Kiltartan, like the natives of the region of Lady Gregory's brain.

Friday, January 27.   Seeing by all the papers that Lord Dunsany's play in two acts *King Argimenes and the Un-*

known Warrior was a success on its first production at the Abbey last night, I was sadly disappointed on seeing it to-night to find it a crude, ill-digested piece of work with a really fine speech for "Argimenes" in the opening act, splendidly given by Fred O'Donovan. If a speech could make a play, this one would have done the trick. But, alas, the author let the comic element creep into the second act to spoil all, and so what promised big things degenerated into burlesque. . . .

Lord Dunsany arrived looking radiant; he beamed with delight over the first night success of his play. . . . Yeats came on the scene, discarding his overcoat and looking as shifty as usual. . . . Robinson hovered around silently, and then passed away having the same effect on my mind as a telegraph pole seen through the windows of a rapidly moving train.

Thursday, February 16.   *The Land of Heart's Desire* by W. B. Yeats was tried for the first time by the Abbey Company [1] and failed completely to convince. Were it not for the beautiful playing of Sara Allgood as the be-witched, newly-made bride, "Maire Bruin," the piece would be hopeless as a stage play. . . .

Sara Allgood has refused to play "Widow Quin" in *The Playboy* anymore, and Robinson says they will compel her to play it, and they have the press with them in Man-chester and won't they make her smart through it! What a little puppy this elongated essence of conceited impu-dence must be.

Thursday, March 30.   It was a great night at the Abbey. The excitement of an important first night was visible on every side. The theatre rapidly became thronged; even the stalls could not have held another. . . . The event was the first production of a play in four acts by St. John G. Ervine, a young Belfastman, son of a minister, entitled *Mixed Marriage.* [2] The subject was topical of the moment and had a spice of actuality in it. . . . The piece took well and is a clever topical discussion with about ten minutes real drama in Act III, rather than a living play from first to last. It must be written down a propagandist play with too much reiteration. . . . Robinson came in with Mr. Ervine, the author of the play, and made him known to Henderson who handed him a letter. Mr. Ervine is very young in appearance, and resembles a sort of pocket edition of Lord Dunsany. . . . The rock on which the young dramatist strikes is "talk." He has got the modern idea that talk makes drama, whereas it is action and action only that keeps an audience illusioned. Talk may entertain for awhile, but it can't make a play of itself.

Thursday, December 7.   *Red Turf*, Rutherford Mayne's new one-act play at the Abbey to-night, proved merely a crude essay in melodrama plus bad language. . . . The play saddened me when I thought of Mayne's comedies *The Drone* and *The Turn of the Road*—both pieces of sheer delight. . . . The "damns" are having their day at the Abbey.

1912

Tuesday, January 2. I visited The Hermitage (St. Enda's) and was in town with P. H. Pearse. We spoke of the reception of the Irish Players in America. He is very tolerant of everyone's views and never hisses. The Abbey is a freak theatre and should be treated as such; if you don't like it, stop away. Pearse admires Yeats for his splendid pluck. He thinks Yeats the greatest talker in Ireland. Ireland has always had such men as Shaw, Yeats, Martyn, Russell, and Moore—irresponsible beings that help to keep life fresh. . . . Pearse thought the Abbey was run too much on Ascendancy principles. He often saw Lady Gregory enjoying her own pieces and laughing at her own jokes. Yeats does the same. Truly they were both like little children in their ways. It would be fine for someone to burlesque the whole Abbey movement, and get the Abbey Theatre and produce the burlesque there with someone got up as Yeats to run up and down the stairs, etc. A young man like Yeats should not have accepted the pension, and he always professing nationalist principles also. He made a fine speech on Wolfe Tone; he was a great speaker, but had no sincerity at the back of anything he said. . . . Pearse did not rightly know whether Yeats was a man of self-consciousness or childlike simplicity. Much they thought artistic was eccentricity. . . . Pearse did not believe all the Irish were as bad as the Abbey plays would have us believe. He maintained that those who did not hold with the Abbey and its doing should stay away; he believed in freedom for all.

I suggested that Yeats and Lady Gregory were so near-sighted that they would allow freedom of thought to no one; everyone should think as they did. Their conceit is colossal and tyrannical.

Wednesday, January 17.   All the players of the Abbey Company were arrested in Philadelphia on ground that *The Playboy* is an immoral production. Later they were bailed out on a sum of $5000, and have to appear before the magistrate on Friday to answer the charge.[1]

Friday, March 29.   Lawrence came in and told me about last night.[2] He sent a telegram to Boyle in my name. He met D. J. O'Donoghue there. He was also speaking to Colum; the latter was doing notice for *The Manchester Guardian.* The queue was the longest Lawrence had ever seen at the Abbey. Some wondered at its length until told Boyle was a power in the land. Yeats was present looking as glum and unhappy as could be. The crowd for Boyle sent him thinking. At the end there were great cries for author which made Yeats uneasy, and at last he went behind as the calls continued. Sinclair it was who answered that the author was not in the house, and thanked the audience for the reception of the play and their work. Lawrence thought Sinclair quiet and artistic in the play, and Annie Walker gave a remarkable portrait of an old maid—as perfect in its way as the mother in *Birthright.* The first act was perfect, but the others fell away and became improbable.

Saturday, April 7.   Received the following letter from John Guinan:

13 VICTORIA ROAD
RATHGAR, CO. DUBLIN
Saturday

Dear Mr. Holloway,
You will be interested to know that *The Cuckoo's Nest* has been accepted at the Abbey. . . . If the piece has any success I'll owe it largely to yourself.

Only you liked it. I might possibly have burnt it long ago. As it is, I think when it is pruned down a bit, it ought to go. They told me not to touch the Ms. at all — that everything will be done at rehearsals. May be whenever they come off you'll be able to give a look in.

Yours sincerely,
John Guinan

Thursday, April 11. The Home Rule Bill was introduced into the House of Commons, and *Patriots* was played for the first time at the Abbey.[3] I hope the first mentioned will be the success that is hoped; the latter is nothing to boast of as a play. The first act is dull, the second interesting in patches, and the third fell to pieces.

Thursday, April 25. I am a play-goer before all. If a play comes across the footlights with dramatic illusion, then all is well. If not, all is ill. That it is literary does not matter a straw if the dramatic instinct is absent. Most of those who judge the plays at the Abbey are literary critics pure and simple, and have little sense of the theatre — hence the puffery of literary craftsmanship and the belittling of true dramatic work. To be successful as a dramatist on the Abbey stage is to be despised by the highbrows. Boyle and Casey, who know how to write successful plays and draw audiences as well, are no class with the high and mighty type of non-theatrical critic brought into being by the production of undramatic literary plays. They can only see merit in the unactable. If the turn of phrase pleases, then its dramatic worth may go hang.

Wednesday, June 19. I received the following letter from T. C. Murray.

WOODVILLE, RATHDUFF, CO. CORK
17 / 6 / 12
Dear Mr. Holloway,
It was very kind and thoughtful of you to send me *The Express.*[4] You must have been somewhat surprised to see the altered title. The Abbey people — or at

least Robinson—objected to the original title. Maunsel's didn't care for it either. So I adopted that of *Maurice Harte*—the name of the central character in the play. I was very disappointed at its non-production in Dublin, and but for Yeats I doubt that it would have been rehearsed on tour. I think your friend Father Brown will like the play.[5] The whole atmosphere of it is Catholic and Irish in its best sense. In the *American Ecclesiastical Review*, I read an article by Rev. George O'Neill, in which he states that the Abbey plays were either non-Catholic or anti-Catholic. This is a notable exception. Four priests—three of them on the Dublin mission—have read the Ms. and have given it as their opinion that it is elevating and that it introduces for the first time perhaps the true note of Irish Catholic life on the Abbey stage. . . .

> Yours very sincerely,
> T. C. Murray

Tuesday, July 2.   Brinsley MacNamara came into tea about the proposed book on the Abbey.[6] . . . I received the following letter from William Boyle.

> 56 CRESCENT LANE
> CLAPHAM S. W.
> 1 *July 1912*

My dear Holloway,
   Thanks for your kind card. The play[7] went remarkably well considering the atrocious way in which it was produced. Few of the players were at home in their words, and the whole thing was done in the slowest manner possible, speeches left out here and repeated there in a way to make many of the retorts pointless. . . . Clearly, it had not been rehearsed half enough, and no one seemed to care whether the words spoken were mine or the actor's own "make-up" on the spur of the moment.[8] . . .

> Yours very truly,
> W. Boyle

Friday, August 30.   I met Padraic Colum at Webb's on the quay where he was trying to dispose of some of his books, and ultimately did for 3/-. . . . I said I was sorry that Sinclair did not produce his play at the Coliseum, but it was the old lady's fault.[9]

He exclaimed sarcastically, "Poor old lady, she is blamed for everything, and she has no one to take her part."

"Never you bother; she is well able to take care of herself," said I.

"She is, indeed," said he. "I only spoke sarcastically just now."

He struck a hard bargain with Webb, extolling each book as being "great." "*The Black Prophet* by Carleton with illustrations by J. B. Yeats—a splendid book," he said, "with remarkable illustrations. Rhys of Everyman's Library said all the world would be reading it, had it been written in Russia."

Webb merely said he found it difficult to dispose of a few hundred copies of the book he had for three years at 1/6 a copy. Two hundred copies of *Irish Fairy Tales* with introduction by Yeats took over four years to sell at 2/- a copy. He thought a year or two would see them all gone.

Thursday, October 17.   There was a big house present at the Abbey for the first night of St. John G. Ervine's one-act play of Belfast life *The Magnanimous Lover,* which had been so long shelved for lack of an actress to fill the role of "Maggie Cather," the girl who had fallen away, owing to the coarse expressions put into her mouth. Mrs. Mair (Maire O'Neill)[10] volunteered to play that part, hence its production to-night, and the mild excitement it caused amongst Abbey first nighters. . . . The play's only merit is its unsavouriness—this is always the side that appeals to the Directors.

Wednesday, October 30.   Lawrence dropped in the following letter . . . from Frank Fay.

3 CAMBRIDGE TER.
SUNDERLAND
Sunday (Oct. 27)

Dear W. J.,

Thanks for letter and enclosure, which I return. I am glad your book [11] is so well noticed. England is too busy money-grubbing to have time to devote to thinking about the right way to put before the public the work of her greatest son. I am, I must tell you, very jealous of anyone writing about the Abbey Theatre. I alone know how it originated because the idea was mine. If you want any information for your article, I can give it to you. I hope you have counted, and will publish, the number of times the pieces of that selfish old lady have been played.[12] I viewed her entrance into our movement with distrust from the first. It is astonishing that Dublin can allow an outsider like Monck to be placed in the position that either Will or I should have.[13] It will interest you to know that on the Monday morning following the production of *The Playboy* Lady Gregory referred to Boyle as a "rotten branch." When speaking to me about his letter to the press severing his connection with the theatre, Synge also wrote me a letter (which, *at his request,* I burnt) in which he said a Yeats-Gregory Theatre would be no use to anybody. . . . I want to get back to Dublin. . . .

Yours sincerely,
Frank

Monday, November 25.   As I passed by Essex Street, I saw an extremely long queue of wretched, hungry-looking men ranged against the wall in two's awaiting to get relief from the Dublin Distress Office in the corner house. Numbers of others, as hungry-looking as themselves, stood looking in from the other side. It was a picture of Dublin I had not seen before, and it distressed me very much when I thought of the hundreds of poor wretches that stood shivering and hungry lined up in the street awaiting help.

1913

Saturday, March 22. . . . Yeats is a fascinating talker [1] —good to listen to even if one does not grasp all he says. He always invites questions at the end of his lectures for fear some would go away without understanding him. His answers, as a rule, are more mystifying than his original statements. He is so full of musical words that his sentences form themselves into rhapsodies of speech rather than clear explanations of basic fact. A poet has a right to cloud his words in obscurity. At any rate, Yeats takes the opportunity. He couldn't say yes or no to anything—a flood of words comes forth as sure as he opens his mouth to form a simple yea or nay. He is a wonder truly. What would Dublin do without its Yeats? Why, empty of distinction. . . .

Saturday, April 19. I met James Stephens in Eason's, and I said, "I was pleased to see such a glowing notice of your book *The Crock of Gold* in *The Daily News* of Thursday."

He said, "Someone sent the notice to me. It means a sandwich or two more to me and a bottle of stout."

Thursday, April 24. . . . George Fitzmaurice's one-act play *The Magic Glasses* . . . knocked *The Full Moon* out of the place of honour, as the silliest production ever attempted on the Abbey stage.

Friday, May 2.   Arthur Sinclair came over after the
matinee and had tea with us. He spoke of Brinsley Mac-
Namara and his playing the role of self-appointed advance
agent to the Abbey Company in the States [2] in order to
touch people, until he became such a nuisance that the
company made up his fare and something over and sent
him back to Ireland. Now he is turning and rending them
in the press for their kindness. He may have talent but he
is very lazy. A play of his was refused at the Abbey. He
was on *The Boston Transcript* for awhile. On the first
tour he was engaged as understudy, but when he was
called up to play Morgan's part in *The Image*, it was
found he hadn't learned it at all. Sinclair also told us that
why he didn't come to us the evening we asked him
before the company left for the States was because he
thought Sara Allgood was coming, and he didn't want to
meet her as they had not been on speaking terms for
years. She was very hard to pull with.

Tuesday, June 24.   We spent the evening at Colum's at
2 Belville Avenue, Donnybrook. William Boyle had arrived before us, and M. Bourgeois soon followed. . . .
Colum has a snappy way of interjecting queries in others'
conversation that invariably hauls up the speaker with a
rush and stops the flow of talk for a time. . . .

When Colum repeated, "What the hell!" Boyle po-
litely intimated, "There are ladies present." But God love
them, they didn't mind a bit, the dears. Irish drama has
made them used to it. . . .

What a strange and wonderful head is Colum's with its
big, half-dome-like forehead and large, velvety soft sad
eyes under curved brows with long straggling locks of hair
falling anyhow over forehead and ears and covering the
abnormally large sweep of skull at back of head. His nose
is delicately formed and his mouth regular, with rounded
sweep of chin. A strikingly delicate face, with thin hollow
cheeks and drawn sad expression. A poet to the eye! A
little scrap of humanity with pathos clinging around his
personality. . . . Eileen said to Mr. Boyle, "Colum is

quite like a poet in expression," and Boyle replied, "Yes, but he is far too clean and washed. Thompson, who sold matches on the Embankment, rarely washed."

Thursday, July 10.   When I was downtown in the early part of the day, I saw AE looking into Greene's library window and scanning the backs of the books with his nose nearly touching the glass. He was looking well and more tidy than usual. He had discarded his old overcoat, and had his hair and beard trimmed. Dr. Gogarty motored past with a lady in the motor, as I stood at the door of No. 6, St. Stephen's Green, and I thought of George Moore's description of him in *Salve* as the wit of Dublin. To me he always looks like an overgrown schoolboy who would like to be thinner so that he could more readily take part in games.

Saturday, September 6.   . . . I again went down to the Abbey in the evening, and again the house was very slack owing to the strike and the stoppage of tramcars in the evening.[3] . . . A fellow of the Labour-leader type, half-seas-over, waited to see the new manager, Wilson. . . . Morgan came out to enquire if a parcel had come for Mr. Wilson. I enquired, "What sort of a parcel was it?" And he said, "It was made up of bottles, if you want to know." It had not come, and he retired again. Henderson, as we took our tea, said, "What a change has come over the theatre of late. All the old bohemian spirit has fled from those connected with it."

Thursday, September 11.   T. C. Murray's revised version of his first essay at playwriting, *The Wheel of Fortune*, entitled *Sovereign Love*, played for the first time at the Abbey to-night, proved a great success. It is a merry little comedy of country matchmaking, full of fine characterisation. . . . In speaking to Padraic Colum after its enacting, he said, "The comedy was excellent, but it would afford a little pruning here and there. The characterisation was fine. I could not hear what the girls said, the others chattered so noisily round the table."

I said, "That was the fault of the producer and not of the dramatist who never saw his piece rehearsed. Robinson should have subdued the men so that the girls' talk could be heard clearly; that was his business."

Friday, September 19.   Arthur Sinclair came in early in the afternoon and stayed on till after 7:30 when we both walked into the city together. . . . He spoke of Yeats taking him up at first and praising him, and he drinking it all in, so that when Yeats told him to do this or that, he copied as well as he could the poet's gestures and erratic instructions. He remembered once Yeats telling him that he should show in his expression of face the idea contained in the phrase that followed the one he was speaking at the time. Irving did it, Yeats told him. Yeats brought him up to the rehearsal room, and at last he said Sinclair had got it and that would do for today, and Sinclair went down in glee to the Greenroom and said to the Fays that Yeats had said he'd got it.

"Got what?" inquired they.

"I don't know what, but Yeats says I've got it!" was his reply, and they both laughed heartily.

Next morning Yeats again called him up to the rehearsal room and put him through the lines, and in despair said, "You have lost it; stop the rehearsal."

And Sinclair said, "How could I have lost what I never knew I had!"

Yeats and Lady Gregory knew nothing whatsoever about acting. Robinson is smarter than he looks; he always agrees with them in everything. At rehearsals he merely holds the book and lets them get along at their own sweet will.

1914

Saturday, May 9.   Wilson is a rough diamond, always grousing about something or other in a rich flow of literary language in which the sanguinary adjective repeatedly rears its head. He is never at a loss for something to grumble at when Abbey actors are the topic.

Sunday, June 7.   Post card from Sinclair from Court Theatre, London: [1]

> *June 6th, 1914*
> COURT THEATRE, LONDON
>
> Got your card. *The Supplanter* came on Thursday night. It went pretty well, but was not the theatre piece Mr. Yeats led one to believe. The notices were fair. I will send you a few later. Lennox Robinson severs his connection with the company this week. He has been with us since 1910. A. S.

Robinson made himself so unpopular with everybody that he never will be missed. He leaves unwept, unhonoured, and unsung. A sad way for anyone to part company with others. He wrote one powerful acting play in *The Cross Roads*. His *Patriots* was only good in spots, like the parson's eggs. He was an understudy of Yeats in depising the public and forcing on them what they didn't want, and now the public has the laugh on their side in seeing him get the kick out. Wilson, the Scotchman, has worked his point and got Robinson out of his way. He has the old lady on his side just at present because he cleverly caters

to her extreme personal vanity of personal achievement.
Some day he'll be found out too. Then he'll get the run
and pretty quickly too. The reign of any under Yeats or
Lady Gregory is short and usually inglorious. . . . Robinson was but a simple country schoolboy when his one-act
play *The Clancy Name* was produced at the Abbey, and
his manner was simple and unsophisticated. Later on
when he got his nose into the Abbey, he became a conceited cad of the most overbearing and kickable type.

Sunday, July 26.   This day will be remembered as Dublin's Sunday of Blood, when a company of the King's
Own Scottish Borderers fired on a crowd of people who
followed them up the quays, killing three and wounding
dozens. The Irish Volunteers had successfully landed
arms at Howth, and on their way into Dublin were
stopped by some companies of soldiers . . . and Dublin
Metropolitan Police (some of the latter refused to obey
orders). However, after some shots being fired and some
volunteers and soldiers being wounded and less than a
score of 3,000 imported rifles captured, the volunteers
dispersed, and a hostile crowd followed the soldiers into
town. Some stones were thrown at them in O'Connell
Street, and on Bachelor's Walk the soldiers turned on the
crowd and bayonetted and fired on them with deadly
results, and their cowardly action rings through the world
and will forever more. May the cowardly brutes all swing
for their ruffianly deed, and the cur who gave the order be
drawn and quartered for the brutal puppy he is!

Monday, July 27.   I left two pictures at Webb's to be
framed. Great crowds were examining the bullet marks on
opposite side of the quay near Liffey Street where the
soldiers murdered the people last night. . . . My private
opinion is and always has been that it is no use in looking
to England for justice for this country until we are in a
position to drive it to heaven or hell.

Thursday, August 27.   . . . McHugh's farce *A Minute's
Wait* proved an amusing little piece, and the author was

heartily called at the end. . . . The setting was novel—a railway platform with the audience supposed to view the platform from the train—and successfully carried through. . . . The dressing and playing of some of the characters were bordering on the stage-Irishman type, and ought to be avoided as much as possible on the Abby stage. Like in Jack B. Yeats's pictures, a convention is rapidly creeping into the Abbey plays, and all characters are attired as tramps or such-like, instead of attired as in nature we find them. McHugh complained of this, and also Murray when he saw his *Sovereign Love* staged.

Monday, October 19.   . . . I walked as far as the Pillar with Hughes, and we spoke of Wilson and his rough treatment of ladies. He never could be a gentleman, and he shows it at every turn. He takes violent dislikes to people, and then hasn't a good word to say for them. Farrell Pelly, Una O'Connor, Eileen O'Doherty have all fallen victims to his displeasure. O'Donovan was too able for him, and Sinclair has won him over from enemy to be a friend of his. Wilson has a good business head, but is too full of prejudices. . . . Personally I like Wilson with all his faults, and I think he'll make a success of the Abbey. At all events he is giving young playwrights a great big chance that they never had before.

Friday, October 23.   . . . In O'Connell Street I passed Thomas MacDonagh with a salute. He was with his brother and another gentleman. Shortly behind, Edward Martyn with a young man followed on. MacDonagh hailed me and said, "We have just been speaking of you and the interest you take in theatricals." They were just coming from a rehearsal of Martyn's new play which was to be produced at the theatre, 40 Upper O'Connell Street on the first week in November. He intends sending me on a ticket for the first night. . . .

Then I stopped and talked to Martyn for a few minutes, and he introduced me to his young friend as Mr. Fagan, one of their coming dramatists who had written *The Walls of Athens* (a play that had appeared in *The*

Irish Review and was reprinted, a copy of the reprint
being given me by Joseph Plunkett some time ago).
MacDonagh asked me had I read it, and I said, "Yes, and
think the character of the old beggar woman very clever."

He said, "I mightn't have asked you that question, for
you read all plays."

"Yes, all I can clap my hands on," I replied.

Martyn said he heard I was a sort of Sainte-Beuve in
taking notes. "Why don't you publish some of your memoirs?"

"Perhaps I might some day."

MacDonagh said, "It would be hard in such a wealth of
matter to know what best to retain."

I then said, "I hope if ever my notes will be published
the people about whom they are will not be offended. I
said to Martyn that I hoped he'd come up some day to see
my collection when the worries of his new play would be
over, and he said he would be delighted; he had heard it
was a wonderful collection.

Tuesday, October 27.   John Guinan came in early with
his play *The Plough Lifters* for me to read and tell him if
I thought with Yeats that it would be better in two than
three acts and generally to see if Yeats's charge of its
obscurity in places holds good. . . . I read the play carefully and began to get a little puzzled in Act ɪɪ, and
thought Act ɪɪɪ was too drawn out, and might with advantage to the play be telescoped into Act ɪɪ. . . . Yeats in
his communications wisely counsels Guinan to clarify.
Guinan suffers from a love for too many complications in
his plays, and sometimes gets into black knots, as Wilson
expresses it. On August 23, 1914, Yeats first writes to
Guinan from Coole Park, Gort, Co. Galway, about the
play—a typewritten letter, signed by himself. It runs thus:

> *Dear Guinan,*
>   Lady Gregory has just read out to me your play.
> The first act was excellent, and there is the material of
> a good play. Speaking first of the general defects, the

acts are rather short; at least III is and Act I. I doubt if
there is matter for more than a two-act play. Your third
act is most of it reminiscence of what we have already
seen upon the stage. It seems to me to contain only one
piece of dramatic material, Garry and Jerry putting
themselves right with the Plough-Lifters. That could
quite well follow at end of Act I with some re-writing
of the other part of the act, re-writing which is necessary in any case, as the act is very obscure. It was only
when we got the passages of reminiscence in Act III
that Lady Gregory and myself got some vague idea as
to why Garry's plan had miscarried. Even now I am not
quite sure that we are right. We suppose it miscarried
because someone said that Shawn got up the plot. But
even then Winny's attitude in the whole thing is obscure, and the attitude of everybody else upon the
stage. I suggest that you clear this matter up. Make the
sympathy of the Plough-Lifters turn round to Shawn
and the girl; make them turn, when Shawn and the girl
are off the scene, violently upon Garry and Jerry, then
make another twist by Garry professing to have
brought it all about through the goodness of his heart.
Do what you like, however, so long as you make the
action perfectly clear, and rid the latter part of the play
of all telling over again of what we already know. That
Rooney song must go out, she would never begin singing under the circumstances. Your dialogue is often
very good, but sometimes it loses the peasant and becomes conventionally romantic; some of Winny's
speeches, for instance. In the first act, I thought it the
closest dialogue you have done, in that act you don't
waste words, every word gets something done.

Yours,

W. B. Yeats

Guinan told me he had re-written the play since he got
this letter, and Winny's romantic turn of speech which
he had wittingly given her was since translated into ordinary speech and the Rooney song omitted. . . . Another

letter (this time written by Yeats and most difficult to
decipher), dated October 3, 1914, from Stephen's Green
Club, Dublin, came to him.

> *Dear Mr. Guinan*:
> I have spent two bewildered afternoons over
> your play. Act I is excellent, but Act II seems to me
> from Shawn's first words after the entrance of the
> Plough-Lifters to the exit of the Plough-Lifters to begin
> a drifting conversation. I do not understand the motive
> of anybody. I didn't know till I had read it a dozen
> times what confirmed Shawn in his belief in thinking
> of treachery, and I do not know now when or why he
> discovered the truth or when the Plough-Lifters did. I
> have only read the text of the play rapidly. I see a good
> deal to criticise (still too much retelling of what has
> already happened before our eyes). Before I examine it
> carefully I want you to send me a scenario of the play
> from the return of the Plough-Lifters in Act II unto the
> end. This scenario should be about as long as you can
> get onto two sheets of note-paper. The sort of thing I
> want is "Shawn there questions Winny and is con-
> firmed in his belief in her betrayal of him by her
> knowledge of plot" and so on. Every conversation must
> have its clear motives. Your dialogue is good, and your
> humour is good and your own, but you lack logic—archi-
> tecture! As I suppose you have another copy of the play
> I shall keep the copy you have sent until I hear from
> you. Please write to my London address: 10 Woburn
> Buildings, Upper Woburn Place, London, W.C.
> > *Yours,*
> > *W. B. Yeats*

From 10 Woburn Buildings, Upper Woburn Place,
W.C., on October 23, 1914, Yeats again wrote to Guinan
thus:

> *Dear Mr. Guinan,*
> After keeping this back with the idea of making
> an analysis for you of the obscurities, I have come to

the conclusion that the best thing for you to do is to read the second and third acts to some person of average intelligence and get them to stop you whenever they cannot understand why a particular sentence is used. You constantly assume that the hearer will guess why a thing is said whereas he will only know what is said. Remember that in a play there is no time for inference. Winny should cross-question in Plough-Lifters like a lawyer and rub in the points. I wish you would read a few Molière plays and notice how simple it all is. Then again nothing in the last act seems to me of dramatic nature except Jerry putting Garry right, and this would be more telling if he succeeded with the Plough-Lifters at least. Make it all simpler. I mean the whole play, and put every motive into dialogue, leave nothing to be inferred.

Yours,

W. B. Yeats

Tuesday, November 3.   Wilson's three-act slum play *The Slough* was a complete success. It somewhat resembled *Mixed Marriage* in having a strike for background, and like Ervine's play it is chockful of human nature. All three acts are excellent in their way, and the whole play gripped. The story of manly "Tom Robinson," a mechanic, and his love for the delicate "Annie Hanlon," who dies on learning he is arrested and hurt in trying to rescue her father from the fury of a riotous mob of angry strikers, is poignantly pathetic and brought tears to the eyes of many to-night. . . . A reverend gentleman seated near me remarked at the end of Act I, "It seems like a skit on Larkinism." [Larkin was the Irish Labour Leader of the period.] And he wasn't far wrong, for the "Jake Allen" of the play, forcibly enacted by the author, is in very truth drawn from Jim Larkin, and the realistic committee room scene in Act II I have little doubt is very like the real thing too. On the stage it appeared so at all events, and easily out-distanced the Board Room incident in *The Bribe*, the street preaching episode in *The Prodigal*,[2] or the League meeting in *The Casting-Out of Martin Whelan*.

Thursday, November 5.   After the dreariest of wet days
during which I didn't stir out, I went down to see Edward
Martyn's satirical play in five acts entitled *The Dream
Physician* in which he gets it back at George Moore for
his treatment of him in his book *Hail and Farewell,* in the
character of "George Augustus Moon" in the play. I must
confess that until "Moon" came on, I could hardly get at
the hang of the first three acts. To me they seemed crude
preposterous piffle . . . and then farce entered with him,
and the fourth act which takes place in "Moon's" sitting-
room was of the material out of which "screaming farces"
were made fifty or sixty years ago. This act would make a
good music hall sketch if snatched bodily from the play,
with very small alteration. . . . The play was crude and
unconvincing as drama, but the egotistical antics of
"Moon," and the fantastical conduct of an eccentric musician called "Beau Brummell" [3] introduced an element
into the play that one could laugh at and not at the play's
expense, as I had been doing up to their entry.

The managers of the Irish Theatre are Edward Martyn,
Thomas MacDonagh, and Joseph Plunkett. "Three messrs.
(messers) and no Mismanager," as I said to Jeffs, who sat
next to me, when I saw the curtains behave so unruly—in
low comedy fashion in fact, and witnessed the poor stage
management. . . . John MacDonagh, drolly made up à la
George Moore, amusingly filled the role of "George Augustus Moon."

1915

Friday, February 12. . . . Robinson has written an interesting play, if rather a morbid one, round Emmet and his rising,[1] in which he makes almost all Emmet's followers out to be drunkards and worthless creatures. I heard a young lady near me say, "The play interests me very much, but it is too gloomy and unrelieved by patriotic figures to give a true picture of the time. The Irish were never all worthless drunken ruffians." And the lady who was with her said, "You know the Abbey is the place to see morbid, unpleasant pictures of Irish life. . . ." What a reputation for a theatre calling itself a National one to have earned. . . . The entire play makes you feel the utter hopelessness of ever making this country anything but a country of slaves or drunken brutes.

Thursday, April 8. . . . With all its many faults, *Shanwalla* is the best three-act play Lady Gregory has yet given us. . . . The drama was well acted, but Acts II and III fell flat after the high promise of Act I, but loud and continuous applause, with cries for author, followed the ending of the piece, and at last Lady Gregory appeared on the stage, attired in black with a mantilla of lace on her head . . . to bow her acknowledgement. *Shanwalla* is melodrama run to waste in a choking tangle of unnecessary words.

Saturday, April. . . . Wilson spoke of the *Freeman* cri-

tique [2] to Lady Gregory, and she said she supposed Holloway wrote it, and Wilson said I didn't—it was a man
named Kelly who did so.

"Well, Holloway had a hand in it anyway, I'm sure,"
she said.

Wilson said, "Yeats and Lady Gregory do love you,
Holloway."

Yeats came to him just now and said, "I see Holloway
again in the house." And Wilson said, "He likes the play
well." "Oh, indeed," was all Yeats replied on hearing that.

Then Sinclair said to me, "I think, Holloway, you are
the villain of the piece in the Directors' eyes." . . .

Wilson told us of Yeats and Lady Gregory making out
the programme for the London season if it came off, and
Lady Gregory started by saying they should have no
gloomy plays on, and then commenced reading out the
plays she considered should be done, starting with Synge's
Playboy and *Riders to the Sea* and *In the Shadow of the
Glen*. . . . Wilson queried, "What about gloomy plays?"

"Oh, they must be done," she said, "and *Deirdre of the
Sorrows* as well." Wilson murmured at this. By then her
Ladyship passed on to Yeats and mentioned *Cathleen ni
Houlihan* and *On Baile's Strand*. "Cheerful works also,"
Wilson interjected without avail. Again her Ladyship
murmured, "They must go on."

Then she came to her own work and said to Yeats, "I
suppose *Shanwalla* must go on the opening week." And
Yeats said docilely, "It must!" Wilson objected, but her
Ladyship (who is top dog at the Abbey) said, "It must!"
That ended the matter.

She said to put a query after *Mixed Marriage* and
Patriots, and Wilson suggested, "Why not *The Dreamers?*" And she said, "It isn't a good play; I don't see it."
She supposed they would have to put on one of Boyle's,
but she didn't like his plays. But for Sinclair's sake, Wilson might put on *The Eloquent Dempsy* the last week.

Thursday, May 6.   . . . I said to Sinclair I supposed he
was busy studying up the role of king in *Deirdre of the*

Sorrows for the London season, and he said he wouldn't play the part. He had another letter from Lady Gregory re *Shanwalla,* and he had written consenting to play in it at a special matinee in London. He gave me her Ladyship's letter to read and afterwards presented it to me for my collection.

> COOLE PARK
> GORT, CO. GALWAY
> *Monday, April 25, '15*

Dear Mr. Sinclair,

I received your letter this morning, and read it to Mr. Bernard Shaw. He said, "Like all fine actors Sinclair is a fool. What is it to him if the play is liked or not while he plays the part so very finely as he does. He will be a success in London in it anyhow."

Mr. Shaw had already told me how very good he had thought you in it. I had written this to Mr. Wilson. He was especially struck with your playing of the last scene, but said there was not a moment that was not good in your part. He also says it is the best ghost play he ever saw, and must certainly go to London, that it is a very interesting play.

I don't know what you mean by a fiasco in Dublin. It got plenty of applause. The *Freeman* and *Independent* abused it, the *Express* and *I. Times* praised it, but one never gives much heed to Dublin praise or blame. I have seen very good notices in some English papers, I have no idea by whom they were written. They merely show that some people liked it.

I am glad we have been able to arrange for London, it will be interesting trying a new theatre there.

> Yours, etc.
> A. Gregory

Thursday, May 27.   . . . Wilson promised to come to tea to-night.[3] He told me he had a terrible row with Yeats over the production of *Deirdre of the Sorrows.* He refused to put it into rehearsal, as there was no money in it, and the company could not rehearse it or *On Baile's Strand* in

London. They had plenty of plays that could be put on without any rehearsal. Yeats said, "Synge has left us a glorious heritage, and I have worked to make the theatre a Synge theatre." Wilson asked him, "What about the Irish Dramatic movement?" He was dumb to this, but called the company together and began to speak to them "about the glories of Synge," and that "Wilson said they would not rehearse *Deirdre of the Sorrows.*" Wilson, who stood by, broke in with, "I did not mention anything about the company at all, but I won't rehearse the play. There is no money in it, or in any of Synge's work."

The upshot was that Wilson sent in his resignation that evening, giving a month's notice. The Directors took three days to consider it, and then wrote accepting it, and accusing him of a breach of orders in refusing to do legitimate work in not rehearsing Synge's play. He told Lady Gregory they were trying to make out a case against him, but it wouldn't go, as the time they first spoke of producing this play in London was on Easter Monday, and he had produced three new plays at the Abbey that week, and left Dublin the next. Hence he had had no time since to rehearse any play at all.

Wilson suggested, when Yeats was holding forth on Synge, "Why not include *The Tinker's Wedding*?" But Yeats did not say anything on the point. Wilson then said, Yeats wasn't fair to the company in producing non-drawing plays and robbing them of their livelihood; Yeats and Lady Gregory had their homes and didn't mind, but it was different with the players.

Yeats shouted and said, "I was never spoken to so before in my life!"

And Wilson merely added, "It is about time that someone spoke to you and told you what most people think of you." . . .

Wilson spoke of Yeats in rehearsal, speaking to one of the supers in *The Green Helmet* and telling him he did not come on right; he should walk on as if he were taking part in some great ritual, as if inspired by some great religious emotion, etc. The super couldn't understand the poet, and no wonder. So Yeats turned to Wilson with, "Let you explain." Wilson merely said, "Walk on and pause a moment; then proceed as if you were attending your grandfather's funeral!" The super understood, and Yeats had got the effect he in vain had sought to explain.

Again, in *Shanwalla*, Yeats started speaking to Hutchinson thus: "Victor Hugo in one of his books writes of Napoleon 1 going into Russia in an ecstasy of hope and returning utterly crushed and defeated. I want you to look like Napoleon did then, as you say these words." Hutchinson looked at Yeats, tried to do something, but didn't please the mighty man of words, and he appealed to Wilson to explain. Wilson said to Hutchinson, "Arise suddenly as if to go, and then sit down again and look at the footlights till the end of the scene." He did so, and Yeats's Napoleonic look was realised.

Again, Yeats addressed Miss Drago, who is a great actress but not burdened with intelligence to an excessive degree, and started by saying, "Balzac in one of his books says so and so, and so and so, and so on. Now I want you to realise that on the stage just here." She kept saying, "Yes sir! Yes sir!"—not understanding one word he was saying. Again Wilson was called to the rescue, and in a few commonplace words put matters right. Between Lady Gregory, Yeats, and Robert Gregory, the actors had a lively time of it at rehearsal, with those three eternally in disagreement over all points and disputing them as the actors stood idle and listened.

Sunday, July 25. . . . I showed Lawrence a letter from W. B. Yeats quoted in "Pigeonhole Paragraphs" in *The Irish Monthly*, July, 1891, in which Yeats administers a rebuke to a journal called *The Gael*. . . . He had contributed a poem, and many misprints occurred.

23 November, 1887

 Dear Sir,

  I write to correct a mistake. The curious poem in your issue of the 19th inst. was not by me, but by the

compositer who is evidently an imitator of Browning. I
congratulate him on the exquisite tact with which he
has caught some of the confusion of his master. I take
an interest in the matter, having myself a poem of the
same name as yet unpublished.

Yours faithfully,
W. B. Yeats

Monday, November 8.   . . . The Abbey re-opens this
week (Wednesday) with two of Murray's plays, under the
management of St. John Ervine—an unhappy choice I
imagine, if all I hear be true. . . . Those who know him
give him two months at the Abbey, as he is self-willed and
cocksure, and is likely to get at loggerheads with the
Directors.[4]

Wednesday, November 10.   . . . I saw Eileen to the
door and then went on to the re-opening of the Abbey. I
found T. C. Murray leaving his hat and coat in the
vestibule and St. John Ervine in evening dress talking to
someone near the box-office. Mr. Nally joined us, and I
introduced him to Murray as a fellow dramatist who was
yet awaiting the production of his plays. Nally told us that
his play, *The Spancel of Death,* had been accepted, and
Yeats declares it a very powerful work and promises production about January next. He has signed a contract as
regards it. He had an interview with Ervine about its
production, and the parts are being typed. Ervine had
written to him asking whom he should like cast for the
parts, and he had come down to-night to see the company
play and then he might be able to offer suggestions,
although he'd prefer leaving it to Ervine himself, all the
casting and producing, but certainly would like to attend
rehearsals as Evrine had asked him to do. . . . Ervine
wrote to Nally to meet him at the United Arts Club over
a bit of dinner and have a chat over his play. Ervine is
going the right way about making himself popular with
the Abbey playwrights, at all events.

Tuesday, November 30.   St. John G. Ervine's tragedy in four acts, *John Ferguson*, was played for the first time on any stage at the Abbey before a crowded and very distinguished audience, and met with much applause and a call —a double one—for the author at the end of the play; but, nevertheless, I thought the piece straggling and lacking in grip and extremely reminiscent of other Abbey plays. T. C. Murray, who sat beside me, saw at once a paraphrase of his *Maurice Harte* in the opening act, while I am almost sure that Lennox Robinson who was in the stalls thought during the enactment of the final act that he was witnessing his play *The Clancy Name*, with the motive of the mother's grief transferred from the "nannie" to her son. Then our old friend "Shawn Keogh" merely changed his name to "James Caesar," and "Mikeen Whip-the-Wind" from *The Casting-Out of Martin Whelan* merely changed his name to " 'Clutie' John Magrath" and the whip for a tin-whistle. The tragedy is over-laden with much talk; and, though here and there are excellent lines and much cleverness on the whole, it just missed being interesting and gripping. The interest always faded away in talk or anti-climax when it should have enchained our attention.

Thursday, December 9.   . . . To judge by the audience to-night, I should say that Ervine as manager is the right man in the wrong place. It doesn't do to fall out with the press and patrons . . . as he has done. . . . Ervine is a clever writer, but seemingly a damned bad manager of a theatre.

1916

Thursday, January 27.   On my return from seeing the first episode of the second series of *Exploits of Elaine,* called "The Serpent Sign," I found William Boyle seated by the fire in the half-dark; he had come up from Louth this morning and had been at the Abbey and seen Ervine there and left his comedy *Nic* with him to read, and was impressed by his manner and communicativeness. He was the first person connected with the Abbey from which Boyle had ever received any civility. . . . Ervine took the comedy and said he'd read it and tell him what he thought of it to-night, and Boyle could read it to the company in the morning. Boyle thought this strange as the play had not been yet seen and approved of by Yeats, and he told Ervine so. It hadn't struck Ervine so before. . . . Lately Ervine got in a four-act farce, the last act of which occupied only half a page of Ms. Half a minute in action on the stage!

Thursday, February 8.   . . . To see Kerrigan play the travelling tinker in *The Coiner* [1] is to see him at the top of his art as a character actor. His spontaneity was as casual as nature, from the time he enters the cottage to the moment he escapes in the darkness, and his singing of the ballad about the devil and the woman he makes off with, as he sits by the fireside with old "James Canatt," was one of the most deliciously droll and artistic moments I have ever witnessed on the stage. Kerrigan has often played a tramp before, but never a droller or a more lovable one than "Tom McClippon." How the author, who sat in the stalls, must have enjoyed himself hearing the audience roar with laughter. . . . As played to-night, *The Coiner* proved one of the best short pieces ever presented on the Abbey stage.

Easter Monday, April 24.   An eventful day in the history of English misrule in Ireland. I was in blissful ignorance of anything unusual happening in the city till I went out after dinner at 2 o'clock to attend the matinee of *Shall Us* at the Empire. Just as Ellen the maid called me to dinner, some trams stopped opposite the house as if there was a breakdown on the line, and the end one of the string of cars reversed the trolly, and the passengers got off, and it moved off towards Ballsbridge as I went into dinner, and I thought no more about it. All trams were cleared ere I had finished my dinner.

When it was time to go into town, I started to walk in. At Mount Street Bridge and down towards Grand Canal Street end, knots of people had collected and were chattering earnestly and excitedly, and a man inquired of a woman as he passed, "Is there anything up?" And she said, "It is them Sinn Feiners, or whatever you call them, are about."

All down Mount Street people collected in groups, and I began to notice no trams passed and many people with children and baskets of eatables passed me walking from the city. Dark, threatening, ominous clouds hovered all around in the sky, and something oppressive was in the air, and I couldn't tell what. Very few cars or motors were to be seen about, and most people chatted in groups along the way. Somehow I soon felt something unusual was happening, and, as I passed along Merrion Square, a series of noises resembling the falling of corrugated iron from a great height lasted for about a minute and then ceased, and I thought for the time being it was something falling over at the new science building. Now and again as I walked along Nassau Street, I heard the same strange sounds. I knew by this time that there was something out of the common in the air. At the printseller Howe's window in Nassau Street as I passed, a man with two ladies looked in at a bas-relief of a nude infant marked 7/6, and he was saying, "I would think it worth 7/6 if it were real."

At Grafton Street corner and all down towards O'Connell Street and up Grafton Street, crowds spoke excitedly, yet I walked on towards Dame Street. An odd soldier could be seen about, but never a policeman, and it was not till I came to George's Street corner did I enquire what was happening in the city. And a youth said, "Firing is going on in many places, but you are safe where you are." Then he added, "I know as I am one of them."

I went on and found the Empire doors closed, and a few in front talking. I asked a man at corner of lane, "Will there be any matinee?" and he said he didn't know. There was one advertised for 2:30, but it was that now and no doors open. So I went down the laneway, and at Essex Street corner I saw three of the actresses chatting to people at the corner in an excited state. From Anglesea Street I went on to the quays and found them deserted. No trams, no cars, and but few people about.

I passed a hoarding and read a Proclamation pasted up which caught my eye at once. It had a Gaelic heading and went on to state that Ireland was now under Republican Government, and they hoped with God's help, etc., etc., to do justly to their own countrypeople. It was signed by seven names including T. J. Clarke (who headed the list), Thomas MacDonagh, Joseph Plunkett, P. H. Pearse of St. Enda's, James Connolly and two others in Gaelic characters. It was a long and floridly worded document full of high hopes.

Having read it, I went on towards O'Connell Bridge and saw great crowds up the street especially near the G.P.O. [General Post Office], and as occasional shots were to be heard I did not venture up, but went round by Marlborough Street. Seeing Ervine and O'Donovan outside the Abbey chatting, I went over to them. (I had previously met Mr. Mannix and his wife and the bell porter and pit-entrance keeper of the Abbey near the Metal Bridge, and they it was who first told me of some of the happenings of the day. The Abbey was closed for matinees. They said the G.P.O. had been captured early that morning and companies of Volunteers were entrenched in Stephen's Green and Westland Row Railway Station was in their hands also. Some soldiers—Lancers— had been shot on O'Connell Street and their horses as well. All the windows of the G.P.O. were smashed, and Kelly's gunshop broken into and looted. The police had been called off the streets and one shot dead at the entrance to the Castle [Dublin Castle, hub of British government].) Ervine and O'Donovan told me more or less the same thing over again. As we spoke, two men passed up old Abbey Street leisurely, one with a pair of new ladies' boots under each arm, and the other with two boot boxes under his. On seeing them, we surmised looting was going on. (Afterwards I heard it was Tyler's at the corner of Earl Street and also Noblett's.) Down Abbey Street towards Earl Street, rushes took place every now and then, and I decided to face home. . . .

It was rumoured that the mysterious stranger who was taken in Kerry was Sir Roger Casement, and that a cruiser full of Germans had been sunk off the coast. . . .

Most of the Volunteers felt that the Government intended suppressing them, and they thought it as well to take the bull by the horns, and take their oppressors unaware, and give a blow for Ireland before they died. No matter when for Erin dear they fell! They had been ridiculed as tin-pike soldiers, but they would show the world that they were boys with hearts undaunted in the cause of Ireland's liberty. . . .

I met Charles Dawson, Jr. and a big friend of his with him. They were going in to see what has happened in the city. All sorts of rumours were about. The big one said, "If they wanted to fight, why didn't they go out to fight Germans?"

I said, "Because they are Irish!"

And he replied, "Anyone with a stake in the country is against the Germans. If they got uppermost, they would take everything."

I said, "It is only fighting for one plunderer to keep off another." Those who were ready to die today preferred to die on Irish soil for Ireland! Of course, he couldn't see it in that light, being an Imperalist. . . .

I met Tom Nally and his sister-in-law going in towards town. . . . Nally wondered what the fate of his play would be, and I added, "Now two stirring events are taking place at the same time!" [2] I walked back with them into town and heard shots now and then as we went towards town. . . . All was quiet and we walked as far as O'Connell Bridge, and then Nally said he'd like to see the Proclamation, and I took him on to read it. Quite a number were doing the same. . . . A drunken soldier loitered about the quay, and a crowd rushed over the bridge. We parted at the corner of Westmoreland Street, they to go home by Great Brunswick Street, and I to go on to Eileen by Marlborough Street. . . .

As I came out of Eileen's, I met Jim Moran and his wife. . . . They had been all around and walked quite close to the G.P.O., and saw the muzzles of the guns pointing out, and mere youths of fifteen or sixteen behind each of them. They were also up at the Green. There was a barricade across at the Shelbourne, that gave them to understand that the hotel was in military hands. They spoke to a policeman at Store Street, and he said, "We're not very likely going out with only batons to be shot." At Stephen's Green a woman had asked one of the Volunteers, "What are you doing there?" And he said simply, "Defending Ireland!" . . .

On parting I met Father Dinneen and a friend chatting at the corner of O'Connell Street, and while lamenting the course things had taken, Father said they were more or less driven to it by the action of the Government towards them. . . .

On parting I came home by Marlborough Street and found it strewn with boot boxes and boys and women in every direction with pairs of boots or boxes. A rush came up Earl Street into Marlborough Street and I went by, and I saw Mannix and his wife go towards the Abbey, which was all in darkness as I passed. The quays were quiet. I crossed Butt Bridge and looking towards O'Connell Bridge saw all the lights dancing gleefully in the water, long jagged swords of various colours, and I thought of the slaying of good Irish youth on the morrow.

Tuesday, April 25.   I didn't sleep a wink all the night, and through the night and early morning shots were being continually fired very close at hand. I counted over thirty at least, and some of them seemed right under the window. Ellen came up to tell me there was no gas in the stove or jets, and I concluded that the firing had been around the gasometer. Shots were fired from Haddington Road corner, and also from Schools at bridge at a soldier in a motor going into Dublin. In fact, Mr. Cussin's house [3] had been commandeered, and two machine guns mounted ready for action in the drawing room. The Armstrongs cleared away next door. . . .

There is an omnious silence over all things. Nothing to be heard save the occasional whiz past of a motor cycle or the footfalls of people walking past, with sounds of shooting emphasizing the silence frequently. Poor brave fellows, it is sad to think that those who serve Cathleen ni Houlihan must give her themselves, must give her all.

Lawrence came in on his way from town and told me he had been out all the morning. . . . Nally's play has been postponed till next week. The military occupy the Shelbourne Hotel and are firing volley after volley into the Green on the Volunteers therein. The Countess Markievicz is with them in the Green. Lawrence saw one of the Volunteers lying dead near the railing inside the Green. Many of the shops in O'Connell Street are being looted by the populace. Sheehy-Skeffington has called on the citizens to form into a body of special constables and guard the people's property. . . . Those entrenched in the Green commandeered all sorts of things—motors, etc. They ordered one old cabman to stop, and when he didn't shot his horse, and he soon fled away leaving all after him.

After dinner I left home and went over to 5 Cavendish Row to stop with Eileen till the trouble was over. . . . All day excitement ran high in O'Connell Street, and several shops near the Pillar were looted, and Lawrence's set on fire. It was a day of dread and suspense.

Wednesday, April 26.   This was a day full of dread happenings with firing kept up all during the night, and the terrible booming of cannon was to be heard shortly after eight with the whizzing, prolonged, weird, wave-like sounds of the machine guns coursing through the air. We afterwards heard it was a warship in the Liffey blowing up Liberty Hall, the headquarters of the Citizen Army. Early in the morning, O'Connell Street was cleared of all people, and soldiers fired on anyone who crossed over by Parnell Monument and succeeded in taking down a poor woman at the foot of the Monument and also a man near the pathway. Two men rushed out and carried the woman off the street, and an ambulance removed the man. And as they did, I saw a man rush out and take a snapshot. A terrible fusillade of rifles was kept up each minute in the day almost, and the cannon boomed afar off, and the machine guns zigged out their cargoes of death and destruction frequently. The Republican flag floated over the G.P.O. through it all, and, when darkness came on, the din of firing died down, and almost ceased altogether during the night. The sharp pong-pong of the rifles at intervals only made the dread silence after the din earlier in the day all the more terribly impressive. The sun shone out for the most part of the day, and the twitter of birds could be heard amid the noise of strife.

Thursday, April 27.   The birds twittered in the eaves, and the sun came out early, and the bells tolled for 7 and 8 o'clock Mass, and shots were constantly being heard afar off. Things were fairly quiet till close on the stroke of

twelve, and then came the most awful ten minutes or so
of cannonading and shooting, I am sure the ears of human beings ever heard. Afterwards dead silence followed
for a long time, with occasional volleys of shots to punctuate the silence. Scarcely anything was astir in the streets
after the awful din—save a boy coming along past the
Rotunda whistling shrilly, and a pigeon alighting on the
roadway in search for a meal. . . . Looking down the
deserted O'Connell Street with the dead horse lying as it
was shot under a lancer on Monday last, one thought
desolation had come on the city so gay and normal but a
few days ago. It was awful to contemplate what was
happening and which of your friends were in the thick of
the fray.

I write this as I sit in the parlour at No. 5 Cavendish
Row, from the window of which room I can command a
view of O'Connell Street and can see the flag of the Irish
Republic still floating over the G.P.O. Please God, out of
all this carnage and destruction may come good, and that
it may open the eyes of England to the fact that there
must be something rotten in her government if this country can make such a thing possible in the twentieth century and in the midst of England's troubles abroad. That
hundreds of young men were willing to sacrifice their
young and valuable lives to drive this fact home is an
arresting condemnation of power misapplied. They died,
poor misguided youths, for an ideal; where, to my mind,
they would be far more useful to the country alive. I
always hated warfare and bloodshed, and never more than
at the present moment, and was always against the use
of arms in this country. But Carson's armed forces up
North were the only thing that made the arming of the
rest of the country possible, and the blind eye being given
to Carson's seditious utterances and the persecution of the
Irish Volunteers for the same cause clearly proved to the
latter that there was one law for those who hated and
another for those who loved their own land. . . .

At a quarter to three, an awful din filled the air all
around, and, as Eileen went down to see about dinner, I
noticed a company of soldiers scaling the rails of the

Rotunda opposite, and by the aid of step-ladders reaching
the roof of the new annex and vestibule, and I called
down to Eileen, "What is happening?" And a sort of
panic seized us all, and dinner was soon forgotten, and we
all at last got into the doctor's study at the back of the
house, as the safest retreat from the fusillade all round.
Earlier the officer told me to get away from the window as
he gave orders to his men to "Fire up the street!" And
from that forward the noise was terrifying, and the booming of cannons close by was the most appalling sound I
ever heard, I think. For the rest of the day all was chaos,
and poor Eileen almost became hysterical with fear every
time William left the room in dread he might look out
and get shot. We all spent an awful afternoon. . . .

A lull came with the dark, but during the night repeated dull booming shots were fired, as if they were
blowing in the entrance of the G.P.O. which seemed to
withstand all attempts to shatter it.

Thursday, April 27.   . . . O'Connell Street about the
G.P.O. and opposite is in a state of total wreckage, and
several houses are on fire. Nobody is allowed up the street
as firing is continually going on. . . . I am so depressed at
my poor dear native city being laid in ruins that I can
write no more just now.[4]

Friday, April 28.   . . . After a day of most awful noises
—musketry, cannon, machine guns, etc., etc.—about five
o'clock the roof of the G.P.O. took fire, and then the
shooting had begun in real earnest. Regiments of soldiers
had been passing through Parnell Street during the afternoon on their way to surround the Henry Street block for
fear of any of those taking part in the G.P.O. escaping, so
that when the place went on fire and they saw some of
those in the building hasten away as if to make their
escape behind, the military instantly set to work to set the
whole block on fire, and succeeded in doing so, and a fire
the like of which was never seen in Dublin before was the
result. Some hours later, the roof of the G.P.O. fell in
with a crash, and a mighty cauldron of flame rushed up

into the skies. All the while through the smoke, every now and then, the little green flag still waved from its post defying the flames to demolish it. The firing, deafening and terrible, continued all the while, and from the Rotunda and the National Bank a continuous fusillade was kept up. The glare from the G.P.O. lit up the heart of the city. Cannon went noisily rumbling along, and an armoured car hastened out of O'Connell Street and up Parnell Street towards Capel Street, and all was excitement and bustle with the military. We wondered what was really happening, and if any of those who were in the G.P.O. escaped alive. The Rotunda had become the Military Headquarters for the time being, and Cavendish Row became within its area. I was almost maddened by depression. Just as darkness closed in, I saw that the little flag had disappeared, and the fire still burned fiercely within the grey stone shell of the ruined building. All of us thought that with the darkness would come some spell of restful silence, but, alas, no, such was not to be. Volunteers were discovered to be in the YMCA building near the top of O'Connell Street, who had been firing on the military, and a cannon was mounted at the corner of the street opposite and boomed away continually for some time amid continuously kept up rifle fire. It was a night of horror and noise. There was a great blaze afar, looking across the Rotunda.

Saturday, April 29.   On looking out next morning, one could see the damage done by the cannon's thrilling booms. . . . Fierce fires raged up near the G.P.O. in O'Connell Street, and an engine of the Fire Brigade passed the sentries on duty at Cavendish Row. . . . One old man on being put back said, "Damn it all, man, you've beaten them. What more do you want?"

To a poor woman the sentry said, "Get on the other side." But she didn't know what he said and murmured, "It's a lovely Saturday.". . .

Later on as I went to bed, I looked out and saw the flame tipped urn on top of the Parnell Statue silhouetted against the glowing sky. All the block from Middle Abbey

Street to Liffey Street was ablaze it seemed. Towards evening a company of Volunteer prisoners arrived and took their stand beside the Parnell Statue to have their names taken down by an officer. They were twenty-two in all, some of them mere boys and most of them starved, hungry looking poor fellows. One was a stout middle-aged man. None wore uniforms, but a sturdy little boy had on the cap of the Citizen Army. . . . Shortly after, another company of prisoners came marching down O'Connell Street, and, having laid down their arms in the middle of the street, ranged themselves along the Rotunda side of O'Connell Street in single file to have their names taken. Later on a big company of Volunteers bearing a flag in front came along in fine marching order, and, halt being called, they stood at ease, and, dropping all their guns and trappings, retired to the pathway this side of the Gresham Hotel. It was a most dramatic moment when they marched down the street. . . . I wonder what they thought as they stood there in the street and saw all the destruction that had come in the city since last Monday at noon.

Wednesday, May 3.   . . . Pearse and MacDonagh were shot today.

Monday, May 15.   Sir Roger Casement's trial for High Treason opened in London today. I remember seeing him once with Colum in the vestibule of the Abbey—a tall, distinguished looking man with jet black hair and beard. Colum looked a timid little rabbit beside him.

Monday, May 29.   About eight o'clock I strolled down to the Abbey to find the doors had just been closed, and some small knots of people were standing about in eager conversation, and a boy in front of the stalls entrance handed out handbills to the people as they arrived at the theatre. The slip read, "To the Patrons of the Abbey Theatre. The Players regret having to disappoint their Public this week as they will NOT APPEAR at the Theatre under the present Manager, MR. ST. JOHN ERVINE. Full particulars will appear in the Press.". . .

From the first Ervine hit his head against everyone he came in contact with in Dublin. He promised everything and fulfilled nothing. He had no idea of what the truth is in his statements, and all will think he would be a good riddance from the Abbey. He had the art of being unpopular, and as a manager, producer and actor was a dead failure. When asked was this the last of the Abbey, I said, "Not at all. The Abbey has come to stay. No Ervine can slay it. . . . Had it not had nine or more lives, it would have been slain long ago by the vagaries of Yeats and Gregory, but the public refused to let it die."

Sunday, September 24.   I received the following letter from Frank J. Fay.

> NEXT WEEK C/O MISS BAILY
> MELVILLE HOUSE, ABBEY ROAD, TORQUAY
> *Saturday*
>   *Dear Joe,*
>   . . . It is rather exasperating that the Directors of the Abbey Theatre, when they want a manager, have never given Will or me the offer, but any outsider, completely ignorant of the work the theatre was started for, is good enough. Now they have lost their old company and what remained of our traditions, how can a man trained in quite different traditions bring back what made the company famous.[5] It never occurs to the Directors that the reputation Will and I made in Dublin and the friendliness of the audience to us is an asset to the theatre: and that if the acting of the Abbey Theatre is to be the ordinary acting that one gets much better done on the regular stage, then the Abbey Company has no *raison d'être*. Ireland cries out when her people leave her, but she doesn't trouble to get them to come back. . . .
>   *Yours,*
>   *Frank*

Thursday, September 28.   . . . On leaving Eileen's, I went on to the Abbey where I found a queue, extending into Marlborough Street pit entrance, and great business being done in the vestibule. Long before eight o'clock, the theatre was packed, and people being turned away.[6] I had a long chat over a cup of tea with Mr. J. Augustus Keogh, who asked my opinion of things, as he said he valued it.

And I said, "As a play-goer I know I am going to have a fine time of it at the Abbey, but I fear all the traditions of the theatre will be ignored by you, and a repertory theatre of excellent quality set up to replace the old Abbey stuff. I can see that by the production of Shaw's Irish play, where many of the characters, such as 'Patsy,' were grotesqued by over-playing. The naturalistic style of the Fays' creating, whether good, bad or indifferent, which brought fame to the Abbey Players, was about to be ignored and acting of the usual showy kind to take its place."

My remarks seemed to nettle Keogh, who retorted, "The Abbey acting is not acting at all, and some of the company are appallingly bad, such as O'Rourke, whom I wouldn't have in a company of mine at any price. Sinclair is simply a clown of a comedian who can make people laugh. What I want is people who can act, and not people who can only act woodenly and talk disjointedly and carelessly through an ill-staged peasant play. Why I'd put on *Othello* to-morrow if I could get the right people to play in it; and I feel I easily can in Dublin because all people here are actors.". . .

He pointed to Frank Fay's portrait by J. B. Yeats on the wall, and said he had asked Fay to come back, and he'd have liked him to be in the theatre for poetic plays as he could speak verse well. He couldn't act, and Keogh would have no use for him only to teach verse speech. The Abbey tradition was not to act at all; he would make his company act. He came into the place with only the four walls provided; he'd have to re-make everything, and he intended doing so by making the theatre pay. He intended laying out over £300 on the outside, putting up big signs with "Abbey Theatre" thereon and hundreds of electric lights.

"Like any picture palace!" I said.

Thursday, October 26. . . . Acts I and II of *Nic* went like wildfire, but Act III from one cause or another acted on the others like a damp squib. It spluttered and went out. The players weren't so sure of their words or their meaning, nor was the matter given them to say so brilliant. The idea of the coming of a technical instructor into a contented country home and causing chaos throughout and raising discontent amongst others, was most amusingly carved out by the author.[7] The big acting success of *Nic* was undoubtedly the "Mrs. O'Carroll" of Maureen Delany; she was delightfully explosive.

Wednesday, December 13. . . . I saw the first performance of Lennox Robinson's comedy in three acts, *The Whiteheaded Boy,* played before the United Arts Club [8] and a few stray people who patronise the Abbey since the revival of *The Playboy* a little while ago. . . . The comedy went real well up to the end of Act II, but, alas, Act III soon tumbled all that went before into chaos, and the unruly curtains completed the confusion. The author was called and came and bowed, looking more bored than ever, if that were possible, and as he retired from the stage hands were seen trying to push him on again, and, as the curtains refused to close on the stage Robinson came sheepishly to one corner of the stage near the footlights and said, "I have been speaking to you for two hours and a half and don't know what further I can say to you. You on that side of the footlights (meaning the audience) haven't missed one of your cues all night." This effect at speech-making was just like the man—ever superior and insolent.

I was pleased to see that Breffni O'Rourke, who showed no aptitude for comedy or character acting in the parts he had already filled at the Abbey, was at home in the straight part of "George Geoghegan," the stay-at-home drudge in Robinson's comedy and made good by his angry outbursts and demeanour generally. He should never try to play any other sort of part, save guileless ones like that

of "George.". . . . He hasn't the gift of sustaining character, but has of playing himself.

It was a delight to old Abbeyites present to see Eileen
O'Doherty back again at the Abbey and playing a part
like old "Mrs. Geoghegan" that suits her style of playing
so well and brought back echoes of her great playing of
"Mrs. Morrissey" in *Birthright*. Maire O'Neill as old
"Aunt Ellen" got a good deal of fun out of the part as
well as playing it cleverly. . . .

In the opening acts the characters were individualised;
in the last act they certainly were not. They became
merely talking machines without life or interest. It was
sad to see how a play that promised so well should have
become such an utter failure in the end.

1917

Saturday, January 6. . . . Higgins[1] queried, "Why is it that one author in Dublin hasn't a good word to say of another behind his back?" I couldn't answer him.

Wednesday, March 25. . . . Of course, Mr. Keogh, like all stage folk, is full of his own importance and thinks himself the last word in stage producers, etc., etc. His fetish is Shaw; all other dramatists are as naught . . . and when I chanced to remark, "We have had far too much Shaw of late at the Abbey, and many are saying so to me," he nearly had a fit and rushed away from us . . . almost in a tearing rage—which was only emphasized when I suggested that why the Irish plays failed to draw was that they were not well played, as the Irish acting did not take kindly to the English methods. Keogh lost his head on hearing this, and railed about my absurdity in thinking the Irish players could act, and belittled Sinclair, etc., as poor actors, querying, "How could Sinclair act 'Hamlet'?" and other silly questions like that. He thought there was one good Irish actor, Fred O'Donovan, in the company. I said, "He is a great actor." But I maintained my point that the English method destroyed Irish acting, and gave as my examples Sara Allgood, Maire O'Neill, Frank Fay, and Willie Fay, who returned but poor artificial players after their contact with the English stage. . . . When I said that the Gaiety or the Royal were the proper places for Shaw's plays and not the Abbey, Keogh could have slain me on the spot. . . . Keogh and I parted as good friends as before the tiff.

Tuesday, April 10.   Michael Willmore² called at 3 o'clock and we had a delightful chat at the fire. He is a youth with real talent who has played in *Peter Pan* and other plays and studied art in the Slade School for three sessions. He has a fondness for Jack B. Yeats's work and produces some very clever imitations of his style in colour, but with a more refined line that emphasizes the crudeness of the method he mimics. Some of his black and white designs are really beautiful and clever, and all his work in whatever medium is full of imagination, such as those who talk of the Celtic Note and Celtic Twilight worship. . . . He has all the modesty of an artist and is a nice-looking, unaffected boy with curly lightish hair and all the enthusiasm of youth. . . .

He fears that Jack B. Yeats is a bad one to try to form one's style on, "as there can be only one Jack B. Yeats." I agreed with him; as a rule, it is only the crudities without the life and animation Yeats puts into his work that is apt to be developed by those who take after him. . . . Yeats's very crudities of colour and draughtsmanship are the things his worshippers admire most in him. It is the action in his sketches I like best.

Willmore wore a soft hat and with his portfolio had the air of an artist about him. He is a clever youth who is likely to go far.

Wednesday, May 9.   Received a letter from W. J. Lawrence from New Brunswick, N. Y., and replied to it as follows.

> *My dear Lawrence,*
>   Yours of the 15th of April to hand today. It is too bad that America is not agreeing with you and that you have been laid up. I hope when all the trouble is over that you may find your way back to Dublin again! I cannot tell you how I miss you personally. You will

be surprised to hear that J. A. Keogh has got his walking papers from the Abbey; a love of Shaw and a hatred
for Irish drama and Irish acting were, I am sure, the
cause. Keogh from the first wanted to make it a sort of
Shaw playhouse, and not caring a tinker's curse for the
traditions of the little theatre. . . . As an Irish theatre,
the Abbey reached its lowest ebb under the reign of
Keogh. . . .

Thursday, June 14.   . . . "The Abbey closed its doors
for the season on Saturday last, not re-opening till September. They play in Coliseum, London, in August—
O'Donovan is now Manager. . . ." [3]

Saturday, September 22.   I finished reading James
Joyce's crudely compiled book, *A Portrait of the Artist as
a Young Man*, in which he succeeds in introducing more
downright coarseness of language and filthy expressions
than any book I ever came across.

Saturday, October 20.   William Butler Yeats, the poet,
was wed in London to Miss Georgia Hyde-Lees, the only
daughter of the late Mr. W. G. Hyde-Lees of Pickhill
Hall, Wrexham, and of Mrs. Henry Tucker, 16 Montpe-
lier Square, London. The wedding was a quiet affair. He
was born 52 years ago, and was only 24 when his literary
talent began to blossom. What will poor Lady Gregory do
now?

Wednesday, December 5.   . . . "Here in Dublin were
it not for the little Abbey Theatre and its interesting plays
and players, we would have nothing to go to in the way of
plays. Our theatres have fallen into the hands of show-
men, who have turned them into music-halls or worse in
their craving to make money, till at last they have succeeded in killing all taste for the theatre in the old play-
going class, and even the people they attracted to the
fifth-rate variety stuff they provided have got tired of such-
like rubbish, and are rapidly deserting such-like perform-

ances for the Pictures, where they can see lurid melodramas, set in beautiful surroundings, capably enacted on the screen, to music from a more or less orchestral accompaniment.

I was at the Abbey last night where an amusing comedy, *Fox and Geese*,[4] was revived with success, with *In the Shadow of the Glen* as a first piece. The Abbey Company under Fred O'Donovan is becoming quite a good repertory company of very capable players. . . . Next week we are promised a new slum play by Dr. Oliver Gogarty, which may, by all accounts, create talk and controversy." [5]

Tuesday, December 11.   . . . Not for years has such an audience been inside the Abbey as assembled tonight to see the first performance of *Blight*, a play of Dublin slum life by A. and O. (Dr. Oliver Gogarty and Joseph O'Connor, Heblon of *Studies in Blue* fame). To me the audience was quite as interesting as the play. In the vestibule before eight were grouped together Con Curran, Conroy (the Gaelic writer), Susan Mitchell and her sister, George Russell, Mr. and Mrs. Darrell Figgis, Mrs. Stopford Green, Seumas O'Sullivan, Estelle Solomons, Lady Gregory, Mr. and Mrs. James Stephens, George Roberts and Mrs. (*née* Maire Garvey), and crowds of other well-known figures. . . .

The theatre was abuzz with excitement before the play began; it had got about that the play might be suppressed after the first performance—that, in fact, it was very "hot stuff." So all rushed to be there; just as the Royal was crowded before twelve o'clock on Saturday morning to witness *Ghosts* in the hope of being shocked. In both cases those who went with that intention must have been sadly disappointed. *Ghosts* merely proved very dull as a stage play, and *Blight* quite interesting to Dubliners, as it discussed a problem sincerely that eats into the very heart of our city, and treats it with a certain amount of crude realism . . . but, nevertheless, brought home its lesson— that the evil of slums can never be checked by charity nor

extensions of hospitals, but at its own roots alone. Check
the evil that creates slums, and slums vanish and all the
evil they create. Such is the lesson to be learned in witnessing *Blight*, a tragedy of Dublin.

On meeting Conroy in the vestibule on coming out, he
summed up what he had seen as, "A discussion with
interruptions." "From the audience?" I queried.

"No, from the characters," he replied. . . . The general opinion was that the piece was more a discussion than
a play, and that the characters argued rather than con-
versed.

Saturday, December 22.   T. C. Murray's letter ran thus:

> GORTBEG, 136 S.C. RD.
> KILMAINHAM
> *21 / 12 / 17*

Dear Mr. Holloway,

My new volume of plays was published today.[6]
It comes very opportunely to bear my message of good
will for Christmas.

> *Yours very sincerely,*
> T. C. Murray

P.S. You will see that I have given myself the pleasure
of dedicating the little volume to you. T. C. M.

1918

Tuesday, January 29. . . . I went into town in the evening to see the first production of *Hanrahan's Oath* by Lady Gregory at the Abbey. . . . Byrne (editor of *Sport*) and his wife were present, . . . and he was indignant over the "blasphemous blather" he had just listened to. I said, "It is up to you to say so when you record your views in *Sport*." And he said, "I will."[1]

Kelleher,[2] who left the theatre with me, felt inclined to call out, "Ring down the curtain," but thought it might give the piece an "ad" if a disturbance were created. I thought as I listened to such drivel that it was a sad thing to think that the concoctor of such wearying balderdash was the one who chose the fate of pieces sent to the Abbey. . . . Oh, the dreariness and the blasphemy of it all! After this "comedy," an Abbey audience can stand anything. . . . On seeing *Hanrahan's Oath* with the involved artificial dialogue that gave none of the actors a chance, I wondered how it ever came to pass that Lady Gregory wrote that little gem, *The Rising of the Moon* or the tragic incident, *The Gaol Gate*. Just as I continue to marvel at each fresh effort I see of Edward Martyn's how he wrote *The Heather Field*.

Sunday, February 3. . . . Monty dropped in the following letter from Frank Fay. ". . . I didn't make any fuss about going away. I never do. If Dublin doesn't choose to give me work, I must seek it here. . . . The Abbey Theatre could have retained me had they wanted to. I have letters from Lady Gregory which made me believe they wanted me and were delighted to have me; but I suspect the company got at her and rather than risk another rebellion there she let me go. . . . Dublin is and I fear will remain largely an amateur city. One can only learn from people who know more than you do, and I can honestly say there's no one in Dublin who knows more acting than me. Besides, I seem to have very few friends in Dublin now. . . ."

I replied to James Montgomery in returning Frank's letter: ". . . It reads like a letter of a disappointed man, soured with the world, because it hasn't taken his newly formed and mistaken notions of things. The fact of the matter is, playing with cheap melodramatic companies has ruined his originally beautiful natural style of playing, and has only been replaced by artless theatricality, which, alas, he has come to look upon as the quintessence of the player's art, and anyone who dares tell him so is his enemy and one to be despised. O'Donovan told him he was anxious to have Frank play as often as he could at the Abbey, but found him impossible to get on with. . . . Oh, the pity of it all, that a great natural player whom we all loved and admired should descend to this. . . ."

Tuesday, February 19.   To-night was a big night at the Abbey, when Lennox Robinson's strangely interesting play, *The Lost Leader*, was first played before a packed house and a brilliant one as well.[3] . . . Act I was arresting; Act II continued more or less so, and Act III halted somewhat, and the tragic death was slightly marred by the prolonged delay . . . in dropping the curtains. The death itself was a quite thrilling moment, realistically enacted; the lighting of the matches was quite artistically introduced. The whole thing struck me as a big achievement; a great framework erected around a central idea with almost perfect result. It is undoubtedly the most ambitious political play yet presented to the public.

Saturday, October 26.   . . . I went down to hear Shaw's discourse on "Literature in Ireland" at the little theatre.

. . . His discourse was quite Shavian in his findings, and
he kept nagging all the while he spoke; he afterwards said
he knew he was nagging, but once set going he couldn't
stop. Only those who don't succeed in art or literature
make good critics was his opinion; therefore, he was no
critic. He didn't read critically. It was only when they
went to Paris Irishmen could write, and then he spoke of
George Moore's and Joyce's works and their indecencies.
He also said that Synge got his local colour in Paris, and
that there is nothing Irish about *The Playboy*. The central
idea is that the worship of crime is universal; in fact, the
Irish people don't understand it. Then he went on to say
that the Irish should be conscripted out of their own
country so that they would learn to know what Ireland
was really like. He also said they could never get anything
until they ceased to have a grievance. Nobody liked people with a grievance; they were generally bores. The man
who didn't leave Ireland wouldn't write like Synge. The
plays that were written by Irishmen who never travelled
were generally those that lacked poetic outlook and were
sordid and abusive in character. . . . Shaw is always stim-
ulating and entertaining and never dull. He mixed all he
said with a very nimble wit, and his words came ever ready
to his lips. He speaks excellently well always, and his
delivery is clear and telling! . . .

Murray, who was at the meeting of the Drama League
in the United Arts Club by invitation from Robinson,
told me all about his feelings of amusement at those
present posing as bohemians à la the Latin Quarter. For
instance, Boyd addressed the meeting sitting down till
some Philistine called out to him to stand up. Robinson
spoke between puffs from his cigarette. The League proposed to give plays of an "unsavoury" nature such as
Joyce's *Exiles*, etc. Those present were asked to put their
names down and form a committee—each paying a pound
subscription for five performances. Murray did not put
down his name. . . . The air of artificiality was over all
the proceedings. Robinson seems the prime mover of the
movement; only four names were in the circular sent out
—Yeats, Boyd, Stephens, and Russell.

Sunday, November 3.   . . . The city in darkness and fog looked intensely gloomy and very few were about. . . . The war is setting its deathly seal on the world now with a vengeance. May God have mercy on the souls of all its victims. . . . Dublin is now a City of Terrible Night!

Tuesday, November 19.   ". . . The peace rejoicings in my city ended in the soldiers forming themselves into a mob and breaking windows in the Mansion House and elsewhere, and so ended the peace carnival in useless destruction of property. . . .

One of our most brilliant young writers and dramatists, Seumas O'Kelly, died suddenly of heart failure last week,[4] and was given a public funeral on Sunday last—a most solemn, impressive affair. T. C. Murray, T. H. Nally, Seumas Connelly, and I walked in a row. We all dearly loved the poor fellow for his gentle ways and kindly manner. He was only 36 years of age and had written *The Shuiler's Child*, *The Bribe*, *The Parnellite*, and several other plays of ripe dramatic merit. . . .[5]

Friday, December 6.   . . . Con O'Leary told . . . some stories of Yeats's absent-mindedness. One day Yeats was passing through the Abbey, and seeing the charwoman at work, he said, "Good morning, Miss Allgood, that's a splendid make-up."

"I'm not Miss Allgood, but Miss Martin," said the charwoman, and Yeats, putting up his right hand palm outward, repeated as he walked away, "A splendid make-up."

Another was told of when Ervine was manager, and his wife was rehearsing, and Yeats called out to Ervine, "What is that sack doing on the stage?" . . . And Ervine said, "That is my wife," and Yeats moved off.

Lately he was heard to say, "I hear that all the old Abbey Company have left the theatre."

Saturday, December 7.   . . . O'Donovan said he was thinking of going to America, and asked me what would be his reception on his return to Ireland, and I said, "Probably you will be forgotten, and have to build up a reputation again." And he sarcastically thanked me for my very flattering and encouraging opinion, but said it never would be realised as once he left the country he'd take jolly good care never to return. He had missed the tide twice before, but not the third time if he could help it!

He asked me whether I liked operas or plays best, and my reply was that "I like all sorts of stage work provided it is good of its kind."

"It is wonderful how you never tire of the theatre."

And I said, "At present I am as enthusiastic as ever; when the enthusiasm vanishes then I will cease theatre-going."

"That won't be till you are laid in Glasnevin," was O'Donovan's opinion. And perhaps he was right.

1919

Wednesday, January 8. . . . I walked home and met Edward Martyn in Clare Street, and had a short chat with him. He was gotten up like Tree as "Demetrius" in *The Red Lamp*. . . . He believed in the psychology of a play and not its dramatic significance. When the Abbey was subsidised by Miss Horniman, Yeats could experiment with interesting drama; the box-office wasn't the test of good drama to his mind. Of late years the Abbey had to play pieces that drew audiences, hence the failure to produce good intellectual plays.

They were starting a society to try to produce such, but Yeats, who seldom makes a mistake, did so this time in not selecting plays and insisting on them being subscribed for. He didn't do that, and chaos had come to the Drama League—everyone wanting his own selection. A theatre where intellectual dramas were played should be the taste of one man—like the Irish Theatre—where the plays given were to his taste.

Wednesday, January 22. . . . In the evening I went up to Con Curran's. . . . Kelleher and White came, soon to be followed by Stephen McKenna (who said that looking for a clean collar delayed him). He was speaking of his wondering where Lennox Robinson got his extraordinarily large-rimmed hat and how he had the courage to inquire for such in a shop. AE arrived just then and said his old hat had served him for the past ten years; he loved old clothes and hats. . . .

Willie Dawson was also of the party. He told me he attended two meetings of the Drama League and decided not to join. He didn't like their way of ignoring Martyn and his efforts altogether, and when Murray called attention to the fact James Stephens stood up and declared the discussion closed. Dawson is of the opinion that a small group wants to see fad dramas staged and wish others to pay for their pleasure, without interfering with the box-office receipts of the Abbey. . . .

AE joined us at the folding doors, and leaning against a half-opened door joined us in our conversation—just then about Yeats and the Psychical Research discourse promised for next Sunday—and he told many strange and droll incidents of Yeats's adventures in search of "spookish" experiences. . . . AE has the saving grace of humour to keep him sane and cool on such subjects. He thinks they must be very ill-informed if they can't give clearer messages from the Unknown than those. . . .

AE also told of his first meeting with James Joyce. One night at 11:45, a knock came to the door, and he opened, and a figure outside asked, "Are you AE?" And Russell owned up that he was. "My name is Joyce, and I want to see you. Is it too late to come in?" "No," said AE, and in he came. He sat on a sofa with his legs crossed and, pipe in mouth, began to smoke and await what Joyce had to say. For awhile he seemed confused, but afterwards thawed and showed the most utter contempt for everybody and everything, and spoke slightingly of Yeats and all others. His arrogance was colossal in one so young.

Joyce some time later read some of his poems to Yeats and himself, and when Yeats expressed an opinion that he liked them Joyce merely said, "Your opinion isn't worth anything more than another's. It doesn't matter whether you or I like them; they and your work will all be forgotten in time."

He asked Yeats about some of Yeats's poems, and the poet went into an elaborate explanation of their meaning, and all Joyce said was, "You're past developing; it is a pity we didn't meet early enough for me to be of help to you." Joyce at the time was the condensed essence of studied conceit.

AE says Austin Clarke visited them several times, but he seems so shy and reticent, and sits on the edge of the chair ready to run off affrighted at any moment. . . . I was sorry to have to leave such good company.

Friday, March 7. The morning was wet. I went into town and called at Cavendish Row, but Eileen was out. Mr. Tighe in the bank was asking me about O'Donovan's leaving the Abbey and what was the theatre going to do. I replied, "The remnant of the company's reply to that was the production of a new three-act play by Brinsley Mac-Namara, called *The Rebellion in Ballycullen* on Tuesday next." . . . I was speaking to Dr. Larchet as he stepped off the car at Haddington Road, and he was saying O'Donovan treated the Abbey very badly, though well-treated himself even up to the present minute. When Shaw heard he was leaving, he said he didn't think he'd be any loss. Larchet said, "O'Donovan's artistry has fled from him of late, and he plays the buffoon in all comedy parts he attempts. He was out and under as an artist. His touring in the halls with *The Lord Mayor* settles it finally."

Tuesday, March 11. "It wasn't a play at all," said Frank Hugh O'Donnell to T. C. Murray in the vestibule as we came out after Brinsley MacNamara's play, *The Rebellion in Ballycullen,* had ended, and the author had been called.

"It fell to pieces after Act 1," was Sydney Morgan's opinion.

"It was full of clever satirical sayings which the audience took good-humoredly, but no amount of clever sayings will make a play without construction and human dramatic incident," said Murray, and added, "It was woefully badly acted. . . . The prompter had a real big part."

Wednesday, March 26. . . . I told MacNamara that he better rewrite his play and introduce one of the villagers to give their point of view; drama arises out of the clash of ideas; there were none such in *The Rebellion in Ballycullen* as it stands, hence its failure as a stage play. It may read all right, but a play that cannot stand stage production to me is always a failure. . . . Most people who write about plays now have no sense of the theatre at all—like Ernest A. Boyd, for instance. All plays that act to him are melodramas and beneath notice.

Mac, as he sat in front of the fire, his big frame all of a heap on the chair, looked the picture of massive helplessness and dull heaviness. Occasionally he lapses into long silences as he gazes into the fire—a strange, heavy-mannered man.

Easter Monday, April 21. . . . *The Dragon* proved a fanciful, genuine folklore-fairy play, full of homely wit and delicate fancy. The Gordon Craig scenes were used and quaint costumes. On the whole, it was well interpreted. . . . Eithne Magee made a delightful fairy princess, and Barry Fitzgerald a delightfully droll and dry-humoured king. Arthur Shields as the young king was excellent, only for a slight hesitating way of delivery at times that put one in dread of his breaking down. F. J. McCormick made a success as the astrologer, made up like an aged "Shylock." . . . Seaghan Barlow's "Dragon" was quite a success. . . . The children in the audience enjoyed the wonder play immensely. I saw one little fellow jumping up and down in his seat in the stalls with ecstatic delight during Act III. It is an ideal children's play.

Saturday, April 26. I received the following note from Lady Gregory.

COOLE, *April 24*

Dear Mr. Holloway,

Thank you for your note about *The Dragon*. I am glad that it has given pleasure, and that there has been found in it some of the humour and wild beauty

of the folk-tales on which it is built. I think the beautiful acting of this week will do away with an unfounded
impression that the Abbey was on the wane—it is reviv-
ing its youth.

Yours sincerely,
A. Gregory

Friday, August 8. . . . I had a cup of tea with Peter
Judge[1] and afterwards walked as far as the corner of
Grafton Street with him. He plays in *The Coiner* next
week, and is quite nervous as to the result. It is a type
quite unlike any he has as yet played. He usually offers up
a Hail Mary for his success before going on in a first night,
he told me, when he queried and heard I was a Catholic.
It was with Ira Allen he first appeared in the Queen's—in
Father Murphy[2] in a part "specially written" in for him,
and he felt very proud of himself at the time, playing
thirteen performances for £1.0.0. He also played "Beamish
Mac Coul in *Arrah na Pogue* with young Delany as
"Shaun the Post," and remembered that in the arrest
scene when "Shaun" asked to be allowed to kiss "Arrah,"
a woman in the audience shouted out, "Kiss her, man,
and don't stand on ceremony!" to the amusement of the
audience. The Queen's audience is a thing of itself. All
noise and excitement when the play is in progress and as
mute as a mouse during the intervals.

Thursday, November 6. . . . I saw old Standish
O'Grady stand at the corner of Nassau Street awaiting
tram, a glum, set expression on his face. A soft grey felt
hat was pulled down well over his eyes as he gazed straight
before him with nothing but his thoughts at the end of
his vision. . . . A splendid-looking, dreamy-eyed old man
he appeared as he stood in the rain, and I thought as I
gazed at him from the passing tram of the wonderful
heroic stories he had weaved about Cuchulain and the
wonderful people of his time.

Wednesday, November 19. . . . What a very nervous
little man McHugh is; he fidgets about when in the

house, and goes from side to side when out walking. . . .

Peter Nolan came up after rehearsing *The Enchanted Trousers* at the Abbey, and told me that Dr. Gogarty was always changing the text, so much so that they gave him only till tomorrow to continue doing so, as they never could learn and unlearn the various texts by Tuesday next. . . . Yeats has ceased to take any interest in the theatre. Robinson now does take an added interest. It is shyness that makes Robinson so aloof and awkward in his manner, Nolan says.

Tuesday, November 25.   I . . . went to the Abbey for the first night of *The Enchanted Trousers,* a play (or satire) in one act by Gideon Ousley (Dr. O. Gogarty). . . . Starkey in going out said, "I am too full of indignation that the best piece that ever was in the Abbey should have been ruined by bad playing." Most people thought it was a too long drawn out skit with clever ideas and sayings dotted here and there.

Tuesday, December 9.   At the Abbey all the highbrows congregated in great force. . . . Yeats's play [3] was looked forward to with interest and modified excitement owing to rumours of its nature. Its strange story baffles me, while its unfolding is set in so picturesque an environment that it charmed the eye if it didn't wholly satisfy the mind. . . . There is a lot of talk in Act I about the chastity of a unicorn, and in Act II marriage is made very light of, indeed. Willmore thought the play "gorgeous," but neither Starkey nor Higgins had a good word to say of it. It baffled all, but its beauty of setting pleased most, and the acting of May Craig as "Nona" was really fine dramatically; she can get right into the heart of a character and be the person she creates for the time being. . . . Arthur Shields in fantastic character, in out of the way periods and costumes, invariably is quite good. His muddled poet-player, "Septimus," proved to be one of his happiest efforts. . . . Though its purport is wrapt in mystery, its beauty won home.

1920

Tuesday, January 6. Lady Gregory's play in three acts, *The Golden Apple,* for Kiltartan children, was staged for the first time on to-night at the Abbey, and proved full of fantastic wonderment and droll and poetic touches in many instances, but on the whole the many scenes seemed scrappy, and the ending tame and lame. . . . Eric Gorman as a droll old doctor with a conical hat and Barry Fitzgerald as "Simon the Steward," who accompanies "Rury" on his search for the golden apple, were the two comic characters, whimsically enacted and capable of further development on comic lines. As is usual with her, Christine Hayden as the wicked "Witch" allowed discussion to get the better of her and spoke too loudly. . . . Maureen Delany, whose comic art and figure grow apace, made splendid comic capital out of the role of "Bridget," the giant's wife. There was whimsical drollery about all she did in the part, but in the first scene she tried to make bricks without straw and failed to raise laughs by her wealth of facial expression and by-play. When there is nothing for one to do, why try to work overtime?

Wednesday, November 17. . . . "Poor Ireland is passing through a terrible time; may God soon deliver it from its enemies. The savagery that goes on each day is beyond description—women with children in arms and little children of eight years old are 'potted' for the fun of the thing

by the savages from across the water who are well paid to
indulge in such congenial pastimes. But I suppose there
must be an end to everything in the world, so I pray God
there may soon be an end to this sort of thing. . . ." [1]

1921

Thursday, March 17. St. Patrick's Day, a beautiful sunshiny day. The first thing I saw when I got up was a string of lorries, armoured cars, caged lorries filled with Black and Tans, and military all with guns and revolvers on the ready. They were going towards town. . . .

The first production of Lady Gregory's three-act Wonder Play, *Aristotle's Bellows,* was a great success, and the players were called at the end and also the author. It is a whimsical fairy play with snatches of unaccompanied songs interspersed with droll effectiveness. . . . I congratulated Lady Gregory on the success of the piece, and she said, "It is wonderfully well played, and Miss Delany sang delightfully."

I replied, "You are very fortunate in your cast."

I saw Jack Yeats and one of his sisters in the stalls. I went up and had tea with Eileen and the doctor. They had been out towards Ringsend and heard many volleys of shots in the direction of Beggar's Bush while there.

Sunday, March 27. Lady Gregory returned me the copy of *The Warden of Galway* [1] with the following note.

COOLE, *March 25*

> Dear Mr. Holloway,
>   Thank you for letting me see *The Warden of Galway.* It would be interesting to see how such a play

would go now. But I don't think we can put on one connected with hanging for a long time to come—there are too many sore hearts around us.

Many thanks for your kind words upon my play, and I am much pleased at hearing W. Lawrence's opinion also.

Yours truly,
A. *Gregory*

Friday, July 29. Just after dinner I had a visit from Daniel Corkery whom Murray told not to forget to call on me before leaving Dublin; he leaves tomorrow. He was astonished at all the pictures and books, and had a look round, enjoying many of them. He was struck by Tuohy's work. . . . I couldn't draw him out of himself. Whenever I mentioned any of his books, he'd say, "Oh, yes, they have been very kindly received," and leave it at that. He thinks Dublin is coming around to itself again since the curfew was lifted. Cork was harder hit than Dublin, he thinks. . . . Speaking of George Moore wanting hand-made paper, etc., before he'd contribute, Corkery remarked, "Moore has become very exclusive and limited in his editions of new work. Most authors want to be read by many; Moore wants to be treasured in a first edition by a few."

Corkery is small in frame and delicate looking, and his right leg is short, and, though he uses a big soled boot, he walks with a limp of a cripple. His head, like his body, is small, but well-shaped, and he wears a moustache. He is silent, but observant. He expressed surprise when I told him I had been making notes on Dublin events for over forty years. "Oh, my, what a quantity of writing you must have accumulated," was his exclamation on seeing over 1200 pages in a six-months installment. . . . To look at Corkery, you would never imagine him the writer of *The Hounds of Banba* or *The Yellow Bittern*.[2] Though to look at his eye, you know that keenness lurks in its every twinkle, and the soul of the man gets at you in that way. . . . Corkery has a sweet, pleasing smile, with just the slightest hint of cynicism shading off its soothing quality.

Thursday, September 15.   F. J. McCormick called in and had a chat for about an hour and a half. He is not happy playing his part in *Paddy*.[3] He feels little or no interest in it. He sighs for the good and varied parts at the Abbey. If he was offered a good wage, he'd be back again like a shot. . . . The truth is that McCormick is an artist to his finger tips and possesses a keen appreciation of the art he practises so ably, and loves so well. He tells me he is not stage-struck in the way that acting satisfies him. It is only when he is playing worthy parts that he is really interested, parts in which you can let your thoughts run and experiment with. All players who have played at the Abbey have it, and long to play there again. The audience and the atmosphere of the place have a great and distinct charm for all players.

Wednesday, December 14.   ". . . Nobody is satisfied with the terms of the Peace Treaty, as it is only a make-shift and settles nothing. By it, Ireland is as far off as ever from the freedom she has longed through centuries for. It is generally accepted that it was signed to avoid the further assassination by the foreign savage brutes who hold a strangle hold on our beloved land, and not by the delegates' free will. . . ."[4]

1922

Friday, June 30. I just went to Mass and remained in all the rest of the day. Heard a terrific explosion at about 12:30. It shook the city. Afterwards learned by *The Evening Mail* that it was fired from a 60 pounder gun which was brought into action this morning. It shook buildings to their foundations, and plate glass windows were shattered and chimney pots and slates fell. Prior to it, the Four Courts was seen to be on fire in one place. The shell caused a lot of damage in the vicinity of the Four Courts. The gun was again fired at a quarter past 2. At 3:30 P.M., an order to cease fire was given to all the troups about the Four Courts, and immediately afterwards the survivors of the garrison were seen coming out of the building led by a priest and being murdered on Ormond Quay. The building burned fiercely and was enveloped in smoke. Rifle shots continued to be fired all the afternoon and until the night in various parts of the city. . . . Ireland in my time never witnessed such days of degradation as the past three; they shall live forever as an eternal blot on her slave people. The Black and Tans set them the headline, but "they bettered the instruction." . . . The Die Hards ought to be proud of their jackal, Collins, tonight.

Wednesday, August 23. News reached Dublin that General Michael Collins, Commander-in-Chief of the King's own Irish army, was shot dead in an ambush near Bandon, Co. Cork, R.I.P. He served his English masters only too well. Nightmarish Civil War stalks the land. Oh, that the dawn of peace were at hand!

Tuesday, November 14.   The first performance of Lennox Robinson's dainty little comedy, *Crabbed Youth and Age*, proved a most enjoyable trifle, delightfully enacted by all concerned. It was about three men and three maidens and the latter's mother, who was of such a bright, vivacious disposition that she attracted the youths, and the maidens were left lamenting. The whole thing was deliciously conceived and daintily and delicately carried out, and genuinely caught on with a typical Abbey first-night audience. . . . The author was dilatory in taking the call, and Lawrence, whom I afterwards met in the tram, told me he hissed at his delay.

Wednesday, December 20.   ". . . Gloom is over all in Ireland this Christmas; seven Irishmen were shot by so-called Irish soldiers yesterday morning to show the sort of peace and good will to all men those at the head of affairs wish for their fellow countrymen. . . . Those who signed the Treaty last year, wittingly or unwittingly, opened Hell's Gates at the same time, and the worst that that region could produce was let loose on this unfortunate country. The English Black and Tans were saints to the Irish Green and Tans, who at present terrorise the country. . . ." [1]

1923

Thursday, March 8.   On reading of the sudden death of William Boyle on Tuesday evening last at his residence, Herne Hill, London, Ellen recalled the last time he was here and had a chop with me for dinner. . . . It was only last week that his comedy *Family Failing* was revived successfully at the Abbey. I spent some time shortly after the 1916 Rising with him and family at his house at Dromiskin, Co. Louth, built on the spot of the house he was born in, in April, 1853. Then he was happy in his retirement and pottered about the fields and garden, or fished in the river nearby, ever and always with a big pipe in his mouth. Unfortunately he held a different opinion from mine over the War and the Rising, and, as he couldn't brook opposition or silence on matters that moved him strongly, he grew cold to me and never replied to any greetings or good wishes I afterwards continued to send him. It takes two to make a quarrel, and I had none with him. May the Lord have mercy on his soul, amen.

Boyle lost touch with the people of Louth, and when he became a magistrate he grew more and more unpopular, till some years ago he fled his new home in which he hoped, when having it built, to end his days, and returned to England where his end came suddenly on Tuesday evening last. . . .

I had tea with Eileen and the doctor before going on to the Abbey for . . . George Fitzmaurice's new one-act comedy *Twixt the Giltinans and the Carmodys*. The company played it with great farcical spirit, but could make nothing out of it, but poor talky stuff studded with outlandish words and echoing *The Country Dressmaker* at every turn.

Tuesday, April 10.   I walked into town in the morning and at Webb's picked up copies of the *National Story Magazine* and *Maeve* for 4d. each. One of the assistants in the shop referred to the play *The Shadow of a Gunman* by Sean O'Casey. "I know the writer well. He was telling me of its acceptance about a month ago. He had previously sent in plays which were rejected. He had always been fond of playwriting, and even made one about a lame alderman in the Corporation, called Cahill, which caused amusement for those who knew him. O'Casey is not too young. If his first-acted play is a success, he may do big things."

Thursday, April 12.   I saw W. B. Yeats, grey-hatted, walking along with his hands behind his back with a youth past the Kildare Street Club, and Father Dinneen with his head to one side and the usual cluster of papers in his left hand with a young man who walked lame in Nassau Street. I caught up with George Fitzmaurice in O'Connell Street and parted with him at Cavendish Row. He gave up play-going many years ago, he told me, and only goes to operas now. . . . I saw a film picture, Zane Grey's *Roaring U.P. Trail* at the Grand Central before going on to the Abbey and slipping into a front seat in the stalls just as *The Shadow of a Gunman* was beginning.

The scene was a room in a tenement in Dublin during the period of May, 1920, and it proved a bitingly sarcastic study of many types of character during that stirring period of our history. . . . The author, Sean O'Casey, set himself out to character sketch rather than to write a well-knit-together play. What it lacked in dramatic construction, it certainly pulled up in telling dialogue of the most topical and biting kind, and the audience revelled in the telling talk. . . . McCormick was in his element as

"Seumas Shields," and his creation became a memorably humourous one, as was Dolan's "Tommy Owens" also. Both Carolan and Fallon put in splendid studies, and May Craig as "Mrs. Grigson," who could talk the hind leg off an ass, was quite convincing.

Out of the crudeness of this first-acted play by the author, truth and human nature leaped and won the author a call at the end. During the second act, Mr. W. B. Yeats sat a few seats away from me and applauded vigorously the play and the author.

Saturday, April 14. . . . The Abbey was thronged to over-flowing at the evening show of *The Shadow of a Gunman,* and Paddy O'Connery summed it up after it was over as a revue and not a play, and O'Donnell said he liked it better on second hearing. . . . The author is a thin-faced, sharp-profiled man, with streaky hair, and wore a trench coat and a soft felt hat. He followed his play closely and laughed often, and I was told he was quiet-mannered almost to shyness, and very interesting in his views. . . .

Friday, April 27. . . . Sean O'Casey came in, and he and Dolan sat down on the oak seat in the vestibule and chatted over a Ms. of a play he had brought. I afterwards joined them and made myself known to O'Casey.

On the Run was the name he first called his play. He had the subject in his mind for two years, and took three to write it. He felt like a "spectator" at his own play. "The characters seemed strangers to me, but I enjoyed them." He didn't know Yeats when he sat beside him in the seat vacated by Lady Gregory. No author likes to be told his faults, and when Yeats wrote a letter of criticism about one of his plays—he had sent in several before one was accepted—he was so annoyed, he threw the letter aside and put away the Ms. for months, and, when he reread it, he found Yeats had been right and he wrong. He knows now that the Directors were wise in refusing his earlier plays, and thanks them and Robinson for their kindly criticism. He thought the Abbey Company played the piece excellently, and he stipulated that he would have. . . .[1]

There are no critics in Dublin—good criticism could not be dashed off. . . . Speaking of poets, O'Casey said he liked Byron very much, especially his humour as exhibited in *Don Juan*, etc. It was this humour that detracted from him as a poet. Shelley had none whatever, and his poetry is always taken seriously. Shelley was a poet who preached human fellowship, and John Kells Ingram who wrote when he was very young, at the wish of O'Connell, the fine ballad, "The Memory of the Dead," followed his doctrine and was the kindliest old soul O'Casey ever knew.

He hopes one day to write a play called *The Orange Lily* in which he will depict the feelings of a good type of Orangeman who wished well of Ireland, leading up to Easter Week, 1916. It would not be political; it would be more a character study. He was strong on character and weak on construction and could write dialogue with ease. He knew an Orangeman who could stand for his model. O'Casey was once an Orangeman himself and a member of The Purple Lodge, and getting on well till his love for processions and bands got him in disfavour with the members of his Lodge, and he left the body and joined a Gaelic League class and became a Nationalist which he remains.

It was in this way it happened. He always liked to go out to see the annual Parnell Procession to Glasnevin, and usually went up near the cemetery to see it without being seen by his sort. He had a Protestant friend in the Foresters, and one year he was looking on at the procession passing when his friend marched along with a green sash across his shoulder, and O'Casey being in the front row of the sightseers, his friend pulled him into the space beside him to make up a fourth, and he walked along till they came to the Brian Boru pub, and the Forester being a thirsty soul said he was off for a drink, and as O'Casey was a teetotaler at the time, the other said, "Here's the sash," as he took it off and threw it across O'Casey's shoulder. O'Casey, thus decked out, marched on to the cemetery with the procession, and when it was over he took off the green sash and concealed it under his coat. The Lodge called him to account for his marching in a rebel procession to a papist's churchyard and summoned him before them, and he being always of a pugnacious disposition read up about Parnell and defended him and his own action instead of apologising, and he got three years' expulsion from the Lodge and was stripped of all his Masonic trappings. On leaving the hall after the sentence, he told them all they might "go to Hell," and went out and joined the Gaelic League, learned Irish, and became a Nationalist there and then.

(I heard from Kavanagh afterwards that all his people save his mother disowned him after that, but she lived with him on Gardiner Street till she died. The Orangeman in O'Casey's play of *The Shadow of a Gunman* lived in rooms in the same house, as well as others of the characters introduced.)

O'Casey thinks Father O'Leary by far the best Irish writer of all. Douglas Hyde is a good translator, but a very misleading Irish writer. Paddy O'Conaire is out by himself as a writer; in Gaelic he has imagination and power as a writer, and is not afraid of Zola-like realism at times. His writings when translated become but poor stuff. O'Casey thinks Yeats has humour.

"Well, if he has, he shows very little of it," chipped in Dolan.

"*The Countess Cathleen* has glimpses of humour here and there. Humour is not, as a rule, of service to a poet." O'Casey saw *Blight* and liked it. . . .

Dolan spoke of Terence MacSwiney's play as but poor stuff.[2] I said I thought it effective when McCormick played the role of the hero, and Dolan said, "Mac made one fatal mistake in the part; he occasionally played for applause, and thus became self-conscious."

On hearing this, O'Casey said, "Sure, we all play for applause in life, from Jim Larkin down."

O'Casey had never read MacSwiney's "Thoughts on Freedom." "Freedom is a word with many meanings to many people, who all are right in their way. Such books, therefore, don't interest me." . . .

O'Casey in profile and build at first glance very much resembles Mr. Millington, who once was Secretary at the Abbey. He has strong bird-like eyes, and a sharp thin face. He speaks interestingly and well.

Saturday, July 21.   In the evening I had a chat with Dolan, who showed me a letter he just had from O'Casey about his re-written play *The Crimson in the Tricolour*, which he had forwarded on to Robinson. As originally written, Dolan found it impossible. The first scene was outside a convent with people spouting socialism for no earthly reason. Dolan suggested if he wanted his characters to spout such stuff, the bar of a pub would be the most likely setting. O'Casey has acted on his suggestions and made one of his scenes take place in a pub. The play originally seemed written to get off a lot of good things he had to say, without any sense of characterisation or construction. Dolan told him to take *The Whiteheaded Boy* as an example of how a play is built up in interest from the rise of the curtain. "Always keep the interest on the move," was his advice. O'Casey takes kindly to advice.

Tuesday, August 7.   After *The Shadow of a Gunman*, I walked home with Dudley Digges and saw him into a tram at Lansdowne Road. He went down to meet Sean O'Casey at the Abbey, and had a chat with him about his play, as to the advisability of turning it into a one-actor piece for the States. O'Casey said, "You'll have to do so yourself as I am too lazy to do so." . . .

Digges thinks first-night notices a mistake in every way. Why should the public want them? Actors on a first night were taken at a great disadvantage; they were usually very nervous and excited, and many things go wrong, and they have to bear the brunt of all in first-night criticism, which must of necessity be very hastily written. It is a wonder to him how it is usually as good as it is. He remembered the first night of *The Adding Machine*, when in Act II he is on trial and is to address the jury in the pit, and so face the audience. When the curtain went up, he was facing the audience right enough, but no jury was there. Yet despite that he had to go on with the part, the jury filing in afterwards. That incident is similar to many irritating episodes that players have to face on first nights.

Friday, August 17.   . . . The first act of *Maurice Harte* was over before I went into the Abbey. . . . I was speaking to Sean O'Casey who doesn't like Murray's plays because they take too much out of him. Both *Birthright* and *Maurice Harte* distressed him very much in witnessing. He likes his plays with brightness intermingled with sadness. The comedy of life appeals to him most. He once read *Tess* by Thomas Hardy and stayed awake crying all night after it. It had a surprising effect on him though he is not a sentimental fellow in reality; Murray's play has the same effect. O'Casey loves Shaw's work because in the very kernel of tragedy he can introduce something to make one laugh its sting away. Murray never does this; his tragedy is ever unrelieved.

Monday, September 10.   . . . I went on to the Abbey and was just in time to see the curtains rise on *Cathleen ni Houlihan*. . . . Sara Allgood was impressive in the title role. Sean O'Casey was behind me, and I joined him after Yeats's play and had a chat with him between whiles. He told me he had been raided several times lately. Last week he was awakened out of his sleep with hands pulling the sheet off him, and a light full in his eyes, and three revolvers pointed out. He was hauled out of bed and roughly handled, as they queried his name, etc. He knew of a young fellow, a member of the I.R.A., who was on the run, being taken in the middle of the night by the C.I.D. men and brought out towards Finglas and brutally beaten with the butt end of their revolvers, and then told to run for his life while they fired revolver shots after him, taking bits off his ears, etc., and catching up on him again renewed their beating.[3] Next day O'Casey saw the chap and could hardly recognise him, so battered and bruised was he. Such brutality demoralises a country. Flogging demoralises, but does not correct. . . .

O'Casey thinks Casey has put a lot of human nature into his plays. The opening of *The Suburban Grove* is a little slow, but the love of "Dick" for "Una" becomes almost tragic at the end of Act II. Truly the Abbey dramatists try to put nature on the stage, and the players do all they know to interpret it.

Monday, October 1. . . . Somehow or other, despite *Kathleen Listens In* being a good skit, it missed the mark I think and fizzled out somewhat. It was full of subtle touches, most of which didn't fit into dramatic effectiveness. The "O'Houlihans" were trying to keep their house in order despite "The Old Man in Kilts" (The Gael) and all the rest of the pack in search of jobs. It is very hard to make a skit dramatic, and I fear O'Casey has failed to do so. "Kathleen" listens in to all those who clamour for her favours till she almost succumbs, and the doctor recommends complete rest as the only cure. It was types and not characters that made up the cast; therefore, none of the players made their parts live. Perhaps Barry Fitzgerald as "Tomaus Thornton," a neighbour (England), made the best attempt. F. J. McCormick made a brave attempt without much result as "Miceawl O'Houlihan." The fantasy was clever, but proved unfunny. . . . There was a fine audience present, and excitement ran high to see how O'Casey would succeed in his second dramatic effort. The audience was eager to laugh with him, but couldn't, only by fits and starts.

Thursday, November 15. Seeing by the paper that W. B. Yeats had been awarded the Nobel Literature Prize for 1923, I wrote to him as follows.

Dear Mr. Yeats:

Allow me, one of the oldest and earliest admirers of your work, to congratulate you most sincerely and heartily on the great and well-deserved honour that has been bestowed upon you by the Swedish Academy of Science in awarding you the Nobel Literature Prize for 1923.

I *remain,*
   Yours sincerely,
      Joseph Holloway

Tuesday, November 27.   Brinsley MacNamara's racing play, *The Glorious Uncertainty,* proved a winner at the Abbey on its first performance on any stage. It is a play of racing types. It starts a little too talky, but the first act ended up interestingly; the second act rushed up things considerably, and the third to a point progressed well till after the race, when things became complicated and in the nature of anti-climax. . . . This piece is by far the most workmanlike play that Mac has as yet written. It was excellently cast. . . . Barry Fitzgerald was great as "Sam Price," the village better, turned tipster to recoup losses. "What a splendid comedian he is!" remarked Sydney Morgan as he sat beside me, and added, "Some of his methods are suggestive of Arthur Sinclair." This actor also commented on Miss Crowe "as being an actress with wonderful moments."

Thursday, November 29.   I wrote as follows to Lennox Robinson. ". . . I casually heard on yesterday that you had been appointed co-director with Lady Gregory and W. B. Yeats of the Abbey Theatre, and hasten to congratulate you, and to wish the little theatre a very prosperous and highly artistic success under your guidance. . . ."

82 MERRION SQUARE
DUBLIN
November 28, 1923

Dear Mr. Holloway,

Thank you very much for your letter. I am very glad indeed of this honour which will help me here in many ways. I start for Stockholm in a few days.

Yours,
W. B. Yeats

I wrote to Michael J. Dolan, Esq., Abbey Theatre.

Dear Mr. Dolan,

Hearty congratulations on your appointment as Manager of the Abbey. May it flourish under your loving care for many a long day to come; and may you still be able to continue to give us such perfect little character studies as "Simon Swords," [4] without unduly overtaxing yourself. . . .

Thursday, December 6. I saw the announcement of the death of Edward Martyn in the evening papers. He died at his residence, Tulira Castle, Ardrahan, Co. Galway, on yesterday. He had been ailing for a long while.

1924

Wednesday, January 2. . . . The dawn of the New Year is with us. May it prove a happier one for my country than the last; but I fear with a group of incompetent self-seekers at the head of affairs, things can hardly mend. . . . The so-called Free State means Hell for Ireland.

Thursday, January 3. At the Abbey I saw Sean O'Casey who said he handed in a new three-act play last week. . . . He often loves to put in a character he has known into a play without the character having aught to do with the plot. He likes to read Chekhov's plays; Chekhov seems to let his characters speak as they please and get them into his play's scheme. O'Casey is not a racing man and, therefore, didn't much like *The Glorious Uncertainty.*

Saturday, January 19. *The Irish Times* has a lovely, rather flattering portrait of Sara Allgood by P. Tuohy, with the following remarks by Yeats.

Miss Sara Allgood is a great folk-actress. As so often happens with a great actor or actress, she rose into fame with a school of drama. She was born to play the old woman in *The Well of the Saints,* and to give their first vogue to Lady Gregory's little comedies. It is impossible for those of us who are connected with the Abbey management to forget that night in December,

1904, when for the first time she rushed among the stage crowd in *The Spreading of the News*, calling out, "Give me back my man!" We never knew until that moment that we had, not only a great actress, but that rarest of all things, a woman comedian; for stage humour is almost a male prerogative.

It has been more difficult in recent years to supply her with adequate parts, for Dublin is a little tired of its admirable folk-arts, political events having turned our minds elsewhere. Perhaps, the Spaniard, Sierra, who in his plays expounds a psychological and modern purpose through sharply defined characters, themselves as little psychological and modern as Mrs. Broderick herself, may give her the opportunity she needs. I am looking forward with great curiosity to seeing her in his *Two Shepherds*, which is now just going into rehearsal, and one of our Irish dramatists, Mr. O'Casey, has, in his new play, *Juno and the Paycock*, given her an excellent part.

Miss Allgood is no end of a problem, and the sooner our dramatists get that into their heads and write for her the better for them and us. If we knew how to appreciate our geniuses, they would not have wasted her so scandalously.

Tuesday, February 12.   *The Two Shepherds* was put on at the Abbey for the first time here and proved an interesting experiment—though much of the second act missed fire and nearly cancelled the interest created in Act 1. . . . I sat it out alongside Sean O'Casey and W. A. Henderson. The former told me his play has not yet been put into rehearsal though down for production on February 25 (Monday). He likes Dolan best of all the actors in the company, though McCormick acts many parts supremely well and is over-conscientious if anything. McCormick almost annoyed him asking him to explain what he meant "Seumas Shields's" part to be like, and when O'Casey had explained to him over and over again, Mac said he'd carry out his own conception of the part, and did, and was right. O'Casey thinks him really great in the character. He didn't like him in A *Doll's House*;[1] it was beyond the company, he thought.

Monday, March 3.   "It is powerful and gripping and all that, but too damned gruesome; it gets you, but it is not pleasant," is the way Dan Maher summed up *Juno and the Paycock*, O'Casey's new play at the Abbey. . . . The last act is intensely tragic and heart-rendingly real to those who passed through the terrible period of 1922. . . . The tremendous tragedy of Act III swept all before it, and made the doings on the stage real and thrilling in their intensity. The acting all round was of the highest quality, not one in the long cast being misplaced or for a moment out of the picture. Fitzgerald and McCormick as "Captain Jack Boyle" and his bar-room pal "Joxer Daly," an old Forester, make a splendid pair of workers who never work. Sara Allgood as "Juno Boyle," with all the worries of trying to keep everything together was excellent, and in Act III she had great moments of heart-rending sorrow. Arthur Shields as the haunted, maimed boy "Johnny," got the right note of dread into his study from the very first, and Eileen Crowe as "Mary" presented every side of the character cleverly and realistically, and her singing of the duet, "Home to our Mountains," with her mother at the hooley was deliciously droll. Maureen Delany, as the talkative "Mrs. Maisie Madigan" was most amusing, and Christine Hayden, as the sorrowing mother "Mrs. Tancred" sorrowed for her son most touchingly. . . .

In Act III some in the pit were inclined at first to laugh at the tragedy that had entered into the "Boyle" family, but they soon lost their mirth and were gripped by the awful actuality of the incidents enacted so realistically and unassumingly before them. As I left the theatre, cries of "Author, Author!" were filling the air, and I suppose O'Casey had to bow his acknowledgment. He sat with a friend in the second row of the stalls with his cap on all the while, I noticed. He is a strange, odd fish, but a genius in his way.

Saturday, March 8.   I attended the Abbey matinee and there heard that crowds were turned away last night, and that booking was complete for to-night. . . . James Stephens had to be accommodated with a chair last night, by the wish of Dolan. Lady Gregory was up and was astonished at the house.

Tuesday, March 18.   . . . I had a chat with Sean O'Casey in the vestibule. He told me that when he started to write plays he thought he was a second Shaw sent to express his views through his characters, and was conceited enough to think that his opinions were the only ones that mattered. It was Lady Gregory who advised him to cut out all expression of self, and develop his peculiar aptness for character drawing. At first he didn't take kindly to her advice, but afterwards on consideration felt she was right.

He was so poor when he took to writing first that he hadn't the money to supply himself with paper to write his stuff on, and a pal supplied him with paper filched from his employer's store. His first two plays were written in his cramped handwriting, and yet the Abbey directors read his script and expressed sorrow at having to reject both plays, and gave him sound critical advice which he resented at first, but on second thought accepted, and was determined to profit by and did. He was determined to succeed. . . .

He has a small typewriter now. He intends to stick to playwriting; he thinks Robinson has too many irons in the fire to do himslf justice. O'Casey reads Robinson's *Observer* article each week, but doesn't think very much of it. He should concentrate more; only those do who reach the very top. This is the age of the specialist.

Friday, March 21.   . . . I had a chat with lame Maguire.² . . . Speaking of Sean O'Casey, he remembered him as being one of the first to join the Piper's Band and wear the kilt, and an ungainly figure he cut in it. He was more like a country lad than a Dubliner. He

always walked with a near-sighted bend of the head. He
was always strong and energetic, and when he played
hurling he looked a guy in short knickers, and once in a
match in the park—so it is said—he killed a sparrow,
thinking he was swiping at the ball. He agreed with
nobody and believed in nothing. He was strangely distant
and silent always. He wrote for *The Irish Worker* and was
secretary to the Citizen Army. The book he wrote about
the Citizen Army wasn't thought much of by those connected with it. He was a shunter on the Northern Railway
in those days. He was always sore-eyed and took an active
part in the Gaelic movement. He was very energetic in all
he undertook. Now he has struck oil as a playwright, he is
determined to work hard to reach the top in that branch
of literature. His friend out of Webb's joined us in the
latter part of our conversation about O'Casey. It was he
told the sparrow incident.

Friday, March 28.   A bitterly sharp evening with an icy
cutting wind about. I had a long chat with O'Casey in the
vestibule of the Abbey. He thinks the Government is
proving a set of woeful incompetents—egotistical and in-
tolerant of criticism. They are going from bad to worse.
They'll be nobody's friend shortly. He spoke of the hypocrisy over the shooting of the soldier at Cork. "The honour
of Ireland is at stake over it, people say who don't know
what honour is!"

He witnessed terrible deeds during recent years; a friend
of his was riddled with bullets and mutilated in a horrible
way by the Green and Tans, a young Tipperary lad.
Nothing could be more brutal than the treatment he got.
It is hard to think Irish people capable of such savagery.
Savages would be decent in comparison to them. After the
inquest his remains were brought to his digs, and O'Casey
helped to carry in the coffin to his friend's upstairs. Another lad he knew was taken out and tied up by his hands
—his feet dangling some distance from the ground, while
they poured salts through a tin dish down his throat. The
poor fellow was cut down alive, but he is a human wreck
ever since—always shaking, though as brave as ever.

O'Casey believes the oath is the peace destroyer. Irishmen as a whole will never be got to take the oath of allegiance to the King.[3] It is all folly to think otherwise. All oaths should be abolished, O'Casey thinks. Sean Connolly would never take one, yet he died fighting the first day of Easter Week, 1916. O'Casey believes in paying his way and doing without when he can't. "No amount of pledges or oaths will keep a person from breaking them if they have no principle to go by. The present-day creed is to teach all to be dishonest. Hypocrisy is over all."

Tuesday, April 15.   At the end of *The Story Brought by Brigit*,[4] I said to O'Casey who sat next to me, "It was very impressive!" And he replied, "It was almost too impressive for me!" I think that is the way most present felt on the final fall of the curtain. The world's biggest tragedy had been enacted before them with sufficient vividness to touch all hearts. Screens were used as scenes, save in the last scene, by the side of the road leading to Calvary. . . .

O'Casey likes some of Lady Gregory's work, but lately read *Shanwalla* and some others of hers, including *The Wrens*, for which he didn't care. MacNamara likes *The Dragon* and *The Golden Apple*, and thinks she found herself in them.

Speaking of Eileen Crowe, Mac said, "There is a great diversity of opinion about Miss Crowe's acting; some raved about it, while others can't see any merit in it at all." Robinson's word, "Genius," as applied to her acting spoiled her, Mac thinks. "She had a great facility for learning parts without letting their meaning sink into her," he thinks, "that was fatal to her work being ever great, and also her face was very expressionless."

I said, "I think her fine in many parts."

O'Casey didn't like her "Nora" in *A Doll's House*. I did. She must have some rare merit about her work to cause such diversity of opinion.

Mac and O'Casey saw *At the Hawk's Well*; the latter couldn't understand it, he candidly confessed. Mac enjoyed Yeats's speech about the "Noh" plays of Japan on which his play was built. . . . Speaking of Shaw's play

Saint Joan breaking all records at the New Theatre, O'Casey remarked that Shaw could never be repaid sufficiently for his work—which is great.

Mac referred to money-getters like *Peg o' My Heart* and *The Private Secretary* and *Charley's Aunt* slightingly, and I said there must be something in them to draw so long, when thousands of plays that seemed built in the same way have all faded out of sight after short stage-lives. The mystery of a successful stage play is hard, if not impossible, to solve. Facility is the curse of writers, actors, musicians and artists. If you produce easily without much thought or meditation on your work, it usually is of poor quality. Frank J. Hugh O'Donnell has that fault, and he has not yet arrived anywhere.

O'Casey, speaking of the English and Irish, said, "Although I write cynically about the Irish in my plays, I have a much greater opinion of their intellects than I have of the English. I understand English politics, but I never met an Englishman who understood the Irishman's outlook."

Wednesday, April 23.   It turned out a very wet day. Frank Fay called in the afternoon. . . . Fay believes that the old actors were right in sticking as much as possible to the centre of the stage where all could see them. "Why do the Abbey Company now mostly gabble their parts? Is it to be in with the fashion of the English stage for indistinctness of utterance?" . . .

At the Abbey I had a chat with Sean O'Casey in the vestibule during Act 1 of Shaw's play, and I showed him some drawings I had made on postcards, and he said, "You are to me a wonder—a man who takes things easily, or seems to shirk them altogether, yet having a great memory, and very tolerant of other's views and holding very fixed and unshakeable views of your own on many things—very affable to all, and, in fact, a type all to yourself." He hoped I didn't mind him saying so, and I said, "Not at all. But you are wrong in thinking I take things easily, as I am ever and always busy when at home

—reading, writing, drawing, etc. It is only when I am out I take it easily or seem idling time away, and yet all the time I am absorbing material to jot down when I return home. Architecture gave me up before I thought of giving it up. The War killed for the time domestic architecture, and my work ceased to exist in consequence. That was how it was. When it revives, I will probably be too old to resume again."

When I told him I wrote some 2000 pages a year on events and things, he added, "You are hard to understand." . . .

Speaking of a visit to Belfast, O'Casey said he went there with the intention of spending a week in that city, but on being there a few hours he wished for Dublin and returned to the railway station to find no passenger train starting for some hours, so he got on a luggage train that was just starting. He was working on the railway at the time and travelled free. Protestant and all as he was, Papish Dublin was the place for him.

Sunday, April 27.   Lennox Robinson (Paul Ruttledge) made a great personal success as "Henry IV" in Pirandello's three-act tragedy of that name played at the Abbey to-night under the auspices of the Dublin Drama League; in fact, it amounted to almost a triumph. In Act I he gave us such another character study as that of the crafty "Louis XI," [5] all doubled up with his wits astray, and he spoke in tones in keeping with such a character. His stage voice was much stronger and more effective than his rather thin, piping treble which he uses in everyday life. His acting of this part surprised everyone in the theatre, and made many call him a great actor.

Saturday, May 10.   . . . The little theatre was thronged again, and crowds being turned away as I went up at 7:45. . . . The matinee was equal to last Saturday's in attendance. *Juno* has broken all records. . . .

O'Casey told me he came to the rescue of a lady in the vestibule who didn't seem to know her way about, never having been in the Abbey before, and he found out she was a cousin of his he hadn't seen for years. Her father was 89, and as bitter a Protestant as ever he knew, but a fine old fellow if you kept him off his pet subject, hatred of Roman Catholics. O'Casey escaped the narrow environment in which the old man was brought up, having always to work for his living and meeting all sorts of people, and he found all sorts, the good and the bad, in all walks of life and all religions, and his mind broadened to all humanity. . . .

When I mentioned to Sean O'Casey that Frank Fay was to speak on "Dramatic Art" tomorrow, Sunday (May 11) at the Father Matthew Hall, he said, "I don't hold with Fay's views on dramatic art at all, though I admire the enthusiasm with which he upholds such views. It's difference of opinion that keeps the world fresh for people to live in. If we were all of the one opinion, Earth would soon become Hell through monotony."

Tuesday, May 20.   At Webb's I came across Sean O'Casey. . . . O'Casey is amused when he hears people say, who never were in a tenement, that his plays are photographic of the life he depicts. They not knowing anything at first hand of what they are talking. . . . He didn't care for Shiels's play, *The Retrievers;* [6] it was but poor, ill-digested stuff. He was amused when I told him that MacNamara said to me that, "It was a wonderfully clever satirical comedy and far above the heads of the audience." He wondered if it were more subtle than Shaw's plays or Nietzsche's writings, and yet they were easily understood. O'Casey thought Shiels's *Bedmates* and *First Aid* good and understandable satires. But in *The Retrievers* things were too far-fetched and unconvincing. . . .

On his telling me he had purchased a volume of AE's collected poems, I mentioned that he would be writing his next play amongst the stars. Then he told me of the play with the title of *The Plough Amongst the Stars* he had in his mind to write. He also got two volumes of Nietzsche

at Webb's. . . . He regretted the loss of several books he
lent, such as McGill's *The Rat Trap,* a very realistic book.
He thinks James Stephen's *The Charwoman's Daughter* a
very pleasingly written story, but scarcely true to slum life.

Tuesday, June 3.   . . . I met Sean O'Casey looking into
Eason's, and he asked me what way I was going, and I
said any way if he waited a moment till I got the papers.
Then we strolled up and into St. Stephen's Green and saw
the young swans, and sat down near the bandstand and
had a chat on all sorts of topics. I told him of the
reception of the play *Juno* in Cork. He knew Liam
O'Flaherty well years ago when he was a Socialist speaker.
He thought his sketch, "The Hook," splendid. He liked
Kelleher's "Glamour of Dublin," but not his articles or
play in *The Dublin Magazine.*
We spoke of *The Gunman* and "Maguire" and
Knocksedan with regard to the time that should elapse. I
also referred to the pedlar's sleeping out Mass time, and
yet the others acted as if it were a weekday, and O'Casey
said to me, "It was a weekday, but the pedlar went to
Mass each day and was a daily communicant."
Fay wanted O'Casey's earlier plays that were refused by
the Abbey, but he couldn't give them to him or anyone.
He said he destroyed them, but he didn't. He hopes to use
some of the dialogue later on. He thinks Fay's art of
acting is dead. He is pompous and dictatorial now.
O'Casey told me of an evening he spent in one of the
intellectual's houses, where the three or four present
talked art at top speed. He was struck dumb and listened
after awhile for scraps for future plays. Conversation
should be free to roam at will here, there, and everywhere,
and be natural and never conclusive. Everyone have their
say, but none lay down the law.
On Saturday next, O'Casey goes to Coole on his vaca-
tion. He is not enamoured of the idea. He stays for a
fortnight. O'Casey wrote an article for *The Irish Statesman's* "Literature and Life" column under the head of
"Life and Literature" from the workman's standpoint. AE

asked for more. He has notes for fifty articles by him, but is too lazy to write them. He thinks the *Statesman* an interesting paper. The new aristocracy is ignorant and selfish, and he told me of a farmer in a small way who purchased a castle recently vacated by its appropriate owner, who on leaving took the pictures from the frames as the transit of the latter would be exorbitant. O'Casey heard of the farmer writing to a friend to know where he'd get pictures at 2/6 or 5/- to fill the frames. That was the new Irish rich for you.

Friday, July 25.   A continuous wet day. I did not stir out till evening when I went to the Abbey. . . . I was speaking to Sean O'Casey in the vestibule. He spent most of the time when in Galway wandering about the woods of Coole. He found the country people much like anyone else, singing, "Yes, we have no bananas today!" He met one Irish-speaking peasant woman whom he had a delightful chat with. He read *Saint Joan* and thought the dialogue fine and chockful of raps at England. Shaw dearly loves such sallies.

O'Casey told me he has a one-act play nearly finished. He can write dialogue easily enough, having no difficulty in doing so, but construction does not come so easily with him. It is a very long one-act, and he has been cutting it down as much as he can.

Shiels ought to be made to come and see his own plays; he has the gift of drama, but his plots are as complicated as detective stories and get the spectators into black knots; in fact, they "dunno" where they are often. His dialogue is excellent and his character sketching strong and effective, but if he saw his pieces on the stage he could improve them much. He is sensitive in coming up to the Abbey, having only two stumps of legs. O'Casey likes his tramps in *Insurance Money*; they are very poetic, but, like all the tramps in modern Irish plays, are in no way like the real article. Shiels has the knack of writing exciting pot-boiling stories of the wild and wooly west cowboy type. It was in the States he lost his limbs. His American types in *The*

Retrievers are composite ones, Mr. Kelly and others tell me. . . . Shiels is very kindly in his lookout, always tries to soften off all his characters in the last act; he sees good in all humanity.

Thursday, July 31.   . . . At the Abbey . . . I told Sean O'Casey that Colum was anxious to see him. He came in with me, and we sat out the balance of the programme together. He thought *Maurice Harte* a great play greatly acted, and *The Rising of the Moon* was also impressively played by Nolan and Dolan as the Sergeant and the Ballad Singer. Sara Allgood's voice was as richly beautiful as ever as "Cathleen," and her "Mrs. Harte" was the perfection of homely emotional acting. McCormick's "Maurice" was also very fine; he wasn't as fidgety as usual, but gave a very impressive study of the part. Before he went on, he was suffering from a gum boil, and feared he couldn't act at all. Strange to say, the fact was he never acted better.

O'Casey again spoke of *Ann Kavanagh* as real poor stuff. To him Miss Macardle as a dramatist is nil. He looks at strikes from the workman's point of view, and thinks all arbitration biased in favour of capital and the state. The workman has always to fight bitterly for his existence; all the world is against him.

Thursday, August 14.   . . . I witnessed a strange incident last night in seeing W. B. Yeats and Mrs. Yeats being crowded out of the Abbey, and having to seek the pictures to allay their disappointment. O'Casey's play, *The Shadow of a Gunman,* had been staged for three nights with the usual result—that crowds had to be turned away each performance. This and his other play, *Juno and the Paycock,* have wonderful drawing power. The same people want to see them over and over again. . . . And the author stood chatting to me in the vestibule the other night as the audience came thronging in, proud of the fact, but in no way swell-headed, his cloth cap cocked over his left eye, as his right looked short-sightedly at the

audience's eager rush. Certainly he has written the two
most popular plays ever seen at the Abbey, and they both
are backgrounded by the terrible times we have just
passed through, but his characters are so true to life and
humourous that all swallow the bitter pill of fact that
underlies both pieces. The acting in both reaches the
highest watermark of Abbey acting. It looks as if the
Abbey is coming into its own at long last, and it's about
time. In December next it will reach its twentieth year of
existence. Colum was present in the front row of the stalls
last night, and he became so excited during the events in
the second act that he kept unconsciously jumping up and
down in his seat, and even at times went over to the stage
front and placed his elbows on the stage ledge as he gazed
intently at what was taking place thereon.

Tuesday, August 19.   . . . Sean O'Casey told me of all
whom he met with in the old Sinn Fein days, he liked
Mrs. De Valera the best. She was a very bright, unassuming, intelligent woman; he knew her as Miss O'Flanagan,
and heard her lecture very agreeably in Sinn Fein halls.
"It is such as she should represent Ireland in Parliament," he said. The Countess was always in hysterical
terror. Marriage seems to have blotted out publicity from
Mrs. De Valera's life, and more's the pity, O'Casey
thinks.

He told me of a poor girl he knew and liked in the old
days, and does so still, who married, and whose husband is
now a general in the army, and she drives about in a
motor and affects a cockney accent which amuses Sean.
He is friends with her still, as I said, and sometimes when
she is passing in a motor and sees him, she stops to give
him a lift. Lately on one of these occasions, she invited
him "home to tea," and he happened to say, "Now?" by
way of interrogation, and she interpreted it as "No." This
was the last straw, and Sean asked her for God's sake drop
the cockney accent and speak as she used to do in the old
days. The new rich are all beggars on horseback riding to
the Devil!

Saturday, August 23. . . . O'Casey, referring to the way some are flashing money about asked me had I ever been to the Labour Exchange? He had been there lately and tried to get to the hutch his docket was made out for, but the great crush of men in the queue almost made him faintish, and after about an hour and a half of it (and he still hours away from the hutch) he had to try to push his way out of the crowd. It is a terrible sight to see so many men out of work. Some are there from six in the morning though their cards state the hour to apply to the hutch, and if they arrive there before the time specified, "They are told to go to Hell!" He should like to show Yeats or Robinson such sights. Then they would be less ready to advocate the use of the lash.[7]

Monday, September 8.   Since I first saw Irving in the Dream Scene in *The Bells* I haven't been so thrilled by a scene as by Michael J. Dolan's playing of "Owen Keegan" in the final act of T. C. Murray's great play *Autumn Fire* at the Abbey to-night, where the piece was given its first public performance. The little theatre was crowded by a most attentive audience who were completely carried away by the superb playing of Dolan as the old paralysed man. . . . The agony of mind the old wreck of a man goes through in finding the mistake he had made was a wonderful if gruesome piece of acting that gripped one all the while. The stillness of the audience almost could be felt. Murray has written a very strong drama, full of effective characterisation, and, with the exception of Sara Allgood who hadn't her words sufficiently well off to give complete attention to her acting, the cast did remarkably well for a first night. . . .

Murray came in with Bernard Duffy. He was very low in spirits and quite "nervy." He sat out the performance with me in the second row of the stalls, and was all of a tremble during Act I. Sara Allgood's forgetfulness put his nerves on edge, and he moved restlessly in his seat when words failed her, and the prompter was heard. After Act I he brightened up, and went out after Act II and came back talking to Andrew E. Malone (Byrne), the highbrow critic of unacted drama, who told him he thought Miss Crowe too wooden. Murray didn't think so, though not a great admirer of her acting. On this occasion he thought she had gotten into the skin of the character as he conceived it. Malone's idea of acting was Sinclair in *The Heather Field*, one of that clever actor's real failures. So much for Malone as a judge of acted drama.

Monday, September 29.   I went on to the Abbey in the evening and met Mr. and Mrs. Lawrence in the tram going in to see O'Casey's new piece, *Nannie's Night Out.* . . . I left to catch the eleven tram home, and O'Casey's play was in progress. . . . From the bit I saw, it seems very rambling, go-as-you-please dialogue, with little form or story, save the love episodes of three old codgers for the hand of "Mrs. Polly Pender," who keeps a dairy. "Nannie" of the title comes and goes through the piece, in an excited mad way, singing snatches of songs or shouting out wild words. . . . Sara Allgood was fantastic but unconvincing as "Nannie" as far as I saw. Fitzgerald, Dolan, and Fallon differentiated the roles of the old lovers of "Polly" effectively, and Maureen Delany made a popular "Polly." The little piece seemed weighted down with talk. . . . Certainly O'Casey has caught and noted down many Dublin expressions and embodied them in his plays. It is only when you hear them on the stage they ring familiar to the ear. O'Casey hasn't lost his power of strong character drawing, and his power of observation is as keen as ever. I shall be surprised if *Nannie's Night Out* proves as magnetic as either his *Gunman* or *Juno.*

Saturday, October 4.   At the Abbey in the evening, the theatre was thronged, and motors lined up each side of the street. I was speaking to Carolan and Sean O'Casey in the tea room before the performance, and O'Casey told us that the "doll incident" occurred to him when in a shop. The real "Mrs. Polly" was at the performance on Monday and one of the "oul fellas." The man who goes about the city with the fur cap was the model for "Oul Jimmie"; he often presented the real "Mrs. Polly" with jewellery, but begged it back on seeing other candidates in the field for her hand. O'Casey doesn't much care for the farce himself, now that he sees it on the stage. . . . The sentiment of "it is better to feed half-starved little boys before teaching them Irish" was hissed last night and won rounds of applause at the matinee.

Friday, October 10.   Spoke to Sean O'Casey on the inclination of people to laugh at the tragic incidents in life. He told me of an incident he witnessed years ago in the street. A blind man came along and bumped into two men conversing on the kerb, and a little further on a blind man coming from the opposite direction collided with him, and he angrily exclaimed, "Is the town full of blind men today?" O'Casey said he laughed at the incident without considering the terrible tragedy that lay behind it.

Thursday, October 23.   ". . . O'Casey, who is a labourer, has been unable to get work for some months past, and is living on the Royalties he gets from the little Abbey. A man of his natural genius should not be allowed to work at manual labour any longer. It should be made possible to have him allowed sufficient to develop the genius with which he has been endowed. In any other country save Ireland, I am sure this would be done. But here, alas, the new rich only think of motors and dress. Talent and the arts are allowed to starve for lack of appreciation. . . ." [8]

Tuesday, December 16.   I dropped into the Abbey and got a programme on my way up to Parnell Square to hear Lord Dunsany hold forth at the Dublin Literary Society. He had not named his discourse. Hutchinson was in the chair, and read a letter of appreciation of his Lordship's works from A. de Blacam who could not be present to take the chair.

The first thing his Lordship did was to take the plated

tray from under the glass jug and tumbler, and cast it noisily on the ground. He took up his position away from the fire next the piano on which he placed two books. He started by expressing surprise at the letter, saying that the person who wrote that must have read his writings, and he didn't think anyone did in Dublin. Having got his usual sneer off his chest, he took up one of the books and said by way of a start he'd read out a chapter (Chapter 22) and if we hadn't enough of him when he'd done, he'd speak on the drama or almost any subject of an artistic nature we should wish. He didn't name the book he read from (it was *The King of Elfland's Daughter*). At first his lisp almost affected the clearness of his speech, but soon he got into a rhythmic swing that made the glowing prose a live thing and what he read a beautiful prose poem. . . .

When he lay down the book, he at once started off on the drama, and words and sentences tumbled out of his mouth at great speed—sometimes in confusing higgledy-piggledy order—but many wise and sane things were evolved in the process. . . . He loves the beautiful and bright in art; the sordid, the morbid, the realistic are not for him. He thinks the public likes good things when they get them, but financiers being at the head of affairs in threatreland are afraid to break away from the pattern play they know. The beautiful in art, literature, music, and the drama make for the world's happiness. To think all drab is to make life not worth living. Nowadays, the show had captured the stage to the exclusion of the drama. Drama was one of the most valuable of the arts. Tragedy was useful inasmuch as it showed some of the disasters of life. There was something close to life in all the arts, and perhaps closest of all in drama. Drama must be true to life. It must be the essence of life, and surprise must be there. What was called realism of the present-day stage was invariably associated with what was drab in human nature and with passion.

1925

Tuesday, January 20. . . . I was speaking to Sean O'Casey as he passed in. . . . Nesbitt, the publisher, first had his Ms. of plays, and the contract was so tricky when he asked AE about it, he told him he'd better become a member of the Authors' Society and get the Society's opinion of the contract. He did and got an adverse opinion and wrote for his Ms. Macmillan's contract was short and concise and straightforward.

When Sean gets reading a paper and gets on to the political element, he must read it through and compare it with what has gone before. He has no faith in Sean Milroy's blatherskite.

I said, "I call him a mere tub-thumper and nothing more."

He said, "The country is still full of 'Eloquent Dempsys,' but Boyle's specimen had the humour to see through himself. The 'Dempsys' of today are bumpkins without humour."

The last time I was speaking to Sean he said that he had to forage for himself, and when not working didn't effect early hours. He likes Cardinal Newman's *Apologia* and Anatole France's writings. They were both brainy men, but oh so different in their outlook. Men are entitled to their opinions no matter how they differ from others.

Saturday, April 4. . . . Sean O'Casey came later on, and I introduced him to Murray, and they and I had a long chat after meeting in the vestibule until the performance had concluded, and then we walked as far as the Pillar and parted there. O'Casey likes *Portrait* as well as any of Robinson's pieces. He and Murray spoke most about Irish in the schools, and much about the hypocrisy that enters into the heart of the Gaelic movement. Padraig O'Conaire, Father O'Leary, and some few others can write in Irish. Douglas Hyde can't. He can translate from the language splendidly, but not write. Pearse Beasley and Thomas Hayes write hopeless Irish in their plays. . . . Murray said a schoolmaster's life is a very hard one, and sometimes he is worn out after the day. The teaching of Irish adds a new trial to his existence. . . .

O'Casey is very guarded in expressing opinions on acting and actors, as he feels he is not competent to judge. Both he and Murray thought Quinn miscast in *The Old Man* and also in *Portrait*. He is not built for expressing emotion on the stage. Sara Allgood is; she is a great emotional actress, but her tragedy as a stage player is her putting on flesh, which debars her from playing in many parts otherwise suitable to her.

Friday, April 17.   I . . . heard one workman say to another in D'Olier Street, "You're a bloody fool to work for anyone if you can help it." And when I told Sean O'Casey what I overheard, he replied, "Work was made for mugs." He hasn't been working at the new play of late. He is lazy. "I like to read adverse criticisms of my plays," was what he said when I told him of Carey's comments in *Honesty*.

Wednesday, July 22.   George Russell, editor of *The Irish Statesman,* turned down my article on George Sigerson with a typed note as follows.

84 MERRION SQUARE
DUBLIN
July 21, 1925

Dear Holloway,
        There are very interesting things in your memories of Sigerson, but I confess I do not like putting into

the paper statements so loosely made—"The greatest Irishman of his time," "his learning knew no bounds" and similar expressions which to say the least of them are not very critical. I am obliged for the opportunity of seeing the paper.

> *Yours sincerely,*
> George Russell

. . . It is pleasing to consider that AE glanced as far as the third line of my article before rejecting it. That's a consolation in itself. One has to be thankful for small mercies in this world.

Saturday, August 8.   Yeats addressed the House in a short speech about the Abbey and its wonderful accomplishment in the past, and the hopes of a brilliant future now that the Government had made it a grant of £850. It was because it thought of Ireland first that the theatre and its authors, actors, and patrons have succeeded in accomplishing much, was the burden of his remarks. The Irish Parliament at the end of the 18th century accomplished much because its eloquence applied to Irish needs. The literature of the 19th century never reached the really memorable because its first appeal was to outsiders. Even Maria Edgeworth and William Carleton who did such fine work fell short of real greatness on that account. The Abbey plays had been translated into all European languages and many Oriental ones as well. The Abbey was always endowed one way or another since its inception; the actors and dramatists almost accepting nothing for their services at times. . . .

Yeats also said, "Now we can assure you that this Government subsidy and your continued support will enable us to keep a brilliant company, and to offer in the future, as in the past, a means of expression to Irish dramatic intellect. Neither Lady Gregory nor John Synge nor I ever thought of this theatre as an educational theatre in the ordinary sense of the word; we had nothing to teach but clarity of expression, and that for the most part was taught not by us but by the opportunity of the stage and the opportunity that you gave by your critical enthusiasm. The credit belongs to dramatists, actors and audiences. They have been worthy of one another. We have, however, created in this little theatre an assembly where we can discuss our own problems and our own life, and I think we have the right to claim that we have founded an art of drama and an art of acting which are in the first rank. The fame of this theatre has gone everywhere: there is, I think, no European nation where its plays have not been performed, and I am constantly hearing of some new translation of some one or other of our dramatists into some Oriental language. I think at this moment I may be permitted to boast of our work, for without doing so I cannot praise the Government aught for this new manifestation of their courage and intelligence."

At midnight Mr. and Mrs. Blythe were feted at a supper on the stage of the Abbey, given by the Directors and the staff. In replying, Mr. Blythe said he had, when possible, been a regular attendant at the Abbey theatre for the last twenty years.

Wednesday, August 12.   On my way to the Abbey I saw Jim Larkin holding forth to a meeting on Burgh Quay. On first seeing him standing up amid the crowd with his left hand on his hip and his right hand raised well above his head, I almost mistook him for W. B. Yeats.

Thursday, August 20.   On leaving Eileen's, I went on to the Abbey where great crowds awaited the opening of the doors, most of the stall seats being booked beforehand. . . . I met Padraig O'Conaire, drunk as usual, outside the theatre, and saw Michael Willmore alight from a taxi with an armful of his sketches . . . and two others who had photographic appliances with them. O'Conaire went round to the stage door with them. He had been railing against O'Casey's plays not being drama, and told me of a play a mason had written about Aran in Gaelic called *Darkness*. . . . O'Conaire believes he possesses the dramatic instinct, but does not love the theatre. He told me that when Boyle and he saw some Abbey plays Boyle said to him, "I think we could write better than that." "Then," said O'Conaire, "I wrote the play known as *The Building Fund* in Irish, which Boyle translated. Boyle was a good constructionalist." When Boyle fell out with him for something he had done that Boyle didn't approve of, Boyle lost his aid in playwriting and never accomplished anything worthwhile. His *Nic* was a dead failure. . . .

Colum suggested some trifling alterations in the text of *Juno,* and O'Casey informed us that the lines that the "Captain" recites were written by a man named Buckley who thought he could write verse. Buckley showed O'Casey the lines, and O'Casey said, "They are very good," and they were afterwards published in a labour paper. O'Casey introduced the song for "Maisie Madigan" at Miss Delany's request, and he is thinking of taking out Buckley's "poem" and giving the "Captain" a verse of "The Anchors Weighed" instead. Colum advised him not to touch the hooley scene, as it was *the* scene of the play as it stood.

O'Casey, seeing O'Conaire drunk as usual, said, "He has become impossible; all his friends are becoming tired of him. I don't mind a man being drunk occasionally, but I draw the line at . . . one who is always in that state. His Gaelic friends could get no good of him." Larchet called O'Casey away from Colum and me, and Colum went over to speak to O'Conaire who stood in a maudlin condition by the counter in the vestibule. On seeing Colum, O'Conaire took off his hat and threw it on the ground by way of a challenge, and they got into a wordy argument over some difference of opinions they held. On O'Casey's return, Colum joined him and left O'Conaire still maudlin.

Thursday, October 12. . . . The Abbey is playing a revival of Yeats's *The Hour Glass* with Gordon Craig scenery and new costumes this week. Frank Fay is in his old part of "The Wise Man" and plays it most impressively. Mr. Dolan wears a mask on the upper part of his

face as "A Fool," and I can't say that I like the innovation. Little Eileen Crowe is "The Angel," and in Shaw's
comedy *Fanny's First Play* which followed she filled the
role of the light o' love, "Dora Delaney," which Sara
Allgood played last year. From "Angel" to "Dora" was a
big jump, but she cleared it well, realising both roles
adequately. . . . W. B. Yeats and his wife were present
at the Abbey on the first night of the revival of his play.
His raven locks are now silvered, but he still looks distinguished and with his thoughts in the clouds.

Monday, October 12.   The first act of Robinson's new
play was in progress before a fine house of Abbey first-
nighters. *The White Blackbird* proved a long drawn out
play with an ugly suggestion of incest near the end, and
one of the chief characters is a loose woman picked up in
Spain by one of the characters and passed off as his wife.
There was too much talk and too little drama in the
piece. . . . I was home with George O'Brien, the Director of the theatre appointed by the Directors to see that
the grant is properly used. He has to read and approve of
the theatre's new plays, and just got one of O'Casey's
pieces to pass judgment upon and did so by deleting many
mentions of Christ and bad words. He thinks it is a fine
play and likely to be very popular. It is of the 1916 period.
Then he got Robinson's play *The White Blackbird* to
pass judgment on, and though he saw the nasty undercurrent and the suggestion of incest, he didn't like to turn it
down for fear it might be said that the government was
interfering unduly with the liberty of the theatre, and so
let it pass. Though in fear and trembling at what might be
the result. He wouldn't like a row or, for instance, the
Catholic Truth Society to march with banners up and
down outside the theatre, or rows like *The Playboy* ones
to occur inside. . . . I assured him that none of these
things would occur. That the worst that would befall the
piece was a falling off in the audiences during the week.
That the days for rows at the Abbey were over. That the
audience knew better than to make another *Playboy*. This
very much relieved O'Brien's mind.

Saturday, October 31.   I was speaking to Sean O'Casey in the vestibule before the play. He thinks *The Bribe* out of date. One can do anything on the stage, he thinks.

When I said, "The setting of Scene 2 in the Board Room is effective theatrically," he said, "Who cares about theatricality?"

Mr. Thomas went to the door to tell some youngsters to go away from the door, and a little mite of five said to him, "If you don't look out, I'll push you off the street." I saw Sean O'Casey in going out give some money to the little fellow and ask him some questions. . . .

"Some people object to Shakespeare being played before curtains," he said, and I replied that "I'd prefer it so produced than backgrounded by futurist scenery that distracts one all the while. A good actor or reciter can work on the imagination without the aid of scenery, just as a good story teller can make the telling of ordinary events live before one's imagination.". . .

O'Casey's principal characteristic is to take the opposite view to those expressed by the person he is speaking to at the moment.

Thursday, November 12.   "If I were left about £2000, I'd never work again," said Sean O'Casey to Mr. Cummins and me in the vestibule of the Abbey during Act II of *Androcles and the Lion.* "Want has been the terror of my life," he added, and went on to say that "When I was earning 19/8 a week, I was always in dread of being out of a job. I never drank and paid for lodgings and food out of my wages and played football, having joined a Gaelic Club for recreation. When out of work I used to live on a cup of tea at morning and night, and all my little things went in pawn even to keep body and soul together." He thinks he is naturally lazy and wouldn't work if he had means of support; his ideal of pleasure would be to sit by a river and laze away in chat with anyone. . . .

O'Casey would go to London for the first night of his play on Monday next. . . . He has settled up the contract with Fagan over the London season and hopes the play may have a long run. He hears that Fagan is a good producer and he has seen the Abbey show. He'd like Miss Allgood for his new play. Sinclair is cast for "Captain Boyle," and he thinks Morgan is to be "Joxer Daly," but there can only be one "Joxer Daly," and that is McCormick; he lives the part. O'Casey is dead sick of hearing of *The Gunman* and *Juno*, and all his thoughts are now for *The Plough and the Stars*. . . .

Fallon over-worked himself acting in the Drama League and the Abbey, as well as working each day in an office and also writing—two articles of his have been accepted by *The Irish Statesman* to be published shortly. He is very talented, but over-exerts himself quite. O'Casey couldn't conceive how a person could have so many irons in the fire and not wear himself out. He could only concentrate on one thing at a time.

He thinks he could never keep money if it came his way. He has known the pinch of hunger and dreads its return. He regrets that half the population is hungry. . . .

"I hate speaking to interviewers," said O'Casey to me. "You never know what they may write about you in large type, something that may misrepresent what was said altogether. Things one wouldn't mind saying to you both might slip from one also that would be best left unprinted. It is hard to be interview-haunted. It robs life of any pleasure it might otherwise give one."

Friday, December 4.   ". . . We had a very romantic marriage of two players at the Abbey on Wednesday last at Dalkey, when F. J. McCormick (Peter Judge, to give his right name) wed Eileen Crowe. None of the company knew of the coming event until the evening before when they were invited to the wedding the next morning. The young couple are the two most brilliant players that ever came out of the Irish dramatic movement. . . ." [1]

Sunday, December 27.   The 21st Anniversary of the Abbey. Everybody who is somebody in Dublin was there . . . AE, Susan Mitchell, and Con and Mrs. Curran . . . Mr. and Mrs. Harry Clarke, Mrs. Austin Clarke (looking

fragile and all teeth), Mr. F. R. Higgins, the poet, become
as big as the side of a house . . . W. B. Yeats, Lady
Gregory, Gerald O'Loughlin, and Mr. and Mrs. Ernest
Blythe sat in the center. . . . Maire nic Shiubhlaigh
(growing stout like her married sister) and Frank Walker
in the front seat behind Larchet and the orchestra.
. . . A few seats behind were Mr. and Mrs. T. C. Murray. Sean O'Casey contented himself in the balcony. . . .

The plays [2] were very well enacted, Fay coming into his
own again as "The Wise Man"—speaking his lines clearly
and beautifully. . . . Maire nic Shiubhlaigh, in speaking
to Higgins and me, told us that she had offered to play
"Nora," and George Roberts to play "Dan Burke" in
Synge's play, but they weren't required. . . .

It was a great night for a great occasion.

1926

Tuesday, January 5.   I went in and saw Act 1 of *The Would-Be Gentleman,*[1] and laughed heartily at the infantile humour of parts of the pantomime entertainment. After the act I got speaking to George O'Brien in the vestibule. He liked the dressing and blending of colour, and thought Fitzgerald very droll. As we spoke, W. B. Yeats (who had come in in the middle of the act) joined us and said Molière was the Bernard Shaw of his time, and the topical bite of *The Would-Be Gentleman* had evaporated and only the miming remained. He liked the lovers' quarrel episode best; its old conversation delighted him. *The Rogueries of Scapin* and *The Doctor in Spite of Himself* were for all time and hence immortal. *The Miser* he didn't think so well of.

Thursday, February 4.   . . . O'Casey . . . has become far more silent and solitary of late than he was before success came to him; *Juno and the Paycock* will have its hundredth performance on Wednesday (February 10) in London. O'Casey is a very lonely man, ever thinking and brooding over new material for plays. Dublin is agog about his new play.

Sunday, February 7.   I attended the dress rehearsal of O'Casey's *The Plough and the Stars* at the Abbey, which didn't commence till after six o'clock and concluded some minutes after ten. The last act will save the play; the second I am of the opinion is quite unnecessary. On the whole, I imagine, as far as I can judge from such a performance, it is not nearly as interesting and gripping a piece as *Juno and the Paycock*. Will Shields was most indistinct in his utterance. May Craig was consistently good, and Shelah Richards promises to be a big success. I did not care for Maureen Delany, save in the final act into which she got the right note. . . . There are some moments of real drama in Act III. Act II is very badly managed, the bar being placed to one side, cut off from half the house. Ria Mooney's part, a prostitute, in Act II is quite unnecessary; and the incident in Act I about the naked female on the calendar is lugged in for nastiness' sake alone. . . .

Robinson mostly reviewed the rehearsal from the pit, going up on stage every now and then to tell the players what he wanted them to do with this or that situation, and always giving them effective advice. . . . O'Casey was about on the stage between acts and seated alone in the front row of the stalls, and later on with some of the players in the stalls. He seemed anxious, but not excited. He wore his cloth cap and trenchcoat.

Monday, February 8.   There was electricity in the air before and behind the curtain at the Abbey to-night when Sean O'Casey's play *The Plough and the Stars* was first produced. The theatre was thronged with distinguished people, and before the doors opened the queue to the pit entrance extended past old Abbey Street—not a quarter of them got in. The play was followed with feverish interest, and the players being called and recalled at the end of the piece. Loud calls for "Author!" brought O'Casey on the stage, and he received an ovation.

Monty [2] said after Act II, "I am glad I am off duty." Some of the incidents in Acts I and II had proved too much for the Censor in him. Mr. Reddin after Act III said, "The play leaves a bad taste in the mouth." George O'Brien was happy after Act II when he saw it went without any opposition. . . . The dialogue at times

seemed too long and wordy, kept back the action, and will
have to be tightened up. . . . The second act carries
realism to extremes. On the whole, it falls far short of *Juno
and the Paycock*.

F. R. Higgins, Liam O'Flaherty and others were in a
group. Ernest Blythe and Mrs., the Lord Chief Justice
and Mrs. Kennedy, Kevin O'Higgins, Yeats and party
steered into the Greenroom after Act II. Robinson was
about also. T. C. Murray . . . Andrew E. Malone . . .
F. H. O'Donnell. Sean O'Casey contented himself with
standing room on the balcony. . . . I wished O'Casey
luck before the piece. The first-night audience stamped
the play with their approval in no uncertain way. . . .

The street outside the theatre was packed on either side
with motor cars. In Abbey Street a policeman was stalking
after four "Rosie Redmonds" [prostitutes] who flew before him, and I am sure the dispersing audience found no
interest in their flight, although they had applauded
"Rosie" plying her trade in Act II of *The Plough and the
Stars*. The fight between the two women in the pub scene
was longly applauded, yet who is not disgusted with such
an exhibition when one chances on it in real life?

Tuesday, February 9.   The Abbey was again thronged. I
saw . . . Sean O'Casey whom I congratulated on last
night's success (the receipts are heaping up steadily in
London for *Juno*—fell twopence last week). . . . Some
four or five in the pit objected to the Volunteers bringing
the flag into a pub in Act II. Kevin Barry's sister was one
of the objectors. The pit door had to be shut to avoid a
rush being made on it, and two policemen were on the
scene. The audience relished the fight of the women in
Act II and didn't object to the nasty incidents and phrases
scattered here and there throughout the play. . . . Lord
Chief Justice Kennedy frankly declared he thought it
abominable. Kevin O'Higgins was silent until Monty
thanked God he was off duty, and added, "This is a lovely
Irish export." Then O'Higgins owned up he didn't like it.
Meeting Dr. Oliver Gogarty, Monty said, "I hope you are
not going to say you liked it?"

"I do," owned up Gogarty (whose reputation for filthy limericks is very widespread), "It will give the smug-minded something to think about."

Wednesday, February 9. At the Abbey I saw Frank Hugh O'Donnell on the balcony during Act II. He joined Sean O'Casey and a lady in the vestibule. . . . O'Casey was besieged by young ladies on the balcony to sign his autograph in their programmes, and on a gentleman asking him to do so for him, O'Casey replied, "I only do so for young and pretty girls.". . .

A sort of moaning sound was to be heard to-night from the pit during the "Rosie Redmond" episode and when the Volunteers brought in the flags to the pub. (I noticed Arthur Shields unfurled his tricolour, as he came in, in a defiant manner. He usually is out for cheap notoriety, such as repeating dirty remarks in *The Playboy*, usually omitted in representation). . . .

The actors rattle through those interminable word-twisters in a gabbly, inflectionless manner. Miss Delany repeats much she has to say in a loud, monotonous, meaningless way, and Barry Fitzgerald fails to articulate clearly in his longer speeches. When he is silent he is usually drollish; witness his facial expression when asked to take the baby in Act II!

Thursday, February 11. The protest of Tuesday night having no effect on the management, a great protest was made to-night, and ended in almost the second act being played in dumb show, and pantomiming afterwards. People spoke from all parts of the house, and W. B. Yeats moved out from the stalls during the noise, and Kathleen O'Brennan, who came in afterwards, told me Yeats went round to *The Irish Times* office to try to have the report of the row doctored. On his return to the theatre, he tried to get a hearing on the stage, but not a word he spoke could be heard. Nulty was in great *Irish Times* form, foaming against those who objected to the play, and vowing he'd write up Dorothy Macardle, who was one of the protesters to the Volunteers' introduction into the pub on Tuesday last, and accuse her of doing so because of the failure of her play, *Ann Kavanagh*. I reminded him that that would be an untruth, as the play has always been well received and liked.

I am sorry to say that I was incorrect in my judgment as to what Abbey audiences could stand when I told George O'Brien on Monday before Act II that they would stand even the devils in Hell exhibiting their worst pranks in silence sooner than make another objectionable play like *The Playboy* burst into notoriety by their disapproval. But, alas, to-night's protest has made a second *Playboy* of *The Plough and the Stars*, and Yeats was in his element at last. . . .

After Act I was the first I heard that a storm was brewing from Dan Breen, who was speaking to Kavanagh and said, "Mrs. Pearse, Mrs. Tom Clarke, Mrs. Sheehy-Skeffington, and others were in the theatre to vindicate the manhood of 1916.". . .

Few really like the play as it stands, and most who saw it are in sympathy with those who protested. Some of the players behaved with uncommon roughness to some ladies who got on the stage, and threw two of them into the stalls. One young man thrown from the stage got his side hurt by the piano. The chairs of the orchestra were thrown on the stage, and the music on the piano fluttered, and some four or five tried to pull down half of the drop curtain, and another caught hold of one side of the railing in the scene in Act III.

The players headed by McCormick as spokesman lined up onstage, and Mac tried to make himself heard without avail. Then a man came on and begged the audience to give the actor a hearing, and they did, and Mac said he wished the actors should be treated distinct from the play, etc., and his speech met with applause. Then the play proceeded in fits and starts to the end, and the whole house in a state of excitement.

Mrs. Fay protested to me that the play didn't get a hearing. Mrs. Sheehy-Skeffington from the back of the balcony during the din kept holding forth, and at the

same time others were speaking in the pit; all were con-
nected with Easter Week. A great big voice called,
"O'Casey Out!" on "Rosie Redmond" appearing in Act
II. Shouts of "Honor Bright" were heard.[3]

Friday, February 12.   A detective-lined theatre presented
itself at the beginning of the play to-night at the Abbey,
and there was no disturbance up to the end of Act II when
I left for home. . . . I saw O'Casey, Brinsley MacNamara, Liam O'Flaherty . . . and others of the dirt cult in
a group in the vestibule. Mr. and Mrs. Yeats and Lady
Gregory sat at the end of the first row of the stalls. . . .
None was allowed to stand in the passages to make way
for the "G" men, a body of men of evil fame in Ireland.
AE was in the audience.

Sunday, February 14.   On my way to the Abbey I called
over to Darley's and had a chat with them re Thursday
night. . . . The Darleys were pleased at the protest. They
saw Sean Barlow handle roughly and throw a woman off
the stage into the stalls. Fitzgerald had a stand-up fight
with a man on the stage and succeeded in knocking him
over into the stalls. O'Casey was surrounded by a crowd of
questioning women, and his answer to one of them was,
"I want to make money!"—sums up his attitude toward
art.

Monday, February 15.   . . . Mrs. Sheehy-Skeffington's
dignified letter re the protest appeared in *The Independent.* Her letter ran:

> Your editorial misses what was apparent in your re-
> port regarding the Abbey Theatre protest. The demon-
> stration was not directed against the individual actor,
> nor was it directed to the moral aspect of the play. It
> was on national grounds solely, voicing a passionate
> indignation against the outrage of a drama staged in a
> supposedly national theatre, which held up to derision
> and obloquy the men and women of Easter Week.

The protest was made, not by Republicans alone, and had the sympathy of large numbers in the house. There is a point beyond which toleration becomes mere servility, and realism not art, but morbid perversity. The play, as a play, may be left to the judgment of posterity, which will rank it as artistically far below some of Mr. O'Casey's work. It is the realism that would paint not only the wart on Cromwell's nose, but that would add carbuncles and running sores in a reaction against idealisation. In no country save in Ireland could a State-subsidised theatre presume on popular patience to the extent of making a mockery and a byword of a revolutionary movement on which the present structure claims to stand.

I am one of those who have gone for over twenty years to performances at the Abbey, and I admire the earlier ideals of the place that produced *Cathleen ni Houlihan*; that sent Sean Connolly out on Easter Week; that was later the subject of a British "Royal" Commission; the Abbey, in short, that helped to make Easter Week, and that now in its subsidised, sleek old age jeers at its former enthusiasms.

The incident will, no doubt, help to fill houses in London with audiences that come to mock at those "foolish dead," "whose names will be remembered forever."

The only censorship that is justified is the free censorship of public opinion. The Ireland that remembers with tear-dimmed eyes all that Easter Week stands for, will not, and cannot, be silent in face of such a challenge.

Friday, February 19. I was in to town with George O'Brien's mother and her sister. . . . They spoke of O'Casey's reply to critics in today's *Irish Times*, and I went and got a copy before going into the theatre.

A space please, to breath a few remarks opposing the screams and the patter antagonistic to the performance of *The Plough and the Stars* in the Abbey Theatre. In her letter to the *Independent* Mrs. Sheehy-Skeffington does not drag before us the parts of the play that spread irritating thoughts over the minds of herself and her allies, but a talk with some of the young Republican women, which I had after the disturbance, enabled me to discover that the National tocsin of alarm was sounded because some of the tinsel of sham was shaken from the body of truth.

They objected to Volunteers and men of the I.C.A. [Irish Citizen Army] visiting a public-house. Do they want us to believe that all these men were sworn teetotalers? Are we to know the fighters of Easter Week as "The Army of the Unco Guid"? Were all Ireland's battles fought by Confraternity men? The Staff of Stonewall Jackson complained bitterly to him of the impiety of one of their number. "A blasphemous scoundrel," said the General, "but a damned fine Artillery officer." Some of the men of Easter Week liked a bottle of stout, and I can see nothing derogatory in that.

They objected to the display of the tricolour, saying that that flag was never in a public-house. I myself have seen it there. I have seen the green, white and gold in strange places; I have seen it painted on a lavatory in "The Gloucester Diamond"; it has been flown from some of the worst slums in Dublin; I have seen it thrust itself from the window of a shebeen in "The Digs," but, perhaps, the funniest use it was put to was when it was made to function as a State robe for the Mayor of Waterford.

They murmured against the viewpoint of "Nora Clitheroe," saying it did not represent the feeling of Ireland's womanhood. Nora voices not only the feeling of Ireland's women, but the women of the human race. The safety of her brood is the true morality of every woman. A mother does not like her son to be killed — she does not like him even to get married.

The Republican women shouted with a loud voice against the representation of fear in the eyes of the fighters. If this be so, what is the use of sounding forth their praises? If they knew no fear, then the fight of Easter Week was an easy thing, and those who participated deserve to be forgotten in a day, rather than to be remembered for ever. And why is the sentiment expressed in *The Plough and the Stars* condemned, while it goes unnoticed (apparently) in other plays? In *The Old Man* (written by a Republican) during a crisis, the many fall back; only the few press forward. In *Sable and Gold* [4] (played by the Republican Players) a Volunteer, who is a definite coward, is one of the principal characters, and yet no howl has proclaimed the representation to be false or defaming. And are the men of Easter Week greater than those whose example they are said to have followed? Were they all unhuman in that they were destitute of the first element in the nature of man? "Upon the earth there is not his like," says Job, "who is made without fear." Even the valiant Hector, mad with fear, was chased around the walls of Troy. And do the Republicans forget the whisper of Emmet to the question of the executioner, "Are you ready, sir?" — "Not yet, not yet." I wonder do the Republicans remember how Laoghaire and Conall, two of the champions of the Red Branch, ran, as rabbits would run, from what they believed to be the certainty of death; and how Cuchulain alone remained to face death, with "pale countenance, drooping head, in the heaviness of dark sorrow"?

One of the young Republicans whispered to me in admiration the name of Shaw, inferentially to my own shame and confusion. Curious champion to choose, and I can only attribute their choice to ignorance; for if ever a man hated sham, it is Shaw. Let me give one example that concerns the subject I am writing about. Describing in *Arms and the Man*, a charge of cavalry, Bluntschli says: "It's like slinging a handful of peas against a windowpane; first one comes; then two or three close behind him; then all the rest in a lump." Then Raina answers, with dilating eyes (how like a

young Republican woman!) "Yes, first one!—the bravest of the brave!" followed by the terrible reply: "H'm;
you should see the poor devil pulling at his horse!"

As for vanity, I think I remember a long discussion in
The Volunteer over the adoption of the green and
gold, scarlet and blue, black, white and crimson-
plumed costumes of the Volunteers of '82 for the Volunteers of '13; and though these were rejected—they
had to be—there was still left a good deal of boyish
vanity in the distribution of braids, tabs, slung swords,
and Sam Browne belts. And how rich (to me) was the
parade of the stiff and stately uniformed men, "the
solemn-looking dials [faces] of them," as Rosie Redmond says in the play—and they marching to the meeting were serious, very human, but damnably funny.

I am glad that Mrs. Sheehy-Skeffington says that the
demonstration was not directed against any individual
actor. As Mr. F. J. McCormick told the audience, the
author alone is responsible for the play, and he is
willing to take it all. The politicians—Free State and
Republican—have the platform to express themselves,
and Heaven knows they seem to take full advantage of
it. The drama is my place for self-expression, and I
claim the liberty in drama that they enjoy on the
platform (and how they do enjoy it!), and am prepared
to fight for it.

The heavy-hearted expression by Mrs. Sheehy-
Skeffington about "the Ireland that remembers with
tear-dimmed eyes all that Easter Week stands for,"
makes me sick. Some of the men cannot get even a job.
Mrs. Skeffington is certainly not dumb, but she appears
to be both blind and deaf to all the things that are
happening around her. Is the Ireland that is pouring to
the picture-houses, to the dance halls, to the football
matches, remembering with tear-dimmed eyes all that
Easter Week stands for. Tears may be in the eyes of
the navvies working on the Shannon scheme, but they
are not for Ireland. When Mrs. Skeffington roars herself into the position of a dramatic critic, we cannot

take her seriously: she is singing here on a high note wildly beyond the range of her political voice, and can be given only the charity of our silence.

In refutation of a story going around, let me say that there never was a question of a refusal to play the part of "Rosie Redmond" (splendidly acted by Miss Mooney). The part declined by one of the players was the character of "Mrs. Gogan."

Sunday, February 21.   . . . A big queue was outside the Abbey pit also when I arrived and many waiting outside the vestibule. Sean O'Casey was one of them. He would not shake hands with me; he seems very sore over the opposition to his *Plough and the Stars* evidently. He didn't know Professor Oldham. He never read or saw *Dear Brutus.*⁵ In fact, I could see he didn't want to have anything to say to me. I, seeing this, dried up at once. I had a chat with Brinsley MacNamara. He didn't like O'Casey's last play at all, and thought much of its dialogue involved and imitative.

Tuesday, February 23.   In her letter to *The Independent,* Mrs. Sheehy-Skeffington wrote:

In his letter Mr. O'Casey sets himself the task of replying to certain criticisms of his play. Since receiving Mr. Yeats's police-protected "apotheosis" Mr. O'Casey appears to take himself over-seriously, not sparing those of us who decline to bow the knee before his godhead. His play becomes "the shaking of the tinsel of sham from the body of truth"; an over-statement surely, for of the body of truth as portrayed in *The Plough and the Stars* one may only discern a leprous corpse.

As Arthur Griffith wrote nearly twenty years ago, when last police assisted at an Abbey production: "If squalidness, coarseness, and crime are to be found in Ireland, so are cancer, smallpox, and policemen." But because these are to be found it would not be true to claim that nothing but these are present in Ireland. Because Mr. O'Casey has seen the tricolour painted on a lavatory wall he claims the right to parade it in a public-house as typical of the custom of the Citizen Army and the Volunteers. Because indecent and obscene inscriptions are similarly so found one may not exalt them as great literature.

Mr. O'Casey's original version, as is now generally known, was pruned before production. One wonders on what basis certain parts were excluded and others retained. This may, indeed, be the reason for the lopsidedness of some scenes, suffering, as sometimes the picture plays do, from a drastic, ill-concealed cut. Will the original version now appear in London and elsewhere, benefiting by the réclame of a "succès de scandale," a réclame that is usually ephemeral?

As to Mr. O'Casey's ransacking of literature to find soldiers that show fear or vanity, all that is beside the point. Whether the sight of men parading before an action that will lead many of them to their death is "damnably funny," or whether it might be pitiful and heart-rending, is also a matter of presentment and point of view. The Greeks, who knew not Mr. O'Casey, used to require of a tragedy that it evoke feelings in the spectator of "pity and terror," and Shakespeare speaks of holding the "mirror up to nature." Submitted to either criteria, *The Plough and the Stars* is assuredly defective. But no doubt Mr. O'Casey would regard such standards as sadly out of date.

A play that deals with Easter Week and what led up to it, that finds in Pearse's words (spoken in almost his very accents) a theme merely for the drunken jibe of "dope," in which every character connected with the Citizen Army is a coward, a slacker, or worse, that omits no detail of squalid slumdom, the looting, the squabbling, the disease and degeneracy, yet that omits any revelation of the glory and the inspiration of Easter Week, is a *Hamlet* shown without the Prince of Denmark.

Is it merely a coincidence that the only soldiers whose knees do not knock together with fear and who are indifferent to the glories of their uniform are the Wiltshires? Shakespeare pandered to the prejudices of his time and country by representing Joan of Arc as a ribald, degraded camp-follower. Could one imagine his play being received with enthusiasm in the French theatre of the time, subsidised by the State?

I learn that Mr. O'Casey's personal knowledge of the Citizen Army does not extend beyond 1914–15. To those, however, who remember the men and women of 1916 such presentation in a professedly "National" theatre seems a gross libel.

Mourning for the men of Easter Week is not incompatible with sympathy for the suffering survivors. The Ireland that is "pouring to the picture houses, the dance halls and the football matches" is the Ireland that forgets — that never knew. It is the Ireland that sits comfortably in the Abbey stalls and applauds Mr. O'Casey's play. It is the Ireland of the garrison, which sung twenty years ago "God Save the King" (while Mr. Yeats then, too, enforced the performance of *The Playboy* with the aid of the police). These do not shed tears for the navvy on the Shannon nor for the men of Easter Week nor for the sores of the slums.

Mr. O'Casey accords me as a critic in a shrieking paragraph or two the "charity of his silence." Unfortunately for his play, the professional critics are for the most part on my side, justifying my opinion that his latest play is also his poorest. For (pace Mr. Yeats) the police do not necessarily confer immortality, nor is it invariably a sign of a work of genius to be hissed by an Irish audience.

Arthur Griffith wrote thus in *Sinn Fein* of a similar episode: — "Mr. Yeats has struck a blow" (by calling in police and arresting certain members of the audience who protested against *The Playboy*) "at the freedom of the theatre in Ireland. It was perhaps the last freedom left to us. Hitherto, as in Paris or in Berlin or in Athens

2,000 years ago, the audience in Ireland was free to express its opposition to a play. Mr. Yeats has denied this right. He has wounded both art and his country."

May I suggest that when Mr. O'Casey proceeds to lecture us on "the true morality of every woman" he is somewhat beyond his depth. Nora Clitheroe is no more "typical of Irish womanhood" than her futile, snivelling husband is of Irish manhood. The women of Easter Week, as we know them, are typified in the mother of Padraic Pearse, that valiant woman who gave both her sons for freedom. Such breathe the spirit of Volumnia, of the Mother of the Gracchi.

That Mr. O'Casey is blind to it does not necessarily prove that it is non-existent, but merely that his vision is defective. That the ideals for which these men died have not been achieved does not lessen their glory nor make their sacrifices vain. "For they shall be remembered for ever" by the people if not by the Abbey directorate.

Friday, February 28.

To the Editor, *Irish Independent.*

Sir—In a letter on the 15th inst. Mrs. Sheehy-Skeffington said that "the demonstration was not directed to the moral aspect of the play. It was on National grounds solely." Yet in her letter of 23rd she viciously affirms what she had before denied, and prancing out, flings her gauntlet in the face of what she calls the "obscenities and indecencies" of the play. She does more: in the righteousness of her indignation, she condemns, by presumption, what she has neither seen nor heard.

This is her interpretation of the Rights of Man. Evidently the children of National Light in their generation are as cute as the children of National darkness by placing a puritanical prop under the expression of National dissatisfaction, even though the cuteness requires an action that can be called neither fair nor just.

We know as well as Mrs. Sheehy-Skeffington that obscene and indecent expressions do not make great literature, but we know, too, that great literature may make use of obscene and indecent expressions without altogether destroying its beauty and richness. She would hardly question the greatness in literature of Shakespeare (somebody a year or so ago wrote asking if Shakespeare wrote thirty plays without a naughty word, why couldn't O'Casey write them), but in the condemnation of an O'Casey play the green cloak is concealed by the puritanical mantle. Indeed, her little crow over the possible horror of the censored part of the play seems to whisper that the wish is father to the thought, and that, when the play is published, nothing less (or more) will satisfy her than that the united church bells of Dublin, of their own accord, in a piercing peal will clang together—"This is a bad, bad, bad, bad play!"

There is no use of talking now of what Mr. Arthur Griffith thought of or wrote about *The Playboy*. Now the world thinks, and I think so, too, that *The Playboy* is a masterpiece of Irish drama. If these Greeks knew not Mr. O'Casey (how the devil could they?), O'Casey knows the Greeks, and hopes that the Republican Players will one of these days produce one of their works dealing with ancient gods and heroes. At present he himself is interested in men and women.

Mrs. Skeffington's statement that "every character connected with the Citizen Army is a coward and a slacker" is, to put it plainly, untrue. There isn't a coward in the play. Clitheroe falls in the fight. Does Mrs. Skeffington want him to do more? Brennan leaves the burning building when he can do nothing else; is she going to persist in her declaration that no man will try to leap away from a falling building? Will she still try to deny that in a man (even in the bravest) self-preservation is the first law? She may object to this, but, in fairness, she shouldn't blame me.

Langon, wounded in the belly, moans for surgical aid. Does she want me to make him gather a handful of his blood and murmur, "Thank God that this has been shed for Ireland"? I'm sorry, but I can't do this sort of thing.

She complains of the Covey calling sentences of The Voice, dope. Does she not understand that the Covey is a character part, and that he couldn't possibly say anything else without making the character ridiculous? Even the Greeks wouldn't do this. And it doesn't follow that an author agrees with everything his characters say. I happen to agree with this, however; but of these very words Jim Connolly himself said almost the same thing as the Covey.

The Tommies weren't represented without fear; but isn't it natural that they should have been a little steadier than the Irish fighters? Mrs. Skeffington will not deny that the odds were terribly in their favour, and that they were comparatively safe. Sixty or more to one would make even a British Tommy feel safe.

The people that go to football matches are just as much a part of Ireland as those who go to Bodenstown,[6] and it would be wise for the Republican Party to recognise this fact, unless they are determined to make of Ireland the terrible place of a land fit only for heroes to live in.

Sean O'Casey

Monday, March 1.   . . . I had tea with Eileen before going on to the Mills Hall to hear the discussion on O'Casey's play *The Plough and the Stars*. The hall was thronged. I arrived early and was seated before Tom Nally with whom I had a chat before proceedings began. . . . T. C. Murray, Mrs. Despard, Maud Gonne MacBride, John Burke, Shelah Richards, Gabriel Fallon, F. J. McCormick, Arthur Shields, Ria Mooney, Joseph O'Reilly, Mrs. Tom Kettle . . . and many others I knew were present.

Arthur Clery was in the chair and opened the proceedings by merely introducing Mrs. Sheehy-Skeffington to the meeting. Sean O'Casey was received with applause as he walked up the aisle. Others were greeted similarly, especially the Abbey Players.

Mrs. Skeffington spoke mostly about the right to disapprove as well as approve in theatres, and was totally opposed to the police being brought in, and spoke most interestingly in soft, low, carrying tones. She is an easy, agreeable speaker and says what she wants to say clearly and well.

Sean O'Casey got up to propose the vote, and almost immediately felt unwell and broke down, and wished for some other speaker to address the meeting for the time being till he felt all right to proceed with his remarks. Mr. Donaghy stepped into the breach, and became quite eloquent for awhile, and then almost collapsed.

Then O'Casey came forward again, and in a speech put his point of view as a dramatist before the meeting, and then drifted into a sort of Salvationist address at a street corner. Then a young lady spoke and pitched into *Juno and the Paycock* as well as *The Plough and the Stars*, and quoted from a letter from Austin Clarke from London in which he said that plays that defiled the Irish were sure of success in London, or words to that effect. The son of the O'Rahilly spoke, and also Fallon and McCormick as to the position of the players. Fallon objected to the subsidy, the row, and the police equally, and McCormick said players should not be confounded with the roles they are cast for, as a player has to play the parts he is cast for to earn his daily bread.

O'Casey attacked a critic on the *Herald*, and Frank Hugh O'Donnell arose to defend the paper. O'Casey said he had no use for heroes in his plays, and Maud Gonne said she didn't see the play, but from what O'Casey said he had no right to introduce a real hero—Padraic Pearse—into his play, and from O'Casey's own words could clearly see why the protest was made. Donaghy spoke again, and Mrs. Skeffington responded in a very subtle speech, full of sly thoughts and humour, and then the discussion concluded. It had been conducted in the most peaceful way and in the best of good humour, each taking or receiving hard hits in their turn.

The players made it clear that neither Miss Delany nor Miss Craig had been assaulted.

"Well, that is more than some of the protectors can say!" chipped in Mrs. Skeffington. She maintained that a protest was necessary from the nature of the play, and seeing that it would be used in London and America as Irish propaganda.

O'Casey said the script of his play, *The Plough and the Stars*, was in the hands of the Abbey before ever *Juno and the Paycock* was played in London. He didn't write for any stage in particular, but hoped for his play's success; he thought himself that *The Plough and the Stars* was his best play, but that was a matter of opinion. Fallon thought O'Casey the greatest dramatist Ireland ever produced. O'Casey thinks *The Plough and the Stars* an anti-war play, but, "If he meant it as such, his message escaped me," Mrs. Sheehy-Skeffington said.

Saturday, March 6.   I read in the papers that Sean O'Casey, the playwright, has arrived in London for his first visit. He said that his first impression of London was one of sleeplessness: for everything was so quiet last night that he listened for the familiar noises of the tenement quarter in which he lives in Dublin.

Tuesday, March 23.   Sean O'Casey, the playwright, was at the Aeolian Hall, London, presented with the Hawthornden Literary Prize of £100 by Lord Oxford.[7] . . . Ralph Goggins told me that he "had heard that O'Casey has taken a flat in London where he intends to reside for some time."

Thursday, April 22.   ". . . I spent the last Sunday evening with T. C. Murray, whose play has made a great stir amongst the London critics, and very naturally he is elated over his good fortune. It is likely to have a big run there: if so, his name will be made as a dramatist, and some royalties will come his way also. He has been working for years steadily as a dramatist in his leisure hours without much monetary return. Now he may reap a harvest for his patience. *Autumn Fire* to me was always a great play, and now I have my opinion backed up by the London critics. Miss Una O'Connor and Miss Kathleen Drago, both old Abbey players, have made great hits in the play. . . ." [8]

Monday, May 3.   I met Mr. Meldon, and we were chatting about *The Plough and the Stars* [9] when Mrs. Sheehy-Skeffington and a number of women bearing cards on sticks came along on their way to the Abbey. Meldon said, "A lot of that sort of thing is done for self-advertisement; the only way to effectively check a play's progress is to stay away if you don't approve of it. It is the box office that tells.". . . The ladies with placards stood at the kerb in front of both entrances to the theatre with policemen in numbers about, and Maud Gonne MacBride, Mrs. Despard, and Mrs. Skeffington in command. . . . Kavanagh told me some stink bombs were to be exploded during the performance (and they were). Police were everywhere and were busy removing people from the pit and the balcony. . . . Many left the balcony after the stink bombs were thrown, and others in the audience commenced smoking and stood the stink; otherwise, though, it was in keeping with much they witnessed on the stage.

Saturday, May 8.   I went down to the Abbey with the intention of sitting out *The Plough and the Stars*, and stayed in the vestibule and saw the crowd go in. Three plain-clothesmen came in shortly before the performance began, and two went into the stalls, and the man in charge spoke to me and queried, "Do you expect any trouble to-night?" And I replied, "I don't, but one can never tell." Then he spoke of the company being as real as the characters they played; it was a great company. "The actress who played 'Rosie Redmond' was the real thing!"

Then the play began, and on that instant the theatre became full of evil smelling fumes, and the attendants became excited. Lady Gregory had just gone in, and Yeats soon after arrived, and queried, "How are things going?"

And he became gloomy on being told that the theatre was stink-bombed. He went in, but came back into the vestibule, where he wandered about like a lost soul.

Tuesday, June 22.   Arthur Sinclair was married today to Maire O'Neill, widow of the late G. H. Mair, the journalist and dramatic critic, at the Church of Corpus Christi, Maiden Lane. They both were born in Dublin and made their fame at the Abbey. The bride is a sister of Sara Allgood, and the bridegroom's real name is Francis Quinton McDonnell. They are playing at present in Sean O'Casey's play *The Plough and the Stars*, at the Fortune, London. I dropped a postcard to Sinclair.

Wednesday, July 7.   I read in a paragraph headed, "Forsaking Ireland" that

> Sean O'Casey, the playwright, is forsaking Ireland for good and has taken a flat in Chelsea as his permanent home and workshop.
>
> His first visit to London was when he came over for the production of *Juno and the Paycock*, and he has frequently since expressed his liking for the town.
>
> "I am going to write a play about London people, for one thing," he told *The Daily Sketch* yesterday. "Human nature is just the same in a Chelsea environment as in Dublin, but in so many plays about London people one sees only artificial puppets moving. Just as though there was no real tragedy behind the laughter in every life that was ever lived anywhere.
>
> "Probably my first London play will be a failure, but I'm determined to make them see themselves as they are, sooner or later.
>
> "Besides I have to find a place for my feet somewhere, and people don't seem to like me in Ireland anymore. I should not care to write a play about Ireland just now with a possible bitterness in my heart."

I quoted the above from *The Daily Sketch*. In *The Independent* I read:

Sean O'Casey, the Irish playwright, has parted from Dublin more in sorrow than in anger, and has taken a flat in Kensington on a three years' lease.

"I like London," he said to a special correspondent last night, "and London likes me. That's more than I can say of Ireland. I have a good deal of courage, but not much patience, and it takes both courage and patience to live in Ireland. The Irish have no time for those that don't agree with their ideas, and I have no time for those who don't agree with mine. So we decided to compromise, and I am coming here. The English are more tolerant and they believe a lot.

"It may," he added, "mean three years' penal servitude for me, but, begorra, it cannot be worse than Dublin."

Sean, who shunned all interviews, photos, caricatures, artists, etc., when in Dublin, now seems to court publicity at every turn, even if some of it makes him look absurd to us here in Dublin.

Again the Abbey was thronged. . . . I had a chat with Brinsley MacNamara, who had been ill for some time. He spoke about the snobbery of O'Casey and his stage Irishman publicity stunt. Mac thinks that O'Casey's plays lower the tone of the Abbey, the players, and the audience. Now that Ireland is getting re-Anglicized, O'Casey's plays just suit the new class of audience who come to see them. O'Casey is insincere, and holds no opinions of his own, and also is devoid of gratitude for good turns done him.

Mrs. Frank Fay thinks the same about him now. His was the snobbery of humility. When she asked him to dinner one Sunday, he replied he always stayed in bed on a Sunday, and even though his brother was ill he wouldn't get up to enquire for him.

Monty thought this rather callous on his part and said to him, "I am sure if your mother were ill you'd get up to see *her*?"

And he replied, "Not damn likely; why should I?"

Mrs. Fay lost all interest in him after that. Neither Mac nor Dolan has any place for O'Casey as a friend. . . . O'Casey as a depicter of the Irish is only a false prophet with an insincere and distorted view of persons and things.

Monday, August 30.   John Burke remarked, "Last year it was all Sean O'Casey; now it is all shun O'Casey."

Friday, October 8.   I received the following letter from Miss A. E. F. Horniman from St. Jean de Luz (permanent address, 1 Montague Mansions, London).

> *Dear Mr. Holloway,*
>
> It is delightfully kind of you to remember me on my birthday. . . . So the Abbey still lives—will it ever lead to a *real* theatre: I mean with properly paid good actors and dramatists from all the world? I hope so, next century.
>
> > *With kind regards,*
> > *Yours sincerely,*
> > *A. E. F. Horniman*

1899

1. Not to be confused with the Frank J. Hugh O'Donnell who wrote plays in the 1920's. This earlier O'Donnell was an ex-Parnellite who distributed in Dublin his anti-Yeats pamphlet *Souls for Gold*.

2. These "idiotic-looking youths" were fellow university students of James Joyce, who refused to sign their manifesto of protest or to join them. The novelist recalls this episode in *A Portrait of the Artist as a Young Man*.

1900

1. On this date were performed for the first time *Maeve*, a psychological drama in two acts by Edward Martyn, and *The Last Feast of the Fianna*, a play in one act by Alice Milligan. Peter Kavanagh in *The Story of the Abbey Theatre* (New York: Devin-Adair, 1950) incorrectly lists their first performances as occurring on February 21. Lennox Robinson in *Ireland's Abbey Theatre* (London: Sidgwick and Jackson, 1951) incorrectly lists their first performances as occurring on February 22. Lady Gregory in *Our Irish Theatre* (London & New York: G. P. Putnam's Sons, 1913), Andrew E. Malone in *The Irish Drama* (London: Constable & Co., 1929), and Brinsley MacNamara in *Abbey Plays, 1899–1948* (Dublin: Colm O Lochlainn, n.d.) correctly list Miss Milligan's play for February 19, but incorrectly list Moore's *The Bending of the Bough* for the same date. Miss Una Ellis-Fermor in *The Irish Dramatic Movement* (London: Methuen & Co., 1939) lists no performances for February 19, but a lecture by Yeats on *Maeve*.

This remarkable confusion about a matter of easily verifiable facts is a typical instance of the many factual errors permeating the histories and memoirs of the Irish Renaissance. Perhaps the most scholarly and accurate of the above-listed historians is Miss Ellis-Fermor, who in this instance relied upon the theatrical programs contained in the miscellany of clippings and information relating to the dramatic movement that was gathered by W. A. Henderson and is housed in the National Library of Ireland. In this instance, however, the Henderson programs were incomplete, and the files of contemporary newspapers might have been consulted as giving the most accurate information. The present editors have found that Holloway's facts almost invariably tally with reports in the press and with extant theatrical programs; nevertheless, all available reliable sources have usually been consulted when a matter of fact was in doubt, and we have sometimes ventured in notes to correct the occasional factual errors of our predecessors.

2. *The Bending of the Bough* was first produced on February 20. The dates for the first performance given by Lady Gregory, Malone, and MacNamara are incorrect.

1901

1. Although Lady Gregory and Miss Ellis-Fermor both consider Hyde's play the first to be produced in Irish in Dublin, Holloway records a previous Irish play. On August 27, in the Antient Concert Rooms, the Ormonde Dramatic Society of the Fay brothers had produced P. T. McGinley's one-act *Eillis agus an Bhean Deirce* (*Eily and the Beggar Woman*).

1902

1. James Cousins.
2. *The Pot of Broth* by Yeats, *The Racing Lug* by Cousins, and *The Laying of the Foundations* by Ryan were being played.

1903

1. Stephen Gwynn, secretary of the London Irish Literary Society, arranged for the Irish Players to come to London, and on May 2 they presented several productions there. The

London trip was an important step in the life of the company, for the group both won the praise of leading critics and increased the interest of the wealthy Miss Horniman in it.

2. The original title of *On the King's Threshold*.

1904

1. For Miss Horniman's letter of April, 1904, in which she indicates the extent of her aid to the Company, see Robinson's *Ireland's Abbey Theatre*, pp. 44–45.

2. In *The Shadowy Waters*.

3. Robinson and MacNamara incorrectly list the first production as January 25, 1904.

4. Some interesting photographs of this production are included in Alan Denson's *Letters from AE* (London: Abelard-Schuman, 1961).

5. Sponsored by Martyn in June, 1903, this group was one of many that cropped up during the early years of the century in Dublin as part of its theatrical flowering. See Anna I. Miller, *The Independent Theatre in Europe*, 1931, pp. 305 ff.

6. The final bill for the patents amounted to £455.2.10. Miss Horniman's solicitors informed her: "£348.12 of this amount was necessitated by your having to obtain a patent under a very antiquated statute. Inquiring what such rights would have cost in London, she was told from £5 to £10. (Henderson Ms. 1730, p. 37)

7. Joyce used this experience as the climax for his story "A Mother" in *Dubliners*. See M. J. O'Neill, "Joyce's Use of Memory in 'A Mother,' " *MLN*, LXXIV (March, 1959), 226–30.

1905

1. W. G. Fay.

2. *Kincora*, Lady Gregory's three-act play, had been first performed on March 25.

3. In Yeats's *A Pot of Broth*.

4. In Lady Gregory's *Spreading the News*.

5. At another performance of *Kincora* at the Abbey.

6. At another performance of *Kincora*.

7. In the cast list of "The Land" in Robinson's *Ireland's Abbey Theatre*, the character of "Martin Douras" is incorrectly listed as "Martin Couras."

The Land was the last play produced by the Irish National Theatre Society. Peter Kavanagh remarks in his *The Story of the Abbey Theatre* that "By the end of September, Yeats succeeded in turning the Society into The Irish National Theatre Society, Limited, under the *Industrial and Provident Societies Act of 1893*. He and Lady Gregory and Synge commandeered most of the shares, leaving the other members only one share each. Under this reorganization Yeats, Lady Gregory, and Synge became presidents of the Society, Willie Fay stage manager, and Frank Fay secretary." (p. 52)

8. A comedy in three acts by Lady Gregory.

9. Francis Quinton McDonnell, whose stage name was Arthur Sinclair.

1906

1. This entry is a critique by Synge of John Guinan's play *Rustic Rivals* which was rejected by the Abbey. Guinan allowed Holloway to copy Synge's letter. Possibly the play was an early version of *The Plough-Lifters*, produced by the Abbey on March 28, 1916.

2. Lady Gregory's translation of *Le Médecin Malgré Lui* had been presented for the first time on the previous night.

3. At a performance of the revised version of *On Baile's Strand*.

4. In a conversation with Sara Allgood. The play referred to was *The Tinker's Wedding*. It has been performed once in Dublin but never by the Abbey.

5. At a rehearsal of Yeats's *Deirdre* at the Abbey.

6. At a rehearsal of *Deirdre* and of Lady Gregory's *The Canavans* at the Abbey.

7. Cf. W. G. Fay & Catherine Carswell, *The Fays of the Abbey Theatre* (New York: Harcourt, Brace & Co., 1935), pp. 207–9.

8. Maire nic Shiubhlaigh and Edward Kenny in *The Splendid Years* (Dublin: James Duffy & Co., Ltd., 1955) list the first production of the Theatre of Ireland as being on December 6, which is apparently a mistake. The plays presented on the first night were Cousins's *The Racing Lug*, Act IV of Ibsen's *Brand*, and Hyde's *Casadh-an-tSugáin*.

9. At a performance of *The Shadowy Waters* and *The Canavans* at the Abbey.

1907

1. In a conversation with W. G. Fay and W. A. Henderson at the Abbey.

2. "Widow Quin" wants "Christy" to leave "Pegeen" and go with her—"Come on, I tell you, and I'll find you finer sweethearts at each waning moon." And he answers, "It's Pegeen I'm seeking only, and what'd I care if you brought me a drift of chosen females, standing in their shifts itself, maybe, from this place to the eastern world?" It was made more crudely brutal on the first night by W. G. Fay. "Mayo girls" was substituted for "chosen females."—Holloway's note.

3. Ben Iden Payne.

4. Joseph O'Connor, police office clerk and feature writer of "Studies in Blue" as Heblon of *The Evening Herald.* From 1933–47 he was a brilliant criminal lawyer and circuit judge of Cork.

5. Holloway indicates in a note that the "gent" was P. D. Kenny who, under the pseudonym of "Pat" wrote drama criticism for *The Irish Times.* For "Pat's" review, see A. C. Ward's *Specimens of English Dramatic Criticism, XVII–XX Centuries* in the Oxford World's Classics volume, pp. 254–59.

6. *Interior.*

7. On April 20, Holloway noted a lapse of 27 minutes between *The Eyes of the Blind* and Wilfred Scawen Blunt's *Fand.*

8. W. G. Fay.

9. As a matter of fact, he did not leave till the end of the month.—Holloway's note.

10. In a conversation with W. A. Henderson.

11. AE's *Deirdre* and Seumas O'Kelly's *The Matchmakers* were being performed at the Abbey as the opening of the third season of the Theatre of Ireland.

12. Among them, Forbes Robertson in *Caesar and Cleopatra,* Mrs. Patrick Campbell in *Hedda Gabler,* and Martin Harvey in *The Only Way.*

1908

1. Henderson was rehired by Synge on February 3. In his letter to Henderson, Synge wrote, "For the moment I am looking after money matters, and I suppose between us we

could get some system of bookkeeping that we could work. As you know, our arrangements are always liable to change for one reason or another, but if you come back we could offer you the post for certain till the Autumn if that would suit you." (Henderson Ms. 1732, p. 1)

The plays on this night included first performances of *The Man Who Missed the Tide* by W. F. Casey and *The Piper* by Conal O'Riordan (Norreys Connell). Kavanagh and Mac-Namara incorrectly list the first performance of Casey's play for February 3.

2. Elizabeth Coxhead in *Lady Gregory, A Literary Portrait* (London: Macmillan, 1961) remarks, "Short of being actually in the library at Coole with them, one cannot put one's finger on what is his and what is hers. The naturalness and life of the peasant family (even though they do not yet speak with the richness of mature 'Kiltartan') suggest that everything is hers except the symbolic speeches of Cathleen; in a word, that he thought of it and she wrote it; and this is the assertion made to me by the Gregory family, who had many times heard it from her own lips." (p. 68) However, the late Lennox Robinson mentioned to Michael J. O'Neill that Yeats told him several times that *Cathleen ni Houlihan* was the creation of Lady Gregory; his contribution was the poetic polish of the lines. The last line, "and she had the walk of a queen," was suggested to Yeats by Arthur Griffith. Cf. the latter's "Oireachtas Ode" in *The United Irishman* for June 14, 1902, on "the queen full of beauty," "the daughter of Houlihan."

3. Plot of M. Clemenceau's play, *Le Voile du Bonheur* (*The Veil of Happiness*) referred to in Boyle's letter—"A Chinese philosopher who was blind recovers his sight and finds that his wife is unfaithful. He therefore blinds himself again. The old gentleman was, of course, wrong. It may be true that what we do not see does not trouble us, but it is equally true that what we have seen bothers us when we can't see it any more and can remember it." *Referee*, 16/2/08, from "Gossip from the Gay City," by "Percival."—Holloway's note.

4. In Synge's biography, *J. M. Synge, 1871–1909* (New York: The Macmillan Co., 1959), no mention is made of *Le Voile du Bonheur*. The authors, David H. Greene and Edward M. Stephens, remark, however, of *The Well of the Saints* that "Synge borrowed the central idea from a fifteenth-

century French farce entitled *Moralite de l'Aveugle et du Boiteaux* by a Burgundian writer, Andrieu de la Vigne. He may not actually have read de la Vigne's play, but he was familiar with it through an account which Petit de Julleville— whose lectures in medieval literature he had attended in 1896 —gives in the second chapter of his *Historie du Théâtre en France.* According to his diary for 1903 he was reading *Théâtre en France,* and the notebook he was using at the time contains notes on de la Vigne's play, a simple plot summary and short passages of dialogue, all of which he may have transcribed from de Julleville." (p. 134)

5. Allan Wade in his edition of *The Letters of W. B. Yeats* (New York: The Macmillan Co., 1955) prints several letters from Yeats to John O'Leary, and remarks that he found copies of these letters in the Central Library, Belfast, and that the librarian there believed them to be in the handwriting of D. J. O'Donoghue. Holloway's journals make it clear that O'Leary's papers after his death came into O'Donoghue's hands, and O'Donoghue allowed Holloway to include in his journals copies of the letters. As Yeats's hand-writing was at best semilegible, it might be profitable to compare the Holloway copies with the O'Donoghue ones.

The letter quoted was not included by Wade in his collection. The production referred to was one in which Miss Horniman sponsored Florence Farr's productions of Yeats's play, of Shaw's *Arms and the Man,* and of John Todhunter's *A Comedy of Sighs.*

6. This is Holloway's hiatus, for he could not here make out Yeats's handwriting. Probably Yeats was referring to a projected Irish magazine which he also mentions in a letter to Lionel Johnson in the Wade volume. (p. 228)

7. Kavanagh and MacNamara incorrectly list the first performance of this play as March 10, 1908.

8. Frank Fay's long letter to W. J. Lawrence was written on April 7. In parts we have omitted he mentions a plan to play *The Building Fund* in Chicago with Dudley Digges and his wife, and details further royalty squabbles with Yeats and Lady Gregory.

9. Fay did not immediately mail his letter, but added this portion three days later.

10. Sir Thomas Deane the architect's house, opposite that of George Moore, now the Royal Hibernian Academy.

11. Charles Ricketts—Holloway's note.

12. The first Abbey production of *The Scheming Lieutenant*, usually called *St. Patrick's Day*.

13. Poel was visiting the Abbey to produce Calderon's *Life's a Dream*. Holloway remarked of him, "Theatrical cranks make me ill."

14. Henry Irving's famous role in *The Bells* by Erckmann-Chatrian.

15. John Guinan sent Holloway a copy of his one-act play, *The Fairy Follower*, and in it Holloway found the critique by Yeats.

16. They had appeared on November 4, at the Theatre Royal in Hofmannsthal's version.

1909

1. Holloway's niece.

2. Many handsome wreaths were placed on the grave, including the following: "In memory of his gentleness and courage; The lonely returns to the lonely, The divine to the divinity," from W. B. Yeats; "An Irish Cross" from the Abbey Company; "To our leader and our friend—goodbye" from Miss A. E. F. Horniman, London.—Holloway's note.

3. A wandering singer.

4. Connell's troubles began with a letter from him, on April 18, which Yeats told Henderson to read to the Company. The letter has this marginal note by Yeats: "Lady Gregory and I think well of what he suggests."

Connell's letter (Henderson Ms. 1732, p. 67) instructs the Company to make a regular habit of reading prose aloud, thus, "the tendency to gabble and mispronounce will quickly be checked." He concludes by saying, "We are therefore determined to tolerate no artistic snobbishness among the members of our company apart from sheer questions of seniority; all are equal in our eyes and there can be no question, no matter how much we may value his or her performance, of any one actor or actress being starred among the rest, unless the directors decide that it be fitting with regard to some exceptional event."

5. Shaw's *The Shewing Up of Blanco Posnet* was refused a License by the Lord Chamberlain and could not be performed in England. The Lord Chamberlain had no authority in Ireland, so Yeats and Lady Gregory were able to produce

the play despite pressure from Dublin Castle which warned them not to.

6. Joyce did not keep his promise, but later sent Henderson a portion of the *Corriere De la Sera,* Milano (Sept. 9, 1911), with an article "Il Capolavoro del Theatro Irlandese" by Gugliemo Emanuel. The clipping was signed, "For your collection J. J." (Henderson Ms. 1733, p. 235)

7. Joyce had just returned to Dublin a few days previously from a ten day visit to his wife's people in the West of Ireland. The following day he left Dublin for Trieste but returned on October 21, 1909, and remained until January 2, 1910, being involved in opening one of Dublin's earliest cinemas, The Volta, on December 20.

8. Maunsel's, which Holloway called "Won't Sell and Co.," failed to publish *Dubliners* and in 1912 destroyed the type.

9. Lady Gregory's play was first performed on November 11.

1910

1. Fay's letter was written on February 25, at 4 Walkden Street, Mansfield, where he was playing with Allan Wilkie's Company.

2. Martyn's letter was written on March 1, at 5 Russell Mansions, Russell Square, London.

3. This seems a particularly apt point to stress that Holloway's opinions are not necessarily ours.

4. Edward VII.

5. Yeats had arranged with Shaw for Robinson to watch D. G. Boucicault, Granville-Barker, and Shaw conducting rehearsals in London.

6. *The Pot of Broth.*

7. A character in Boucicault's *Arrah na Pogue.*

8. Characters in Boyle's *The Building Fund.*

9. One of Boucicault's famous Irish dramas.

10. On the occasion of a visit to London by the Abbey Company.

11. James Connolly, founder of the Irish Citizen Army, was executed after the Rising of 1916.

12. A play in three acts first presented on September 16, 1909, at the Abbey. The first production of *Martin Whelan* is incorrectly listed by Kavanagh and MacNamara.

13. On October 1, Holloway saw another performance of
the play, which Mr. and Mrs. Bernard Shaw also attended,
and he remarked to them that "Ray's play has hit the public
taste at once, and is a fine thoughtful work full of keen
observation and wonderfully accurate character studies of
peasant types. It is only in his two leading characters that he
fails to convince."

14. The stage name of Annie Walker, the second youngest
sister of Mary Walker ("Maire nic Shiubhlaigh").

1911

1. Malone, Kavanagh, and MacNamara incorrectly record
the first night of this play as January 26.

2. MacNamara incorrectly records the first performance as
January 30.

1912

1. For a full account of the Abbey's trials while on tour in
the United States, see, of course, Lady Gregory's fine *Our
Irish Theatre*.

2. When Boyle's *Family Failing* was first produced at the
Abbey.

3. By Lennox Robinson.

4. The Abbey Company under Robinson's direction was in
London for a five week season at the Royal Court, giving first
productions of *Maurice Harte* on June 20 and Lady Gregory's
one-act comedy *The Bogie Man* on July 4.

5. Stephen J. Brown, S.J. who had edited *A Guide to
Books on Ireland, Part* 1 (Dublin: Hodges Figgis, 1912).
Holloway compiled a long annotated list of English and Irish
plays about Ireland for this volume. No Part 11 was ever
issued.

6. MacNamara proposed to do an edition of Holloway's
journal; wisely or not, he did not persist.

7. *Family Failing*.

8. Frank Fay in a conversation with Holloway on July 4
also held forth at some length on the "fluffiness" of the
Company.

9. The old lady who was saying No was Lady Gregory.

10. Maire O'Neill, Synge's fiancée, married George H.
Mair, dramatic critic of the *Manchester Guardian* who was

attached to the British Ministry for Propaganda in the First World War. He had firsthand knowledge of the dissemination of the Casement diaries by the British government in 1916.

11. *The Elizabethan Playhouse and other studies* (Stratford-upon-Avon: Shakespeare Head Press, 1912).

12. According to Holloway's count, from opening night on December 27, 1904, to September 14, 1912, there had been 600 performances of Lady Gregory's 16 plays and 8 translations, 245 performances of Yeats's plays, 182 of Synge's, 125 of Boyle's, 78 of Casey's, 65 of Robinson's, 47 of Norreys Connell's, and 44 of Shaw's. Holloway notes, "If Shaw and Lord Dunsany's plays be added to the Directors' total, it would leave it at 1257 and all outsiders at 349. Yeats and Gregory 849; all the rest 757."

13. Nugent Monck.

1913

1. Yeats had been lecturing on "The Poetry of Rabindranath Tagore."

2. The Abbey No. 1 Company had just returned from its tour of the United States on May 1. The No. 2 Company had been managed by Andrew Patrick Wilson.

3. There is a good discussion of this important, bitter, and prolonged strike in R. M. Fox's *History of the Irish Citizen Army* (Dublin: James Duffy & Co., 1943). Wilson, who was now manager of the Abbey, had strong connections with the Irish Transport and General Workers Union and wrote many articles for the labor newspaper *Irish Freedom*, under the pseudonym of "Euchan." For a controversy between "Euchan" and Sean O'Casey, see *Feathers from the Green Crow*, ed. Robert Hogan (Columbia: Univ. of Missouri Press, 1962).

1914

1. The Abbey opened at the Court Theatre on June 1, and included two new plays in its repertoire: Lady Gregory's *The Wrens* and J. Bernard McCarthy's *The Supplanter*.

2. Seamus O'Kelly's three-act *The Bribe* was first presented at the Abbey on December 18, 1913. Walter Riddall's four-

act *The Prodigal* was first presented there on September 30, 1914.

3. Holloway did not at the time realize that "Beau Brummell" was satirically directed at Yeats. One incident in the play, in which the frightened "Brummell" begins to pray but instead recites the beginning of *Paradise Lost*, was a well-known Dublin story about Yeats, and some years later Holloway heard it from AE. The character of "Otho" is an egotistic and unbearable young poetaster who is meant to satirize the type of artistically inclined young man exemplified by the young James Joyce. Indeed, "Otho" makes one remark to "Brummell" which the young Joyce in another well-known story is supposed to have made to Yeats: "Ah—I see you are too old for me to influence you."

1915

1. Robinson gives February 10 as the opening night of his play *The Dreamers*, while Malone, Kavanagh, and MacNamara give it as February 2.

2. A disapproving review of *Shanwalla*.

3. The Abbey Company was in London, but Wilson had returned to Dublin to see about a burglary that had just occurred in the theatre.

4. These remarks are from a letter by Holloway to Martin J. McHugh, the author of *A Minute's Wait*, an amusing one-act farce.

1916

1. By Bernard Duffy.

2. Nally's *The Spancel of Death* was to have been produced on this day. Because of the Rising, the performance was called off, and no attempt was later made to stage the play.

3. Two doors away.

4. An extract from a letter to Miss Mary Douglas of New Orleans.

5. After the revolt against Ervine, many of the Abbey actors joined a company formed by Arthur Sinclair. J. Augustus Keogh was the manager appointed to form a new company at the Abbey, and he had written to inquire if Fay would join it. They could not, however, agree on terms.

6. Shaw's *John Bull's Other Island* was playing. Its first night was September 25.

7. William Boyle.

8. Mr. Holloway was being ironic.

1917

1. F. R. Higgins, the poet and later director of the Abbey Theatre.

2. Under the name of Micheál Mac Liammóir, Willmore was co-founder with Hilton Edwards of the Gate Theatre and became one of the finest of modern Irish actors. In 1964 he was conferred Litt.D. Honoris Causa by Trinity College, Dublin. He is the author of several plays in Gaelic and English. His book, *All for Hecuba* (London: Methuen & Co., 1946), is the story of the Dublin Gate Theatre.

3. From a letter to W. J. Lawrence.

4. A farcical comedy in three acts by S. R. Day and G. D. Cummins which was first presented at the Abbey on February 2, 1917.

5. From a letter to Miss Mary Douglas of New Orleans, Louisiana.

6. *Spring, and other plays* (Dublin: The Talbot Press, 1917).

1918

1. He did—in *Sport* for February 2, 1918: "There is no other way of describing 'Hanrahan's Oath,' the latest and worst of Lady Gregory's one-act efforts to, presumably, cultivate and enlighten Abbey patrons. There are half-a-dozen characters, all more or less apparently tainted with lunacy, and the only thing to be said in favour of the piece is that it is sufficiently short to prevent the audience from becoming similarly touched. . . . In the course of the babbling blatherskite one manages to learn that Hanrahan took an oath of silence. It is to be deplored that the authoress did not do likewise—and keep it."

2. Daniel Laurence Kelleher whose play *Stephen Gray* was produced by the Abbey. At this time he was popular as the author of *The Glamour of Dublin* and *The Glamour of Cork*. He was editor of *Ireland of the Welcomes* and originator of the title.

3. MacNamara incorrectly lists the first night as February 9.

4. O'Kelly died on November 14.

5. From a letter to Miss Douglas.

1919

1. Peter Judge, under his stage name of F. J. McCormick, became one of the greatest and most versatile of the Abbey actors.

2. By Victor O'D. Power.

3. *The Player Queen.*

1920

1. From a letter to Miss Douglas.

1921

1. A tragedy by Rev. Edward Groves (1831).

2. A play in one act, first produced at The Abbey on May 4, 1920.

3. *Paddy the Next Best Thing,* a popular comedy by W. Gayer Mackay and Robert Ord, adapted from the novel by Gertrude Page. It was being performed at the Gaiety by Robert Courtneidge's Company.

4. From a letter to Miss Douglas.

1922

1. From a letter to Miss Douglas.

1923

1. The remainder of the sentence is illegible.

2. *The Revolutionist,* first produced at the Abbey on October 10, 1921.

3. O'Casey used this incident years later in the Prerumble to *The Drums of Father Ned.*

4. A character in MacNamara's *The Glorious Uncertainty.*

1924

1. McCormick played "Helmer."
2. Maguire was the proprietor of a book barrow on the quays.
3. A condition of the Anglo-Irish Treaty which established the Irish Free State that all cabinet ministers and government officers had to swear loyalty to the British King.
4. A passion play in three acts by Lady Gregory. MacNamara incorrectly lists the first performance as occurring on April 14.
5. The main character in the play of that name by Casimir Delavigne. In its English adaptation by Dion Boucicault, *Louis XI* was a great success in the repertoire of Charles Kean and Henry Irving.
6. A comedy in three acts first produced at the Abbey on May 12.
7. See "Irish in the Schools," a short story O'Casey published in *The Irish Statesman* on November 29, 1924, and which is reprinted in *Feathers from the Green Crow*, ed. Robert Hogan (Columbia: University of Missouri Press, 1962).
8. From a letter to Miss Douglas.

1925

1. From a letter to Miss Douglas.
2. *The Hour Glass, In the Shadow of the Glen,* and *Hyacinth Halvey.*

1926

1. Lady Gregory's translation of Molière's play was first produced on the previous night, January 4.
2. James Montgomery was the Irish Film Censor.
3. Honor Bright was a Dublin streetwalker who was murdered in the mountains in the winter of 1924/25. A doctor and a superintendent of police were charged with the murder but were acquitted.
4. By Maurice Dalton (Joseph F. Wrenne, M.A., secretary of the Cork County Council and the first Cork County

manager, sometime-acting professor of history in University College, Cork).

5. Being presented that evening by Mrs. May Carey.

6. Annual pilgrimages were made to Wolfe Tone's grave at Bodenstown by various patriotic organizations.

7. O'Casey won the Hawthornden Prize for *Juno and the Paycock*.

8. From a letter to Miss Douglas.

9. *The Plough* was being revived at the Abbey.